8.3X11   1
05/23

SHAPING HOLLAND

All around the world, regions are facing major challenges: climate change, the transition to renewable energy, reinventing the food system, ongoing urbanisation and finding room to sustain biodiversity. These will radically transform our living and working environments. Regional design uses the power of visualisation to unite regional players around appealing spatial development visions for meeting those challenges. It offers a route to new forms of regional governance and planning that match the urgencies of our time. This book exposes the benefits and the pitfalls of regional plans *and* designs.

Shaping Holland gives a unique insight into the emergence of contemporary regional planning and design practice in the Netherlands. This densely populated country in the delta of the Rhine and Meuse rivers is internationally renowned for its urban planning and design tradition. Drawing on first-hand accounts and a rich collection of illustrations, maps and diagrams, the book gives pointers for practitioners, academics and students of spatial planning, urban design and landscape architecture.

Regional design is on the rise in all continents. It provides an answer to a world in which economic activities, activity patterns, urban growth and ecological systems are no respecters of administrative boundaries. Amid the growing number of academic analyses of regional design, this book is unique because it focuses on planning practice and first-hand knowledge. As such it is of interest to a broad international readership.

SHAPING HOLLAND

Regional Design and Planning in the Southern Randstad

Francisco Colombo
Jeroen van Schaick
Peter Paul Witsen

With a foreword by Henk Ovink

First published 2022
by Routledge
605 Third Avenue,
New York, NY 10158

and by Routledge
2 Park Square, Milton Park,
Abingdon, Oxon, OX14 4RN

Routledge is an imprint of the Taylor & Francis Group, an informa business

© 2022 Taylor & Francis

The right of Jeroen van Schaick, Francisco Colombo, and Peter Paul Witsen to be identified as authors of this work has been asserted by them in accordance with sections 77 and 78 of the Copyright, Designs and Patents Act 1988.

All rights reserved. No part of this book may be reprinted or reproduced or utilised in any form or by any electronic, mechanical, or other means, now known or hereafter invented, including photocopying and recording, or in any information storage or retrieval system, without permission in writing from the publishers.

Trademark notice: Product or corporate names may be trademarks or registered trademarks, and are used only for identification and explanation without intent to infringe.

Library of Congress Cataloging-in-Publication Data
Names: Colombo, Francisco (Francisco Felix), 1954- author. | Schaick, J. van (Jeroen), author. | Witsen, Peter Paul, 1964- author.
Title: Shaping Holland : regional design and planning in the southern Randstad / Francisco Colombo, Jeroen van Schaick, Peter Paul Witsen.
Description: New York, NY : Routledge, 2022. | Includes bibliographical references and index. |
Identifiers: LCCN 2021042578 (print) | LCCN 2021042579 (ebook) | ISBN 9781032022628 (hardback) | ISBN 9781032022611 (paperback) | ISBN 9781003182603 (ebook)
Subjects: LCSH: Regional planning—Netherlands. | City planning—Netherlands.
Classification: LCC HT395.N4 C645 2022 (print) | LCC HT395.N4 (ebook) | DDC 307.1/21609492—dc23/eng/20211110
LC record available at https://lccn.loc.gov/2021042578
LC ebook record available at https://lccn.loc.gov/2021042579

ISBN: 9781032022628 (hbk)
ISBN: 9781032022611 (pbk)
ISBN: 9781003182603 (ebk)

DOI: 10.4324/9781003182603

Typeset in Frutiger LT Std and Swift OsF
by Tjarda Hilarius

Publisher's Note
This book has been prepared from camera-ready copy provided by the authors.

Shaping Holland

About the Authors

Francisco Felix Colombo (1954) completed his architecture and urban design degree at the National University of La Plata (Argentina) and his Master in Urban and Regional Design (MTD) at the Universities of Delft and Eindhoven (Netherlands). He has extensive international design experience and has won several architectural competitions in Argentina. From 1993 to 2020 he worked as a senior regional designer at the Province of Zuid-Holland, where he contributed to almost all the major regional spatial visions and policies. His design work has been published in numerous policy documents. His practical experience at the Zuid-Holland Spatial Planning and Mobility department centred on regional planning and design in the South Wing of the Randstad. In addition, Francisco Colombo has worked as a design tutor and mentor in architecture and urbanism for forty years, in particular at the National University of La Plata and Delft University of Technology.

Jeroen van Schaick (1978) completed his urban design and planning degree at the Faculty of Architecture and the Built Environment, Delft University of Technology. He stayed on at the faculty as a researcher in the Spatial Planning and Strategy research group and obtained his PhD in 2011. His thesis, *Timespace Matters*, is on the knowledge gap between social sciences and designers. Jeroen has been working as a strategic spatial planner at the Province of Zuid-Holland since 2010. In recent years he has specialised in futures studies and regional design methods, culminating in research publications on the societal impact of new technologies, the water-food-energy nexus and the book *Kracht van Regionaal Ontwerp* (the 2018 Dutch edition of *Shaping Holland*). His publications include work on the Dutch layer approach to planning, urban time planning and new technologies, as well as the books *Urban Network – Network Urbanism* (2008) and *Urbanism on Track* (2008).

Peter Paul Witsen (1964) completed his urban and regional planning degree at the University of Amsterdam. He is a scholar, writer and consultant on spatial planning. He specialises in regional planning, having been involved in the making of development plans for areas like the Green Heart of the Randstad, National Park Nieuw Land (New Land) near Amsterdam and the New Dutch Waterline military heritage zone. He currently heads his own consultancy firm Westerlengte. He started his career as a planner with the Institute for Traffic, Logistics and Regional Development at the Organisation for Applied Scientific Research TNO. Between 2000 and 2015 he joined the editorial staff of *Blauwe Kamer*, the Dutch magazine on landscape and urban design. His publications include *The Selfmade Land: Culture and Evolution of Urban and Regional Planning in the Netherlands*.

Foreword by Henk Ovink

As with the United Nations 2030 Agenda for Sustainable Development and the Paris Agreement on climate action, we know that complex challenges call for truly comprehensive and inclusive approaches and for truly transformative and innovative solutions. We need to unravel the different interdependent demands and connect these in inspiring and sustainable pathways forward. For this approach and these results, we need systems thinking *and* acting. Our environmental, societal and economic systems are often regional, transcending man-made boundaries, cutting across vested interests and political scales. To bypass these borders and to facilitate and strengthen the regional systems approach, we need design: architecture, urban design and landscape architecture. Design is comprehensive by nature, cutting across disciplines and silos, uniting rather than dividing. Once we understand dependencies – how poverty and health relate to poor infrastructure, how urbanisation touches upon the need for food, energy and water, ignoring jurisdictional boundaries – a design approach informs a way forward that integrates that understanding and identifies opportunities to solve problems holistically.

Design is about both the process and the outcome. In addressing the impacts of climate change, design is inclusive, seeks synergies, looks ahead, and prepares us and our planet for an uncertain future: flexible, adaptive and resilient. Appealing to the imagination but grounded in analysis, design enables us to sketch new futures and determine the steps that will get us there, linking today's conditions with tomorrow's possibilities. A comprehensive plan consists of real, innovative projects to implement and inspire others, kick-starting development and catalysing change. A truly integrated design connects social, cultural, ecological and economic challenges. It connects regional interdependencies, local needs and community assets, not by a trade-off of interests – that is, not by compromising – but by bridging gaps between quality and safety, between economy, ecology and society. Integrated solutions add value across sectors, across scales and through time, building a sustainable business case.

This process of design is inherently inclusive. Design challenges the divisions of our daily lives by drawing all interests, all aspects, all questions and all people into a common understanding and a new deal. It invites us all to contribute, to bring our different needs and demands, and our unspoken dreams and ideas. By making the envisioned tactile and the ambitious practical, the design approach increases everyone's imaginative capacity and helps us make the future tangible and achievable. In this way, design turns complexity into compelling and inspirational ideas, and translates societal issues into shared ambitions and inspiring narratives about our future. Design helps us tell each other stories about what could be – stories that convince, seduce and make us all believe in them. At this level, design is truly inspirational and aspirational, which makes it political: people who have participated in this process will fight for it and what it promises them. This is why we developed the 'Rebuild by Design' approach – to tackle the future and escape the past with vision, by design and in collaboration. It is also why we developed the programme 'Water as Leverage for Resilient Cities Asia'.

This approach demands a free zone, a safe space, or soft space, which Allmendinger and Haughton describe as 'areas where deliberate attempts are made to introduce new and innovative ways of thinking, especially in places where there is considerable resistance to cross-sectoral and inter-territorial governance.' And in my own words, in reflecting upon my work for president Obama's task force, I call on the need for a different culture of working together. The enormous complexity calls for room to experiment, reflect and innovate, time and space where we can step outside existing interests and frameworks, legitimised by the huge challenges ahead. The challenges we face can never be met by our current approach and conditions, our agreed-upon procedures and institutions, rooted as these are in the past.

We need room to experiment, in which we tie government responsibilities to the strength of initiatives in our communities, in academia, by activist groups and by our businesses and investors; room to take risks, make mistakes and learn, to set change in motion. This experiment requires a safe place that frees us from the 'not allowed' and 'won't work' attitudes, based on yesterday's experiences. A place where we can collaborate, where it's all about people, not positions, on a level playing field, space where we can get away from solidified relations and accepted roles. A place where everyone can be vulnerable, where government and communities or citizens and corporations are not on opposite sides, where everyone can change roles and positions. A place where disagreement and even conflict can grow into understanding and better solutions. Here we can organise a truly inclusive and transparent process, rooted in trust and collaboration, a process where individual vulnerability is respected and can grow into a collective force for change.

During the past few decades there has been a rapid increase in the number and complexity of new societal challenges. Design – in its connecting capacity – and an inclusive design approach are now more important than ever: connecting across these complexities, bridging differences globally, forging coalitions and driving transformative solutions we need to meet the challenges we face. Our design culture ensures we do not start from scratch. There is a large reservoir of knowledge and capacity for regional design, of systemic design approaches to the growing societal challenges. The Province of Zuid-Holland holds one of those reservoirs of regional design knowledge and capacity. This book about 'shaping Holland' demonstrates the transformative design experience we must build upon. Its reflective nature and first-hand account of regional design practices will be an inspiration to all of us. By design we can accelerate our actions, scale up, leaving no-one behind. By design we can not only imagine a future, but build a better future for all. By design we must act – now!

Henk Ovink is the Special Envoy for International Water Affairs for the Kingdom of the Netherlands. He is Principal of the Rebuild by Design initiative and was Senior Advisor to the former US Presidential Hurricane Sandy Rebuilding Task. He was both Acting Director General of Spatial Planning and Water Affairs and Director of National Spatial Planning for the Netherlands. Ovink teaches at the London School of Economics and the Harvard Graduate School of Design and holds an honorary lecturer position at the University of Groningen. His book, Too Big – Rebuild by Design – A Transformative Approach to Climate Change, *written with Jelte Boeijenga, reports on his post-Sandy recovery work.*

Shaping Holland

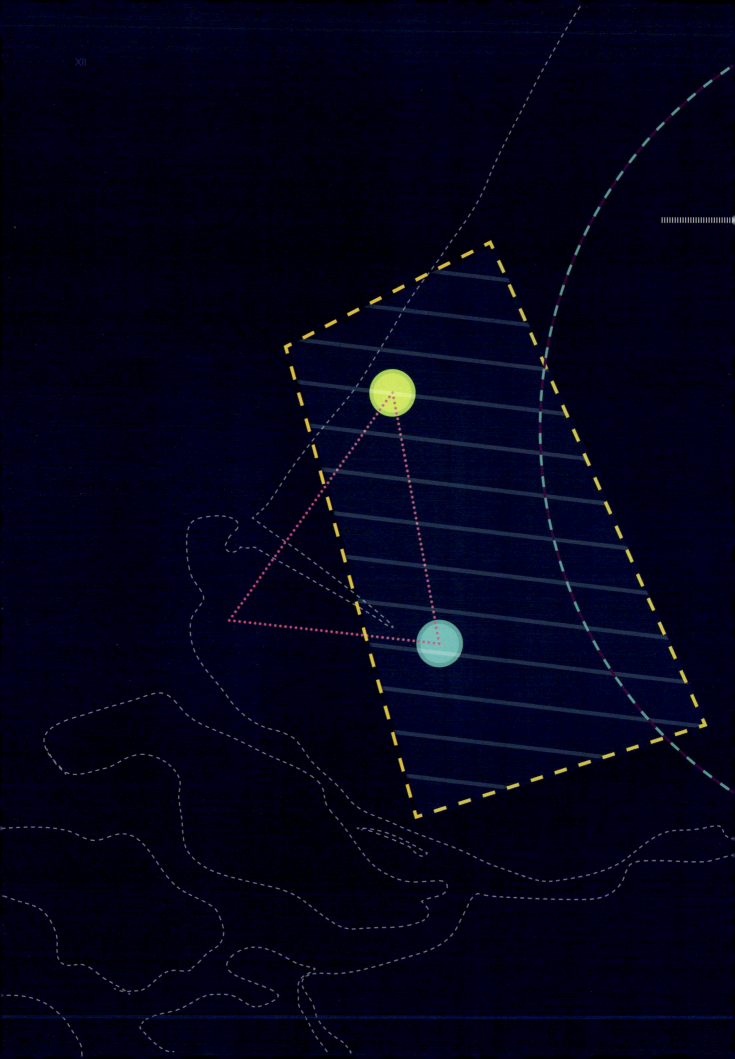

Table of Contents

Introduction **02**

    Why this Book about Regional Design **02**

    Setting the Scene: (Re)shaping Holland Since 1990 .. .. **14**

1 - Coast _ **22**

2 - Urban growth _ **50**

3 - Landscape _ **76**

The Civil Servant _ . _ **108**

The Politician _ . _ **114**

The Director . _ **120**

4 - Corridors _ **126**

5 - Regional transit-oriented development _ **160**

6 - Beyond the port _ **190**

The Researcher . _ . _ . _ . _ . _ . _ . _ . _ . _ . _ . _ . _ . _ . _ . _ . _ . _ . _ . _ **226**

The Advisor . _ . _ . _ . _ . _ . _ . _ . _ . _ . _ . _ . _ . _ . _ . _ . _ . _ . _ . _ **232**

The Academic _ . _ . _ . _ . _ . _ . _ . _ . _ . _ . _ . _ . _ . _ . _ . _ . _ . _ . _ **238**

7 - Regional Design Principles for the Future **245**

Illustration sources **264**

Acknowledgements **270**

Fo.1

Introduction

Why this Book about Regional Design

Regional design: Laboratory for urbanisation and landscape concepts

In the decades to come it will be regional governments that determine the spatial development of urban and rural areas around the world. The boundaries of the traditional city have long ceased to be significant factors in labour and housing markets, while local measures alone will not be sufficient to deal with climate change. The global challenges of sustainable urban development and mobility, developing a new economy, switching to renewable energy and climate adaptive water management are throwing the regional approach increasingly into the spotlight.

Balancing between local and national government, the regions are now in a prime position to shape the course of future development. But what is the 'region'? Regions do not have mayors or presidents. They do not even have fixed boundaries. They may be social, cultural, administrative, political or geographical entities. In this book we encounter regions defined by infrastructure, landscape units, daily urban systems, economic relations and many more parameters. Their geographical boundaries often change as the agenda they serve is reformulated or reinterpreted. Regions are therefore regularly reinvented by researchers, institutes, governments and alliances – and also by designers, and in so doing they give direction to the future, shaping how we live and the environment we live and work in. That may be within a planning culture with strong institutions and legislation or it may be in a heavily market-driven planning culture.

Design is a powerful instrument for regions, which are by nature volatile. Analytical design can be used to investigate intraregional relationships and demonstrate the importance of regional cooperation. Regional design can provide a powerful visualisation of the future, it can cast new perspectives in a visual form and win broad acceptance for them, and it can help to crystallise political agendas and set priorities for detailed planning or implementation.

In the Netherlands it is often the provinces that are the drivers of regional design. Working in a variety of cooperative arrangements they have developed a capability for spatial planning and regional economic development. The way they have done this is unique, but their experience can provide pointers for strengthening regional cooperation in other parts of the world as well. In this book we offer insights into a period during which the Dutch regions underwent rapid develop-ment – from around 1990 to about 2015. In those years the Southern Randstad developed into a coherent urban region (Figure i.1)

Intensification of the spatial interconnections in this area coincided with the growth of admin-istrative arrangements for regional cooperation – or rather, a boom in strategic alliances between government, the market and civil society partners with the common goal of sustainable spatial development. All this happened in a global context and was aimed at strengthening the position of the region in a highly competitive world.

Regional design is an approach to regional planning that gives regional alliances of private and public parties a common platform around which they can pool their interests to shape the future. Regional design is a discipline that shares aspects of spatial and regional planning on the one hand and architecture and urban design on the other. In this book we show how building and cultivating a regional design capability can work as a laboratory for new concepts for urban and landscape development.

This book is unique because we show how regional design works in practice; we open the black box and reveal how opportunities arise to generate new development concepts for the city and the countryside. This is not a theory book. It was born from design practice in the Dutch Southern Rand-stad region, the area around Rotterdam and The

Hague, whose city centres are just twenty kilometres apart. The region is more or less equivalent to the territory of the province of Zuid-Holland.

Regional designing in the Southern Randstad is a distinct branch of a longer and wider international tradition of regional planning. Regional plans have been made in the Netherlands since the end of the 19th and beginning of the 20th centuries. More recently, the landscape architecture design school at Wageningen University and the urban design school at Delft University of Technology have been a rich seedbed for regional design. The marriage of these two design schools was a key step in the emergence of the regional design practice we describe in this book.

This regional design discipline is also a product of the geographical context within which regional design emerged in the Netherlands, and specifically in the Southern Randstad. From early on the geographical realities of the Dutch delta forced government authorities to work together across municipal boundaries on the creation of a unique coastal defence system, drawing on a long history of water management, on its river and peat landscapes where agriculture and horticulture has become increasingly efficient, and on the early development of a polynuclear urban network. In Sir Peter Hall's book *Urban and Regional Planning* (1975) there is a wonderful description of how a polycentric metropolis arose in the Randstad as a consequence of a combination of planning and autonomous development. In 2020 Routledge

published *The Randstad – A Polycentric Metropolis*, an extensive analysis of the Randstad by Vincent Nadin and Wil Zonneveld.

The first regional plans in the Southern Randstad date from the 1920s. At the end of that decade forward-thinking planners in the Netherlands argued for integral regional plans, for example for the Zuid-Holland West region, to provide a framework for local urban extension plans and the construction of infrastructure. This was inspired partly by developments in regional planning in the US, England and Germany, including the 1929 Regional Plan for New York and Its Environs by Thomas Adams. Van Lohuizen, urban planner at the City of Rotterdam, directed a survey in preparation for just such a large-scale plan for the province of Zuid-Holland. This led to the first planning concepts for what in this book we call the South Wing. However, no official policy plan was produced before the Second World War. Some regional sector plans were prepared, though. The IJsselmonde landscape plan, for an island to the south of Rotterdam, plans for greenhouse horticulture in the Westland area to the west of Rotterdam and a plan for a linear city between Rotterdam and The Hague, which was never completed, show that designers and planners in Zuid-Holland continued to look for a regional orientation.

The 1953 North Sea flood provided the next impetus for regional planning: the storm surge devastated the neighbouring province of Zeeland

and part of the Zuid-Holland itself. This flood led directly to the first regional strategies by designers at the Province of Zuid-Holland. They looked beyond the borders of the province, end even beyond the national borders, taking in an area from Amsterdam to Antwerp. The regional design practice that arose in the 1980s and 1990s in the Netherlands, and specifically in the Southern Randstad, is a new phase of regional planning. Instead of regional plans, the emphasis shifted to regional strategies.

We are indebted to a long international history of regional planning and design in both the town planning and the landscape architecture traditions. As Sir Peter Hall said from the perspective of the English-speaking world, regional planning began with Patrick Geddes (1854–1932), inspired by French geographers and sociologists. The development of regional design was taken forward by Ebenezer Howard in his famous book *Garden Cities of Tomorrow* (1898), Idelfonso Cerda with his plans for the expansion of Barcelona (1860), Arturo Soria y Mata with the concept of the Linear City in Madrid (1882) and later by Patrick Abercrombie with his Greater London Plan (1944). Before the Second World War influential Dutch planners and urban designers such as JM de Casseres (1902–1991) and Cornelis van Eesteren (1897–1988) also drew inspiration from the United States and Germany. The international CIAM school (1928–1959), to which Van Eesteren belonged, outlined 'functional zoning' as its paradigm, and had much influence in Dutch spatial planning. In addition, Le Corbusier's

La Ville Radieuse and his Chandigarh vision, with the regional scope and emphasis on the relation between city and landscape in particular, have been a personal inspiration for us.

After the Second World War the Finger Plan for Copenhagen and the Amsterdam Extension Plan put regional design on the regional planning agenda. An inspirational contribution to this regional design tradition was made by the Scot Ian McHarg, whose book *Design with Nature* (1969) combined regional design and natural systems in a single integrated approach. At the end of the 20th century we were inspired by the work of the Frenchman Gabriel Dupuy on 'network urbanism' and especially by Manuel Castell's sociological work on the 'urban question', globalism and flows. Regional planning, including the regional design approach, has developed as a multidisciplinary activity, a combination of art and architecture, urban design, planning, social sciences and economics, engineering, landscape science, landscape architecture and ecological sciences.

More than a hundred years after Patrick Geddes, regional design is gaining ground again in planning practice around the world. It is no accident that the first *Routledge Handbook of Regional Design*, compiled by Wil Zonneveld and Michael Neuman, was published in 2021. This book shows that regional design has also gained a foothold in regional development plans in Asia and North America. Regional design is one of the answers to a world in which administrative boundaries

i.1 – 2004 – The growth of cities in the Randstad area between 1950 and 2010

The Randstad area underwent rapid urbanisation over a period of sixty years. The cities in Zuid-Holland expanded massively and the infrastructure grew in step with this expansion, as did a whole range of industrial landscapes.

are blurred by international economic activities, people's activity patterns, urban growth and ecological systems.

The power of regional design

This book is about the power of design in the Zuid-Holland region over the past twenty-five years. We will show how we used regional design to identify new challenges and put them on the agenda. Regional design helps to forge alliances and pool investments, and translates administrative priorities into a compass for the future. None of this can be taken for granted, and we will not gloss over the pitfalls. Regional design is sometimes liable to break away from the administration it is supposed to serve, or conversely gets overshadowed by unassailable economic and political interests. Its connection with the dynamics of society balances on a fine line. The greatest chance of success is when there is cooperation with stakeholders and other interested parties and the ideas generated are relevant to the administrative and political agendas.

Regional design has played a significant, albeit modest role in the spatial metamorphosis of the province of Zuid-Holland. Significant, because the province had a lot on its plate and regional design proved a means to give structure and direction to these tasks. Modest, because regional design never pretends to have the last word. That is the main difference with urban or architectural designs, which are usually made for smaller areas. Ultimately, the real work has to be done by weighing up options for specific issues and projects, and adopting provincial regulations and spatial plans.

What then is the power that regional design brings to regional planning? This books contains three strands of concrete examples that illustrate the power of regional design to (1) identify and visualise new challenges so that they can be debated in political and societal arenas, (2) create narratives about the interconnections between a plethora of subproblems, scales and interests, and (3) provide a compass for the future.

First and foremost, the power of regional design lies in the identification and visualisation of new challenges. Topical examples are climate adaptation and the transition to a circular economy. By adopting an investigative perspective, regional design maps out possible futures. It connects new challenges with options for political and administrative action, not as a hard and fast plan that must be implemented, but rather as a stimulating idea that invites action. Recent examples included in this book are design research into the relationship between the port of Rotterdam and the Westland greenhouse horticulture complex, and the investigations into the spatial consequences of the energy transition, which are described in Chapter 6 on the logistical-industrial system. This approach to regional design in Zuid-Holland owes a debt of gratitude to design efforts in the late 1980s. The urban development pressure in the area between The Hague and Rotterdam gave rise to a study entitled *Parkstad tussen Hof en Haven?* (Park City between Palace and Port?), which is discussed in detail in Chapter 2. This study investigated a new urbanisation model and put it on the agenda for the first time, with a challenging and well-considered design. Since then, the province has built up a tradition of giving a free rein to research-by-design studies. Initially, the distinction between free, investigative design and planning design was not always entirely clear. An example of this is the design studio in which the Randstad provinces collaborated (vividly described by Luuk Boelens in the interview in this book). From 2005 on, designers collaborated closely with experts and stakeholders in the South Wing Studio (*Atelier Zuidvleugel*) and Xplorelab, where they were given the freedom to range widely and explore ideas. The new challenges and working methods that emerged would fill the regional agenda for the next few years.

Second, the power of regional design lies in pulling together and identifying the connections between a wide range of issues to create a coherent picture of locations, agendas and policy areas. Beside the freedom to explore ideas, Zuid-Holland has therefore always maintained a strong design team. Regional designs with which all interested parties can identify and to which they can all contribute can bring parties together and build mutual trust, making it possible to cluster and coordinate investment decisions. One of the most notable examples of this in this book is the *Stedenbaan* (Cities Line) concept that connected the world of infrastructure and stations to the world of urban development – and therefore also the government to the market. The area around Leiden also provided a powerful example. Design studies for the Leiden–Katwijk Axis and the Oude Rijn Zone created connections between a large number of programmes and projects, both urban and rural. At the intersection between the Oude Rijn river and the A4 motorway in particular, projects were fused together in a sturdy framework of ideas, narratives and ultimately also agreements and investments. Regional designing is a working method that can pull together diverse challenges such as nature development and accessibility by showing that the man-made landscape of water, green space, infrastructure and buildings forms a single whole.

Visualising new development agendas and showing the interrelationships between existing spatial challenges appear in this book as extremes at the ends of a regional design continuum, with many conceivable interim forms. The third power of regional design is to be found somewhere in between these two extremes: providing a compass for the future. We are not talking about rigid blueprints here, but about narratives that are enduring and which provide direction. Chapter 1 on the coast illustrates this changing perspective of regional design. It starts with a comprehensive plan for a Coastal Location (1995) to be developed as a large and distinctive residential and employment area and ends with a number of high-quality civil engineering works at the local level. Apart from boosting the quality of the environment, the main purpose of these works is to reinforce the 'weak links' in the coast. Chapter 4 on corridors describes another example. The narratives about the A4 motorway corridor which forms the backbone of the west of the Netherlands have become stronger and stronger, partly because each addresses a different scale. At one time the entire zone from Amsterdam to Antwerp was the subject to investigation, at another it was all about the routing through a landscape or urban area, or the design of the road itself. The 'compass' provided by the design work on the A4 corridor has continually adapted to the times, which is how the idea came about for a 'knowledge axis' between Dordrecht and Leiden that encompasses not just the A4 motorway but economic and spatial development, social cohesion and accessibility in the area. The design work on the A4 corridor over the years also shows that regional design cannot provide a compass with a single abstract narrative; the key to success appears to lie in the interaction between local narratives and the bigger picture.

__ About this book: Shaping the Southern Randstad

Since the 1990s the Province of Zuid-Holland has positioned itself within the complex regional network of stakeholders as a patron of regional planning and design. The provincial government kept on a substantial team of designers, planners and researchers in a period when many municipalities and other provinces, as well as national government, chose to outsource or considerably cut back their spatial planning capacity. While national planning gained little political momentum and spatial planning responsibilities were increasingly decentralised, steady progress continued to be made at the regional level.

For this book we delved into the experiences gained over the past twenty-five years in the province of Zuid-Holland, an area comprising the Southern Randstad region. As so much happened in those years, this book can only present a selection of the planning and design work during that time, and of course it is coloured by the zeitgeist. Public and private funding resources were readily available until 2008 and the Southern Randstad region experienced rapid growth. This can be seen in the design work by the province, as can the sudden change in direction prompted by the credit crisis of 2008 and the growing urgency of climate change.

With this English edition we want to inspire international readers – professional practitioners, academics, students and anyone else interested in the Dutch situation – to look beyond the confines of the area in which they live and work. The coming decades will be the heyday of urban regions: fluid, networked entities of cultures connecting previously separate towns and cities, industrial ecosystems and clusters of businesses and talent that operate on a daily basis within the orbit of a 90 minute travel radius. Regional design offers planners the means to get to grips with challenges that extend beyond their administrative boundaries. Dutch architects, planners and urban designers have long inspired their counterparts elsewhere. We sincerely hope that the Dutch tradition, as exemplified by the regional design practices in Zuid-Holland discussed in this book, will continue to be a source of inspiration for planners around the world.

The structure of the book

Following an introduction to the regional context for the international reader, this book contains six thematic chapters that take an in-depth look at different facets of regional design and six interviews with key players in regional planning in the Southern Randstad. Each of the six thematic chapters starts with an introduction and main messages from the examples discussed in the form of a list of takeaways for the reader. These six chapters focus on specific spatial structures at the regional scale, a specific area-based agenda, and a specific collection of internationally relevant social issues in spatial

planning. We made a conscious decision to produce a richly illustrated book that gives pride of place to the illustrations. Too many books on design practice do not do justice to the power of visualisation which gives regional design its persuasive force. In this book we also present a visual narrative in which the descriptive texts accompanying the illustrations provide further information on the thematic content of the chapter.

Coasts and deltas around the world are faced with the double challenge of climate change and rapid urban growth. How regional design helps us find answers to this is the subject of the first chapter. Urban growth is the theme of the second chapter. We show how regional design can be an incubator for new models for urbanisation. Regional design as a laboratory for ideas is a recurring theme in other chapters as well. Urbanisation cannot be seen as distinct from the relation between the city and the landscape, which is the subject of the third chapter. Designing the inverse of urbanisation shows how design gives expression to regional values and identity building, as is shown in Chapter 1 on the coast.

In the following three chapters we show how regional design is now not primarily concerned with reserving room for growth, but with designing networks and flows. These chapters, on corridors, a regional approach to transit-oriented development and the logistical-industrial system, show how regional design helps to find a new language for

i.2a – 2021 – *The Netherlands in its wider context of north-west Europe*

i.2b – 2021 – *The Randstad in the Netherlands*

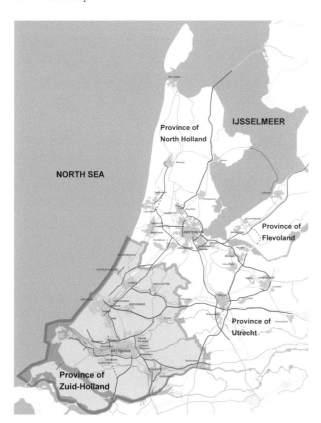

i.2c – 2021 – *The four Randstad provinces with the province of Zuid-Holland highlighted*

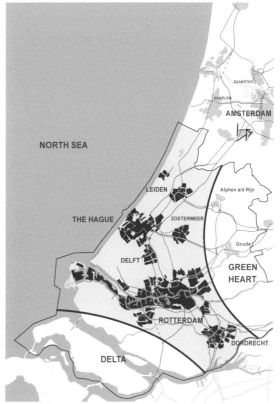

i.2d – *The South Wing of the Randstad highlighted*

regional strategies and alliance forming. The focus of regional planning has shifted from the functional and legal planning of 'spaces' towards a systems approach and is increasingly concerned with the structuring and planning of flows. This shift is one of the central features of the period covered by this book, and as such it sets the tone for regional planning and design in the decades to come.

We end the book with a chapter in which we set out the recurrent themes and lessons from the narratives collected in the book. We attempt to distil from the collective practical experience a set of regional design principles that regional planners and designers can adapt to their own context.

The Netherlands, Holland, the Randstad and the South Wing

The Netherlands is a European nation located in the delta of the Rhine and Meuse rivers, stretching from just north of Antwerp along the North Sea coastline to the Ems estuary in the north (see Figure i.2a). You can drive from the country's eastern border with Germany to the coast in two hours, and in just under four hours from Maastricht in the far south to the Wadden Sea, the intertidal zone of the North Sea, in the north. Amsterdam is the Dutch capital and The Hague is the official seat of government and the Crown. Rotterdam is the Netherlands' second biggest city and the biggest port in Europe. Historically, the Low Countries comprised part of what is now the Netherlands and part of Flanders, the Dutch speaking northern half of Belgium. The basis for the current nation was created during the 16th and 17th centuries when the northern provinces declared independence from Habsburg rule and split off from the Spanish Netherlands to the south (roughly the area of modern Belgium). The term Holland, although often used inter-changeably with the Netherlands, in fact refers to two of the twelve Dutch provinces that are located in the west of the country where the majority of the Dutch population lives: Noord-Holland and Zuid-Holland (see Figure i.2c). Holland is relatively urbanised and contains three of the country's main cities – Amsterdam, Rotterdam and The Hague – and much of the country's economic activity.

The story goes that the Randstad (see Figure i.2b) as a concept was coined by the founder of Dutch airline KLM. When flying over the west of the country he saw a rim of cities around a large 'green heart' covering most of Holland and part of the neighbouring province of Utrecht. Since then it has been a much-debated planning concept, a vision of a coherent spatial structure that many disagree with. Sir Peter Hall brought the Randstad concept into the international spotlight as a metropolitan strategy for fast growing cities in the 1960s: an agglomeration of cities like the Randstad in an open, green landscape would combine economic strength with an unsurpassed quality of life. During the 1990s new concepts such as the 'Deltametropolis' were introduced to reinvigorate this vision of spatial and economic development while maintaining quality of life, with 'nature' nearby. However, the realpolitik of national and regional government relations was more inclined to see recognisable functional urban regions around the major cities. Planning policy divided the Randstad into a Northern Randstad – the North Wing (*Noordvleugel*), the urban region around Amsterdam – and a Southern Randstad – the South Wing (*Zuidvleugel*), the combined urban regions around Rotterdam and The Hague and surrounding smaller towns such as Leiden to the north and Dordrecht to the south-east. During the 1990s a regional partnership of cities and the provincial government came together in a South Wing coalition within the Province of Zuid-Holland, a formal tier of government.

The urban regions around Rotterdam and The Hague had formal spatial planning and infrastructure responsibilities, as did the province. These regional bodies of government were conduits through which national funding for infrastructure was channelled and negotiated. The choice of who to cooperate with, and how, were the subject of a major power play between the cities, the province and national government. Much of the regional design and governance processes described in this book took place against this complicated background of shifting governance landscapes. In 2015 the South Wing coalition came under pressure as national government reconsidered the formal status of urban regions within the Dutch constitutional framework, which contains three tiers of government: national government, provincial government and the municipalities, with a special status for water authorities as regional government entities. The major cities of the Randstad, including Rotterdam and The Hague in Zuid-Holland, repositioned themselves and formed a regional partnership of twenty-three municipalities: the Metropolitan Region Rotterdam–The Hague. The former South Wing coalition continued as a lighter form of network cooperation under the banner of Southern Randstad.

Setting the Scene: (Re)shaping Holland Since 1990

A changing world, a changing region

The year 1990 was marked by major geopolitical shifts. The Berlin Wall had just fallen, heralding the end of the Cold War, and the system of apartheid in South Africa was overthrown. The world wide web was born, setting the stage for a new information revolution. The next twenty-five years would be characterised by globalisation, the rise of neoliberalism, open borders in Europe and the growth of the European Union. Strong economic growth was followed by a financial and economic crisis, while climate change and new wars – and the flows of refugees they created – began to set the global political agenda. It was a bumpy ride.

Lying as it does in the delta of the Rhine and the Meuse, the Zuid-Holland region is particularly sensitive to international trends such as these. Between 1990 and 2015 the volume of goods passing through the port of Rotterdam increased by more than 50% to about 460 million tonnes. Exports of horticultural produce, ornamental plants and flowers from the specialised greenhouse horticulture, flower bulb and arboriculture clusters rose year on year. The Hague welcomed new international organisations in the area of peace and justice, such as Europol and the Organisation for the Prohibition of Chemical Weapons. Universities and businesses became increasingly internationally oriented, attracting talented students and workers to the region from around the world.

At the same time Zuid-Holland ran up against the consequences of this growth and economic globalisation, and especially the effects of climate change. The delta is directly affected by the rising sea level and higher river discharges, as well as by water shortages and heat stress in the summer months. The transition to a circular economy presents challenges to business processes in the port and the agricultural clusters and means changing the way we plan and design urban and rural areas.

Around 1990 internationalisation was a highly promising prospect and the Netherlands was gearing up to it. Major projects were on the drawing board: a new freight railway line from the port of Rotterdam to Germany, a seawards extension of the port, and a high-speed rail connection between Amsterdam, Rotterdam and Paris. All these projects have now been completed.

This global context and the susceptibility of the Netherlands to global changes was the backdrop to a major wave of urbanisation in the Netherlands starting around 1995. Its realisation coincided with landscape restructuring, inner city revitalisation, new infrastructure, new agricultural production and employment landscapes, and a re-engineering of the flood protection infrastructure in this land of rivers and polders. A major housebuilding programme – known as the VINEX programme after the national policy document on which it was based – would reshape the urban landscape of the Netherlands by adding almost 700,000 homes in approximately ten years. It built on earlier waves of urbanisation such as the new town developments (*groeikernen*) and urban renewal of the 1970s and the inner city redevelopment and 'cauliflower' neighbourhoods of the 1980s (so named because of their characteristic street patterns). By 2020 around 800,000 people were living in the new 'VINEX neighbourhoods', of which 30–40% were built as brownfield developments. Approximately a quarter of this building programme was located in Zuid-Holland.

Regional transformation taking shape

Spatial development in the province of Zuid-Holland has always been shaped by the conditions arising from its location in the delta of the major European rivers Rhine and Meuse. This region corresponds roughly with the southern part of the Randstad, the urban ring which connects the four major cities of the Netherlands (Amsterdam, Utrecht, Rotterdam and The Hague). About two-thirds of the province's more than 3.5 million inhabitants live in the urban backbone of the province, while at the same time much of the land use is still agrarian, particularly on the southern islands below Rotterdam and in the Green Heart (the open central area of the Randstad). This dense – and at the same time distributed – mix of

functions and activities is why regional design is needed and has developed here.

Since 1990, the region of Zuid-Holland, the Southern Randstad, has been thoroughly transformed. Rotterdam and The Hague, the two main cities, grew to become the centres of a single green metropolitan region. The rural zones in the south and east of the province remained free of urbanisation and the green zones between the cities were kept open. All this was in line with Dutch planning culture which reflects a deeply rooted desire to protect the countryside against uncontrolled urban expansion. New nature and designed landscapes are integral parts of the metropolitan region.

Rotterdam remained the biggest port city in Europe. Brand new container terminals appeared on a new peninsula reclaimed from the sea and old docks in the city centre have been transformed into vibrant urban neighbourhoods. The Hague, the seat of government and the king's place of residence, became the International City of Peace and Justice, surrounded by numerous towns with their own individual characters. The centres of these towns and cities have come to life, based around their historic churches, market squares and town halls that stand witness to a flourishing trading history. Just a short bike ride away is a modern university campus, leisure complex or

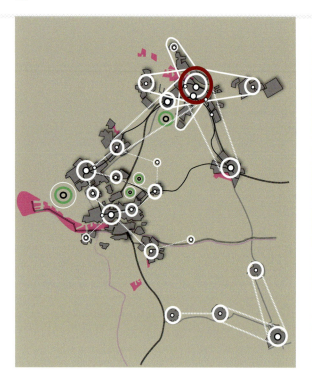

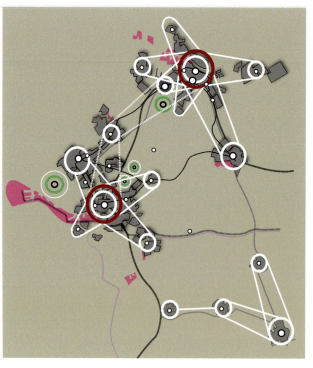

i.3a

- *Metropolitan Region Amsterdam*
- South Wing
- *Brabant Cities*

i.3b

- *Metropolitan Region Amsterdam*
- Metropolitan Region Rotterdam
- *Brabant Cities*

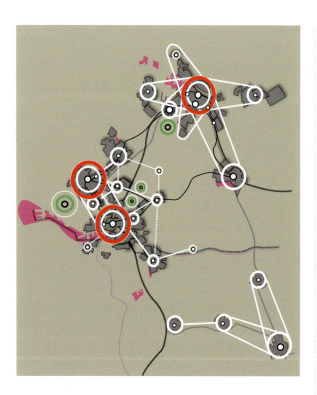

i.3c

- *Metropolitan Region Amsterdam*
- Metropolitan Region Rotterdam - The Hague
- *Brabant Cities*

i.3 – 2010 – Different tracks for metropolitan development in the South Wing

The government's National Spatial Strategy (2006) distinguished between a North Wing and a South Wing of the Randstad. In the first decade of the 21st century the Amsterdam region manifested itself strongly as a metropolitan region within the North Wing, and since 2007 as the Amsterdam Metropolitan Area with a decidedly internationally oriented branding. Around 2010, the cities of the South Wing felt that their position needed to be defined in relation to Amsterdam. These drawings show various spatial models based on different hierarchical arrangements between urban centres in the South Wing. The models differ in the degree of complementarity and autonomy in relation to the Amsterdam region. The Amsterdam region is a clear example of a central-city urban network, with Amsterdam as its centre. The South Wing, on the other hand, is a complex criss-cross urban network, and therefore faces a fundamentally different challenge: the spatial configuration suggests no obvious direction for metropolitan development.

hi-tech delta technology or agri-food complex. New infrastructure is the physical manifestation of the network links between these towns and cities, but that infrastructure is not always really new, as much of the growth in mobility has been accommodated by increasing the capacity of existing road and rail connections.

These developments are the result of more than twenty-five years of working on, thinking about and designing images for the region of Zuid-Holland. The social and economic interconnections in the region have effectively been strengthened. A similar process of metropolitanisation took place in the Northern Randstad, around Amsterdam and Amsterdam Schiphol Airport, but whereas this Northern Randstad region straddles three provinces, the Southern Randstad lies entirely within the province of Zuid-Holland. Moreover, the spatial development visions for the Southern Randstad included in this book should always be seen within their wider context (Figure i.3).

Historical context of planning in the Randstad

After the Second World War regional planning in the Netherlands gained momentum with the birth of the Randstad and Green Heart concepts around 1960. At that time too it was the forecasted rapid growth that prompted the development of a national planning policy. Over a period of thirty to forty years around a million new homes would be needed, as well as many kilometres of new roads, because at that time car ownership was

rising fast. During the 1960s and 1970s regional planning (embodied in national planning) was led by grand visions and visionary concepts. Plans by the national government sought a balanced distribution of growth across the country, which meant steering some of it out of the Randstad to prevent its cities from coalescing and flooding the central agricultural area (the Green Heart) with homes and businesses. Agricultural land parcels were consolidated to make farming more efficient.

Later, during the 1980s and 1990s, a more grounded approach emerged that was embedded in situation and landscape, reflected a re-appreciation of city life and was more responsive to the reality of regional economies as well as new social and environmental issues. Climate change and water management issues became increasingly prominent on national and regional planning agendas. At the same time, increasing conflicts over spatial 'claims' and land use transformation led to a call for integrated design on a regional level that was more specific and more territorial than the conceptual regional planning of the previous decades. The need for regional planning cooperation between municipalities, regions, provinces and national government became more acute. This was the context in which regional design in the Province of Zuid-Holland emerged.

At the beginning of the 1990s the Randstad as a whole was the object of planning and design. However, the question remained whether the Randstad really is the scale at which daily life and the economy function – and thus whether planning at that scale could be relevant and efficient. The environmental, economic and social issues to be tackled did indeed extend beyond municipal boundaries, but did not necessarily operate at the scale of the province or the Randstad (Figure i.4).

The societal challenges facing the Randstad had and still have no corresponding level of government. In the 1990s Amsterdam and Rotterdam attempted to form city provinces that would match the spatial scale of these challenges, but they failed due to local opposition. In the early 2000s it was broadly acknowledged that a tier of government at the Randstad level could not provide effective governance of spatial economic development. The concept was largely abandoned in national planning in favour of an approach focused on the Southern Randstad and Northern Randstad (South Wing and North Wing) and on other functional urban networks throughout the Netherlands. These networks reflect the scale at which daily life unfolds and most regional design operates: somewhere between the municipality and the province.

Changing national governance

For a long time spatial planning in the Netherlands was primarily a national government responsibility. National planning law institutionalised a strong tradition and legal framework of regional spatial plans (*streekplannen*) prepared by provinces and local land use plans (*bestemmingsplannen*),

hierarchically embedded in policy, law and decision-making at the national level. This has gradually changed during the past few decades. Local and regionally operating public authorities and other stakeholders are rapidly becoming the key players in spatial planning. The national government no longer designates sites for new development and has withdrawn from active involvement in nature and landscape policy (except for obligations under international conventions and agreements). National funding for urban redevelopment and urban growth declined, while statutory planning instruments delegated spatial planning and land use decisions as much as possible to the nearly 400 Dutch municipalities. Implementation was increasingly left to the market. Municipalities no longer built houses themselves and the proportion of new homes built by housing corporation for the social rented sector shrunk. The majority of new housing was left to commercial property developers and government-led development was increasingly implemented via private-public partnerships.

The 2008 Spatial Planning Act (*Wet ruimtelijke ordening*) marked a turning point. It put the provinces in a new position. Whereas before, each land use plan had to be approved by the provincial government, now the provinces could only make formal representations just like members of the public. The provinces could still intervene in local planning decisions if regional interests were at stake, but such power play has not been the preferred route; the preference is for area-based partnerships between provinces and municipalities.

Over the past twenty-five years there has been a proliferation of partnerships in all shapes and sizes, sometimes involving complex arrangements. All parties involved needed time to adjust to working in these new administrative structures.

The same applies to arrangements between provincial and national government. The national government has retained its responsibility for projects of national importance, such as the expansion of the port of Rotterdam, the safety of the North Sea coast and the construction or widening of the main transport infrastructure. It acquired greater legal powers to overrule provincial and municipal authorities where the national interest is at stake, but this power is seldom used. Since 1990 the most impressive results have been obtained through cooperation between tiers of government. Regional players, particularly the provinces, have taken the lead in the planning and design of projects with national objectives, but in ways that have also led to improvements at the local and regional scale.

At the national level, the continued decentralisation of spatial planning has now been formalised in the new Environment and Planning Act (*Omgevingswet*), important aspects of which are participation and flexibility for context-specific arrangements at local and regional levels. The Act is being implemented in stages from 2020 onwards. It replaces a range of existing laws, including the 2008 Spatial Planning Act, further strengthening the position of municipalities over provincial and national government in spatial planning matters. The role of the provinces is increasingly to oversee a coherent spatial development and safeguard longer-term regional interests. These regional interests are to be implemented in the visioning stage rather than through control mechanisms for the decision-making stages of plan making. Now that the Dutch provinces are expected to take much more initiative for regional planning, regional design is becoming an increasingly important tool.

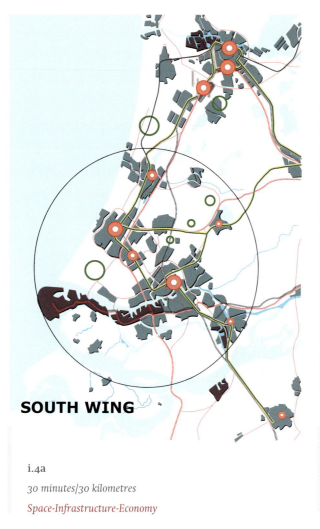

i.4a

30 minutes/30 kilometres

Space-Infrastructure-Economy

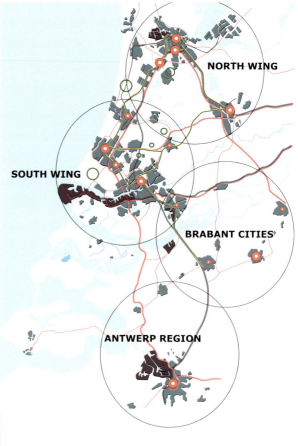

i.4b

60 minutes/up to 100 kilometres

Space-Infrastructure-Economy

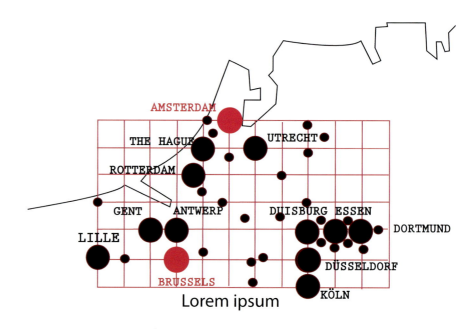

i.4d

100 kilometres to 300 kilometres

Space-Infrastructure-Economy

Shaping Holland   21

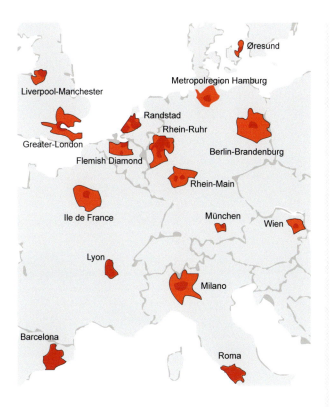

i.4c

up to 600 kilometres

Space-Infrastructure-*Economy*

i.4 – 2002 – Scales of regional challenges: South Wing, Amsterdam–Antwerp, Eurocore and European regions

Contemporary spatial challenges manifest themselves in terms of regions rather than countries or administrative units. The problem though is that regions often lack an administrative authority, making it difficult to make agreements on that level. The South Wing increasingly functions as a daily urban system with a range of 30 km or more, setting new challenges for planning. Relations between Amsterdam and Antwerp via the west flank of the Randstad area and the Flemish Diamond are about functional economic relations such as 'mainports', but also historical and cultural connections expressed in a common language, Dutch. As a megaregion, the Eurocore (a term coined by the design firm OMA) is Europe's most densely populated area. This area encompasses Amsterdam–Rotterdam, Ruhr–Cologne, Brussels–Antwerp and Lille and is Europe's largest delta. A unique characteristic compared to metropolises such as Paris and London is that the area does not contain any large metropolises. At the Western European level, the region functions as a collection of regions. This region of regions is an economic core area for a future European identity. It constitutes the heart of the financial, knowledge and fashion markets – Europe's industrial powerhouse. The challenge here is to look for unity in diversity.

- The South Wing increasingly functions as a daily urban system with a range of 30 km or more (see i.4a) …
- Relations between Amsterdam and Antwerp via the west flank of the Randstad area and the Flemish Diamond are about functional economic relations such as 'mainports' (see i.4b) …
- As a megaregion, the Eurocore (a term coined by the design firm OMA; see i.4c) …
- At the Western European level, the region functions as a collection of regions (see i.4d).

F1.1

COAST

1

COAST

RIVERS

1.1 – 2006 –

Coast and rivers: delta

The Southern Randstad lies where the major Dutch rivers flow into the North Sea. This makes the coast a main element in the identity of the region.

The Coast

If there is one discipline that is responsible for the perception that the Dutch have made their own country, it is water engineering. Water engineers transformed the marshy western part of the Netherlands into habitable and prosperous land. Even so, in 1953 there was a major flood that devastated parts of the south of the province of Zuid-Holland and the neighbouring province of Zeeland. The years that followed saw the construction of the famous Delta Works, a series of imposing dams that close off the sea inlets in the delta, either permanently or when there is a danger of flooding.

The coastal dunes and the Delta Works protect the Dutch against the raw power of the sea, but this sense of security was short-lived. In 2006 Al Gore raised the alarm with his film *An Inconvenient Truth*. By then the Netherlands was already preparing the successor to the Delta Works, called the Delta Programme. It had become clear that the world was warming and that it would not be easy to stop climate change. The melting of the Arctic ice cap would cause sea levels to rise. The Delta Works would keep the sea at bay for some time to come, but the protection afforded by the coastal dunes would soon not be enough.

Given the long tradition of land reclamation it is not surprising that the sea had come into the picture on numerous occasions as a source of additional land for the Randstad. Climate change cast that in a whole new light. The priority was now strengthening the coastline – but not at the expense of the much-loved dune landscape. And the seaside resorts were not to be cut off from the beach, either. Regional design provided a way forward.

'By making space available for morphological and natural processes you can create quality near the city.'

*Arjan van de Lindeloof, landscape architect
at the Province of Zuid-Holland*

__ Takeaways from this chapter

The sea level is rising and the world's deltas are rapidly urbanising, which makes it all the more urgent to develop sustainable systems for protection against flooding. Experience in Zuid-Holland shows the added value of approaching flood protection as a design task. What can we learn from this?

- Technical engineering solutions and high-quality designs for public gathering places with amenity value can go comfortably hand in hand. Nature and good engineering have proved to be perfectly compatible. Building with nature is a revolutionary coastal defence technique which can also be used to reclaim new land.
- Regional and local design can help to combine the different values and emotions found in coastal areas into a unified future vision and lay the basis for implementation plans.
- Regional designs can unite public authorities and other players at all levels around a shared narrative, a common compass. In this chapter we show how the regional authority used 'soft power' to move projects forward, contribute to national objectives for coastal protection *and* add value at the local level.
- Regional designing is not simply or primarily about making a plan, but about helping to determine the political agenda: what conceivable futures are there beyond the immediate solving of an apparently technical problem; what is the real challenge; at what scales and with which parties should we work?

F1.2

1 _Camouflaged innovation

The province of Zuid-Holland draws millions of visitors every year to its coast, with its wide beaches and extensive dunes. People are attracted by the region's natural beauty and impressively restored boulevards, but few are aware of the state-of-the-art coastal management techniques behind all this. From the dunes at Monster, not far from the south beach at The Hague, a sandy peninsula can be seen behind a calm lagoon, where kite surfers, horse riders and other recreationists can often be seen enjoying themselves. Invisible to the naked eye, however, is the way the peninsula itself moves. Sand silts up, is washed away and slowly drifts in a northerly direction along the coast. The shallow water and the sand create a seabed ecosystem that is similar to the Wadden Sea mudflats and which attracts large numbers of seabirds and fish. This is the Sand Engine (*Zandmotor*). It seems a bit of a shame that it will all have been washed and blown away in a few decades, even though that is its purpose. Much of the pumped-up sand will then be on the beaches and dunes of Delfland further north, helping to protect the coastline (see Figure 1.2a–d).

The new boulevard at Scheveningen, at the north beach of The Hague, looks like an elegant, carefully designed coastal promenade. What you cannot see is how the components will separate in the event of a superstorm so that any loose objects are not so heavy that when blown around they will damage the coastal defences. Further north, the row of dunes in front of the boulevard at Katwijk are not particularly impressive, until you realise that there are cars parked inside the dunes. These are world class achievements in the coastal reinforcement projects carried out around the beginning of this century, made necessary by climate change prognoses indicating how much the sea level will rise and what kinds of storms we can expect to batter the coast.

What makes these projects so innovative, though, is the almost casual nature of the actual defences. South of The Hague, the natural defence line of beach and dunes has been reinforced and the Sand Engine keeps replenishing the sand. At Katwijk and Scheveningen the concrete has been carefully camouflaged. At Katwijk, the entrances to the underground car park are the only signs that the dunes are artificial. This seems a logical next step

from the Delta Works, the massive flood barriers along the estuaries of Zeeland south of the Randstad, one which combines safety with other functions. Major civil engineering works were to be part of regional designs and were linked to programmes that would enhance amenity, the economy and nature in the region. However, a roundabout route was needed to achieve this. In the years when protection against the sea appeared to be in order, between around 1980 and 2000, designs for the coastal region looked very different.

2 _ The run-up: Plans for coastal expansion

In 1990 the Province of Zuid-Holland supported the idea of reclaiming land along the Delfland coast between Scheveningen and the Hook of Holland. The Provincial Council adopted a motion to go ahead with a new 'Coastal Location'. This was a political victory for provincial councillor and civil engineer Ronald Waterman, who for ten years had been pushing for an integrated coastal policy based on the principle of 'building with nature', which he described as 'using the forces and materials present in nature'. The practice of beach nourishment in which sand is pumped up from the seabed to recharge the foreshore had taken off in the 1970s; Waterman took this method further, concluding that 'it was possible to shift the coastline towards the sea at certain strategic spots, provided this was in harmony with the natural system of waves and currents.' The Delfland coast was just such a strategic location. The natural sand transport in the sea along this stretch of coast was blocked by a land abutment that reduced wave amplitudes in the waterway leading to the port of Rotterdam, which made the costs of beach nourishment for this stretch of coast relatively high.

But costs were not the only issue for Waterman. His ambitions went further than holding back the rising sea, which he already had his sights on: the Coastal Location was to play a key role in the urbanisation of the Southern Randstad area. In the early 1980s, The Hague was hemmed in between the Westland greenhouse horticulture complex, the Green Heart protected landscapes, the dunes and the Ypenburg military air base, and constrained by the Rotterdam region, with which there was little cooperation at the time. Land reclamation along the coast was an alternative that would create space for tens of thousands of homes, 'clean' employment opportunities and new nature and

1.2 – 2006 – Sand Engine: anticipated development

A joint initiative by Rijkswaterstaat (the government agency for environment, infrastructure and water management) and the Province of Zuid-Holland, the Sand Engine is an example of 'building with nature'. In 2011, 21.5 million cubic metres of sand was pumped up and deposited on the coastline. The sand will disperse naturally across beaches and dunes in the course of a few decades, rendering annual beach nourishment unnecessary. The programme is experimental. The first ten years have been promising.

recreation areas. In the mid-1980s, a steering committee led by provincial executive member Borgman elaborated the idea. Many thematic studies were carried out, which were integrated into three urban planning models. This resulted in a preference for the so-called Wedge or Bar variant, with a surface area of 2,500 hectares of new land and 2,000 hectares of dune lakes, inland seas and lagoons (see Figure 1.3d).

An intense public debate ensued, as many were not convinced by the need for the proposal, or indeed its feasibility or desirability. The confirmation motion by the Provincial Council was not passed until the Dutch government had started preparations for the future VINEX housing districts. In 1994, the minister of transport, public works and water management and the minister of spatial planning voiced their support for a long-term feasibility study. A year later, the study was ready, complete with a new urban design by an external firm, KuiperCompagnons (see Figure 1.3b). The conclusion was that the Coastal Location 'could contribute substantially, both quantitatively and qualitatively, towards resolving issues facing the old land' at costs that were 'within acceptable margins'.

Since 1995, Dutch companies have been reclaiming land and creating islands across the globe, but the Coastal Location failed to materialise because there was no compelling motive. The consequences of climate change were not yet fully appreciated and urban development pressures could be accommodated more cheaply and quickly on existing land, even in existing urban areas. In the past twenty years, land reclamation on this scale has remained limited to Maasvlakte 2, which provides the port of Rotterdam with room for growth. Meanwhile, the coastal visions remain on the back burner. In 2006, the urban design and landscape architecture practice West 8 and the engineering firm Grontmij presented a plan entitled Happy Isles (see Figure 1.3c), a variant on the Coastal Location which extends over a distance of 300 kilometres from Den Helder in the north to Ostend in Belgium. In 2007 the Innovation Platform headed by Prime Minister Balkenende called for an island to be built in the shape of a tulip, analogous to the famous palm island built by Dutch companies in Dubai and intended as a showpiece of Dutch engineering skills. Both initiatives soon fizzled out, but they continued to breathe life into ideas about coastal expansion. The stage was set for the Sand Engine, which came a few years later.

1.3 – 1980-1995 - Designs for coastal expansion

Over the years, numerous plans have been made for coastal expansion. Plan Bhalotra (1995) was commissioned by a public-private steering committee chaired by the province, in which the Stichting Nieuw Holland foundation was also represented. The plan was produced by KuiperCompagnons in collaboration with engineering firm DHV and financial advisors from Coopers & Lybrand. The Stichting Nieuw Holland foundation, with its roots in industry, had revived the first Waterman Plan of 1980, which had been put on a backburner during the economic crisis of the 1980s. In 1995, landscape architects West 8 designed the alternative Buckthorn City plan for the coast, based on the gradual development of an urban island, but without a final plan. Ten years later, West 8 designed another plan entitled Happy Isles, in the style of the Wadden Islands, and MP Joop Atsma suggested the idea of creating an island in the shape of a tulip. These are just a few of the numerous initiatives.

1.3a – *1995 – Duindoornstad (Buckthorn City) by West 8*

Shaping Holland - The coast   31

1.3b – *1995 – Coastal Location: Bhalotra plan*

1.3c – *2006 – Happy Isles by West 8*

Towards an integrated coastal policy for Zuid-Holland

- Primary road with number
- Major highway with number
- Secondary road
- Local road
- Ring road
- Future major highway
- Future secondary road
- Railroad with station
- Tramway in coastal zone development area
- Potential metro
- Canal (>6m)
- Canal with inland navigation function
- Solid seawall element
- Municipal boundary
- Topographic elements
- Ferry
- Building area
- Industrial area
- Potential industrial area
- Silt depot
- Agricultural & Greenland area
- Greenhouse area
- Woodland, park, public green
- Dunes
- Beach
- Tidal flat
- Lake
- Water depths
- Bathymetric contour
- Interesting site in the coastal development area
- Lighthouse
- Port & harbour related activities
- Building site
- Recreation & tourisme

1.3d – *1980 – Waterman Plan*

Plan 1 © R.E. Waterman Topographic map may 1980 - feb 2008

> *'Coastal interventions must be in tune with the emotions evoked by the coast. The Sand Engine moves. Sand, wind and water, the feeling of freedom – it makes perfect sense. The Coastal Location project underestimated these emotions.'*
>
> *Koos Poot, formerly at the Province of Zuid-Holland, currently at the Ministry of Infrastructure and Water Management*

3 _Working in a landscape that has emotional value

The pressure of urban development was not the only aspect about which advocates of the Coastal Location were mistaken. They appealed to a fascination for innovative engineering in the context of the Dutch tradition of living with water and creating land, but for the public, the sea, the beach and the dunes represented the last vestiges of unspoilt nature. The design choices for the Coastal Location were diametrically opposed to this view, employing a design language consisting of geometric residential areas (see Figure 1.3a). Reference images showed high-rise buildings adjacent to high-quality public transport stops. The suggestion that the old coastline would remain intact did not count for much, as new buildings would block the view of the horizon and the waves on the open sea would be replaced by ripples on an inland lake. Wim de Bie, a nationally renowned comedian from The Hague, gave opposition to the proposal a voice in the personage of Wamla le Brinno, chief of the Cananefates. On behalf of the Netherlands' oldest tribe, he predicted an act of divine revenge in the form of a Terrible Spring Tide.

The feasibility study comprised an urban design proposal at the regional scale, but that did not make it a fully fledged regional design. It was limited to the Coastal Location itself and introduced dimensions and a scale that differed from those of the existing coastal landscape. It virtually ignored effects on landscape values, urban development and infrastructure. Commissioning practice and governance (i.e. how responsibilities are divided and how communities are to be involved) were left out of the picture. Laying these conflicts bare, however, is one of the roles of exploratory regional design, which not only investigates the spatial possibilities and financial feasibility, but also puts the desired or expected spatial development into context: the reasons why parties are committed to it and the values that an area represents to society.

In his role as chief of the Cananefates, De Bie put the message across in no uncertain terms: the sea is timeless and inviolable. Nowhere in the Netherlands can the elements be experienced as intensely as along the coast. This unparalleled quality is precisely what is so valuable. Too many permanent buildings would tame and 'civilise' the coast, which is why any such proposals meet with resistance. The Sand Engine, on the other hand, has received almost

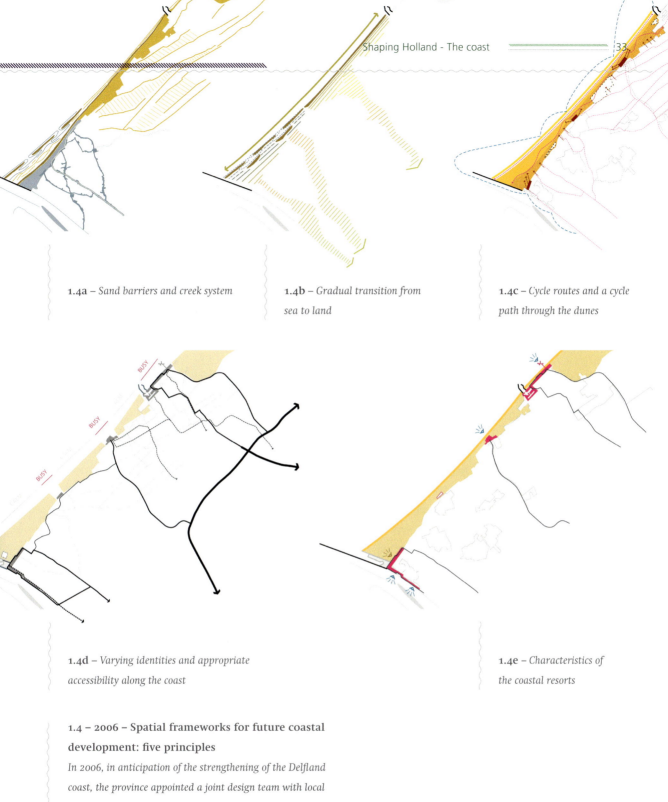

1.4a – Sand barriers and creek system

1.4b – Gradual transition from sea to land

1.4c – Cycle routes and a cycle path through the dunes

1.4d – Varying identities and appropriate accessibility along the coast

1.4e – Characteristics of the coastal resorts

1.4 – 2006 – Spatial frameworks for future coastal development: five principles

In 2006, in anticipation of the strengthening of the Delfland coast, the province appointed a joint design team with local and national government organisations and urban design practice MUST to explore opportunities to raise the overall quality of the coastline. This series of maps shows the basis for the quality uplift: the meeting of delta coast and sand coast in the subsurface, the reinforcement of the gradual transition from sea to land, possible new cycle routes (including a cycle path through the dunes), differentiation between busy and quiet in relation to accessibility, and differentiation in the nature of the various coastal resorts.

'Municipalities, water authorities and Rijkswaterstaat each have their own culture, perspective and responsibilities, and they are not automatically aligned. In its approach to the weak links the province has taken on a very important mediating role.'

Edith van Dam, formerly at the Ministry of Infrastructure and Water Management, currently at the Province of Zuid-Holland

universal praise. It too is a human intervention, but the interaction between sand, wind and water shows how natural forces act upon each other. The Netherlands has been shaped by human society and owes its prosperity to the constant battle against the water, but apparently even the people of the Netherlands feel the need to leave something that engenders a sense of awe and wonder.

4 _A different approach

Laat de Kust met Rust (Leave the Coast in Peace), was the title of a 1997 book in which over sixty people voiced their opposition, in writing and in pictures, to construction along the coast. But even before the ideas for a Coastal Location had receded into the distance, it became clear that the coast was not going to leave us in peace. At the beginning of this century, various locations were identified at the national level where the coastal defences either did not meet the flood protection standards or would fail to meet them in the fore- seeable future. This was done in response to the introduction of stricter statutory requirements and the expected implications of climate change. Six of these weak links were situated in the province of Zuid-Holland. It was the responsibility of the water

authorities to bring these weak links up to the required safety standards, but they were not to be purely engineering solutions; the works also had to bring about a general improvement in spatial quality – the quality of the coastal and urban landscape. National government asked the provinces to take the lead in setting up integrated planning studies for the weak links. It put forward three basic strategies: consolidation (in other words, strengthening the sea defence at the existing location), seaward reinforcement and landward reinforcement.

Having learnt its lesson from the experience with the Coastal Location, the Province of Zuid-Holland decided not to jump straight into working on solutions. Design analyses were required to show the composition of the coast and how it functions, its connection with the hinterland and the interrelationships between seaside resorts and dune areas (see Figure 1.4). The development opportunities could then be deduced from the resulting information (see Figures 1.5 and 1.6). Over the years, such analyses have been carried out at various scales: for the weak links separately, for the coastline in the Zuid-Holland region, and for the entire Noord-Holland and Zuid-Holland coast. The approach to design was consistently

1.5 – 2005 – Integrated development strategies for the coast

This 'framework map' from the study entitled Lines in the Sand (Lijnen in het Zand) visualises the structure of the Zuid-Holland coast. It shows three types of coastline (Delta coast, Delfland coast and Holland's bow-shaped coast). Based on the current spatial and functional situation and accessibility, this map lays a foundation for the future development and use of the coastal zone and for testing the safety options for the weak links against spatial development options. The map shows three options for the future development of the Delfland Coast.

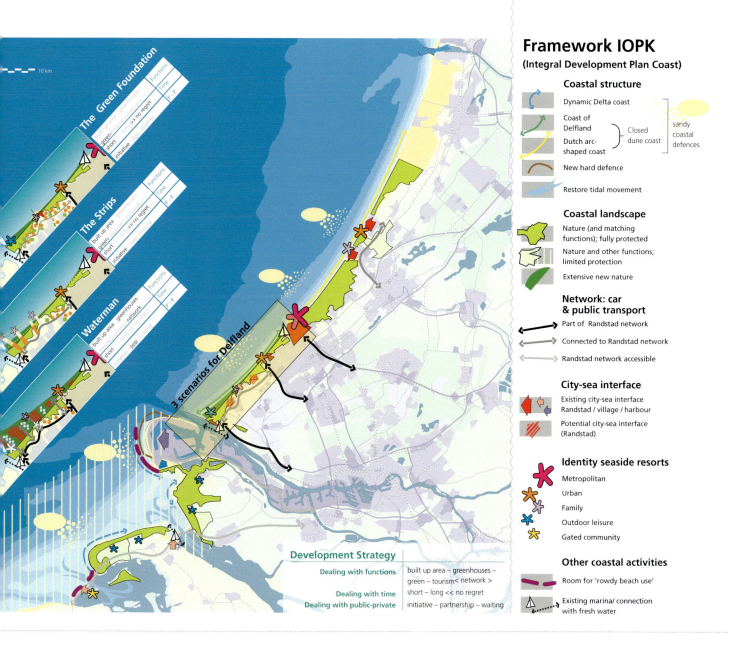

'It's fascinating to see how a city like The Hague has been shaped by the coast in a very different manner from the Westland area behind the Delfland coast, for example. The underlying landscape determines our current approach to coastal development.'

Klaas Hilverda, landscape architect at the City of The Hague

1.6 – 2009 – Possible spatial future for 2050:
Delfland coast

Around 2010, the province was working on Integrated Spatial Projects in various parts of Zuid-Holland. These area-based programmes functioned as a driving force for coordinating local and regional investments and developments. This future vision for the Delfland coastal programme is the result of a scenario study by MUST which explored the possibilities for the development of coast and hinterland taken as a whole.

exploratory. Steering committees and project teams consisting of a range of disciplines supervised the work to ensure that the results were realistic and could count on broad support. The services of external design bureaus were often enlisted and an advisory committee or design studio acted as principal so that conclusions could be announced before provincial executive members and other public officials had to commit to them politically.

Armed with this design and research work, Zuid-Holland set out to tackle its six weak links. Thanks to the insights into the spatial opportunities and characteristics, the province was able to effectively coordinate progress in these areas, showing hesitant municipalities how strengthening the coastal defences could bring local ambitions to fruition rather than frustrate them. It was also able to involve the water authorities – traditionally down-to-earth technical organisations – in an approach that served multiple goals. In Noordwijk, Katwijk and Scheveningen, reinforcement of the coastal defences took the form of a concrete dike. The City of The Hague took the opportunity to build a stepped boulevard, designed by renowned Spanish architect Manuel de Solà-Morales, which reconnected the old fishing village of

'Residents of The Hague who live west of the Laan van Meerder-voort "live on the coast". Elsewhere in The Hague you live, despite appearances, "not far from the coast". So how do we ensure better cross-connections between the coast and the polder?'

Steven Slabbers, landscape architect at Bosch Slabbers

Scheveningen to the beach. In Noordwijk and Katwijk, the dike was concealed beneath new dunes. The economy of the resort of Katwijk in particular received a significant boost from the combination of a wider beach and a car park in the same dune, next to the actual sea wall (see Figure 1.7). On the islands of Goeree-Overflakkee and Voorne-Putten the weak links in the coastal defence were less closely connected to seaside resorts, which meant there was room to raise the existing flood defence in combination with additional beach nourishment.

At the weak link at Delfland, where the Coastal Location had been proposed, it was finally decided to broaden the beach and dunes. In 2006, a study for the House of Representatives determined that while coastal expansion with large-scale new housing might be economically feasible, there was insufficient public support for it. However, there was support for 'seaward reinforcement' of the coastal defences that would benefit nature and provide recreational opportunities. The province concluded from this that the coastal expansion should benefit the local area, not just in terms of increased safety but also the daily life of residents and visitors. The Delfland Water Authority 'improvement plan' provided for additional dunes

with a wet dune valley, the relocation of beach pavilions to the new coastline and the extension and partial rerouting of the beach entrances. The 42 hectares of new dunes was also meant to offset the impact on nature of the new Maasvlakte 2 port area, which was reclaimed from the sea (see Chapter 6). The benefits to residents and visitors came from the province, one example being a new cycle path making the new row of dunes and the coast more pleasant and easier to access.

That cycle path symbolises the new approach. As the primary purpose of the dunes is to provide defence against the sea, a cycle path might not seem to be an obvious development. Recreational use can disrupt sand erosion and accretion processes and the growth of vegetation, while also putting additional demands on maintenance and management. In previous years, however, it had become clear to what extent people valued the coast and felt connected to the coastal landscape. Sea, beaches and dunes are highly valued parts of the living environment – also for people who live in the urban hinterland. That provided sufficient justification for the province and the water authority to make a special effort to make the new sea defences accessible for recreational use.

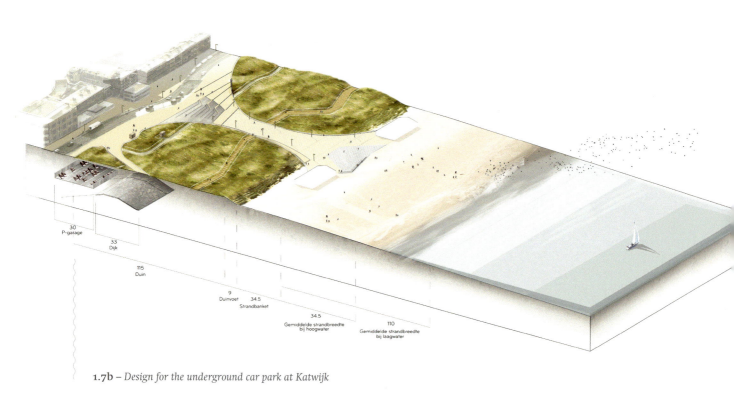

1.7b – *Design for the underground car park at Katwijk*

1.7a – *Masterplan for the weak link at Katwijk*

Shaping Holland - The coast 39

1.7c – *Photomontage of the design by OKRA: Voorstraat*

1.7 – 2016 – Designs for the 'weak link' at Katwijk
After the weak links along the Dutch coast had been identified, integrated solutions were sought that would improve the quality of the coastal resorts and the dunes. The design for Katwijk has become an iconic coastal defence reinforcement project.

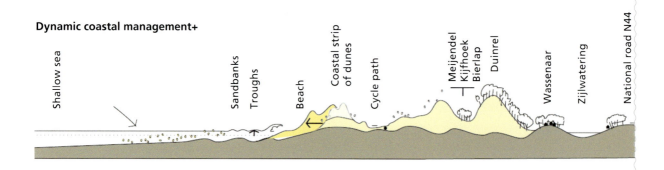

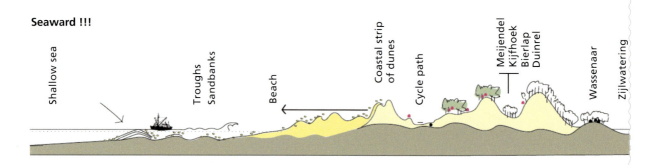

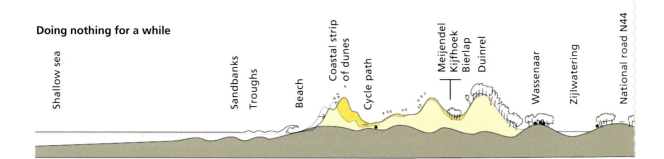

1.8a – *Profiles of the coast for three scenarios*

1.8 – 2011 – Coastal Quality Studio

The Coastal Quality Studio (Atelier Kustkwaliteit) was a collaborative partnership between the Coast subprogramme of the Delta Programme, the Provinces of Noord-Holland and Zuid-Holland, the City of The Hague and TU Delft, and was funded by the Netherlands Architecture Fund. The output from the studios provided input for national policy for the coast. The study aimed to reveal how coastal reinforcement could enhance the quality and character of the 'quiet' landscapes. Three scenarios were developed, each with its own characteristic coastal profile. The three scenarios by the Coastal Quality Studio are a typical example of exploratory and strategic research-by-design. Various area-based challenges are brought together in maps and sketches made of possible development directions. The research set the agenda for a quality-based approach to coastal development.

1.8b – *Coastal landscapes: collage of a dynamic dune area*

1.8c – *Coastal landscapes: collage of seaward development*

1.8d – *Spatial scenario 1:*
Dynamic coastal management +

- swimming beach / undisturbed beach > fully accessible
- dynamic dune landscape > nature to forage about
- drinking-water dunes > nature / sanctuary > limited access
- forested dune landscape > accessible on the paths
- recreational village centres with facilities > fully accessible
- reinforcement of recreational and ecological connections in the hinterland
- amusement parks, golf course, recreation with overnight stays, campsites
- military areas > no access / limited access
- main recreational routes
- boulevards

Shaping Holland - The coast 43

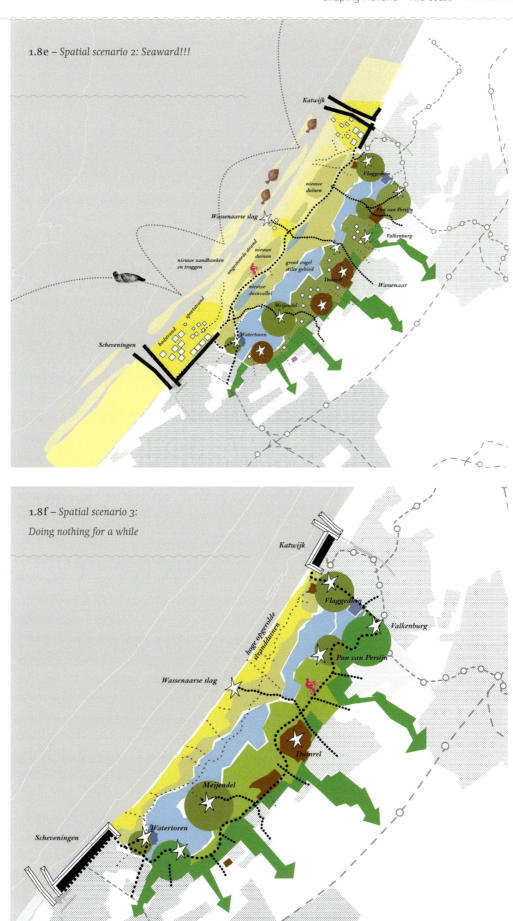

1.8e – *Spatial scenario 2: Seaward!!!*

1.8f – *Spatial scenario 3: Doing nothing for a while*

'The political and public debate on coastal development may give rise to a new wave of regional design, with a new legend. How do we make the dunes and the coast accessible? Should we include tourism and recreation or not?'

Eric Luiten, former provincial advisor for spatial quality in Zuid-Holland

The Sand Engine appeared shortly afterwards as an experimental way to maintain the sand reserves along the Delfland coast for decades to come. The Sand Engine has proven to be the crowning glory of all these efforts. The philosophy of 'building with nature', once the mainspring of the Coastal Location with its 40,000 homes, has now taken shape in an ecologically highly effective way and which undeniably provides an added bonus for residents and visitors alike.

5 _Distinctive quality of the metropolitan area

Sometimes regional design leads to the conclusion that it was unnecessary after all. The integrated development perspective for the Zuid-Holland coast entitled Lines in the Sand (*Lijnen in het Zand*, see Figure 1.5), published in 1975, was an exploratory study by planning consultants Nieuwe Gracht into the possibilities for combining the approach to the weak links with exploiting development potentials and improving spatial quality in the coastal zone. The authors noted that there was 'no reason to consider developments at a level exceeding the scale of the three sub-areas (Delta coast, Delfland coast, Scheveningen–Noordwijk coast).' The options they formulated for various spots along the coast 'mainly

have local effects and can easily be connected to one of the weak links.' And that was how the weak links were tackled – in tune with local values and ambitions and not so much through a process of regional coordination.

This was only possible thanks to the integrated thinking about the coast at various regional scales set in motion by a succession of design studies. The additional investments in spatial quality were considerable and their worth was proven through the combination of local and supra-local significance. The coastal defences are spectacular features in the development of the coast as an extended nature reserve and elongated public space, vital for quality of life and economic development in a large part of the province. Regional design studies have translated this supra-local significance into opportunities and values at the local level, enabling the provincial government to unite parties behind ambitions that transcend separate interests and values.

Coastal defence is ensured again until 2050. All the sea defences meet the current standards. But that does not mean that no more work needs to be done on coastal design. The significance of the coastal landscape for the metropolitan region only seems to be increasing, while the use of the sea is

intensifying, wind farms being the most visible evidence. At the same time, the rate of climate change makes it imperative to look further ahead than 2050. Meanwhile, at the national level, the Delta Programme and Coast subprogramme are ongoing, with a 'look ahead' to 2100.

The Delta Programme includes a national Coastal Vision, the central aim of which is to keep the coast safe, attractive and economically strong for present and future generations. Important building blocks for this vision came from the research-by-design work by the Coastal Quality Studio (see Figure 1.8a–f), a joint workplace shared by a number of government authorities, TU Delft and the Van Oord dredging company set up on the initiative of the provincial governments of Noord-Holland and Zuid-Holland. One of the things it did was to investigate methods for embedding the additional safety task within the integrated approach to environmental quality and how this can be anticipated in the further development of seaside resorts. Sand was to play the main role. It appeared that replenishment and natural sand transport in sea could not only be used to improve safety but also to enhance the natural environment, recreational possibilities and the landscape.

Whereas the 2005 Lines in the Sand vision still led to the conclusion that designing at larger regional scale levels was not opportune, things might well have changed in that respect (see Figure 1.10). Dunes, beaches and the sea give the Randstad area a unique quality. Now that it has proved to be possible to combine coastal protection with improvements to the natural environment, recreation and the landscape, this contribution to the urban living environment can be increased further.

F1.4

Looking ahead to 2100: The Delta Programme

In 2007 the Dutch government appointed a commission of top experts to advise on protecting the country against the consequences of climate change. Besides long-term flood risk management, their brief was also to embody the social value of a climate-proof Netherlands. The threat is not just from a rising sea level, but also from peak river discharges and increasingly erratic weather patterns. In 2008, having explored a number of scientific climate scenarios, the commission recommended making further investments in coastal safety, freshwater supplies and the retention of river water during peak discharges. In the preceding years the Weak Links (*Zwakke Schakels*) programme for coastal safety and the Room for the River (*Ruimte voor de Rivier*) programme to prevent flooding from the rivers had laid the foundation for a more integrated approach. Examples from the Weak Links programme have been given a prominent place in this chapter.

The advice of the Delta Commission led to the Delta Programme, which was given a legislative basis in the Delta Act. The annual Delta Programme has been part of the national budget since 2010. It contains decisions made by the government in close consultation with local and regional authorities on the measures to be taken. The implementation of the Delta Programme is an administrative edifice with (1) key decisions at the level of water systems and flood risk management in the Netherlands, (2) area-based strategies with specific packages of measures and complementary decisions – the North Sea coast is one of nine areas, and (3) delta plans with concrete measures for specific topics. The programme is led by a national Delta Commissioner. Each year the Netherlands invests on average 1.25 billion euros in the Delta Programme for construction work, management and maintenance. These investments will continue until 2050 when the Netherlands will be ready for the extreme effects of climate change expected in 2100.

Shaping Holland - The coast   47

1.9 – 2011 – Strategy map for coastal development

Tackling weak links in the Dutch coastal defences brought the coastal defences up to the desirable level of risk by 2050. The Coast sub-programme of the national Delta Programme looks further ahead to 2100. In 2011 the provincial government established a strategic agenda to set out its position in the creation of this Delta Programme. Three integrated policy agendas came out of this: determining how coastal protection can be delivered in future; designing differentiated accessibility to the coast; and preserving the exceptional natural and landscape qualities while providing room for natural dynamics. The South-West Delta has its own particular challenges.

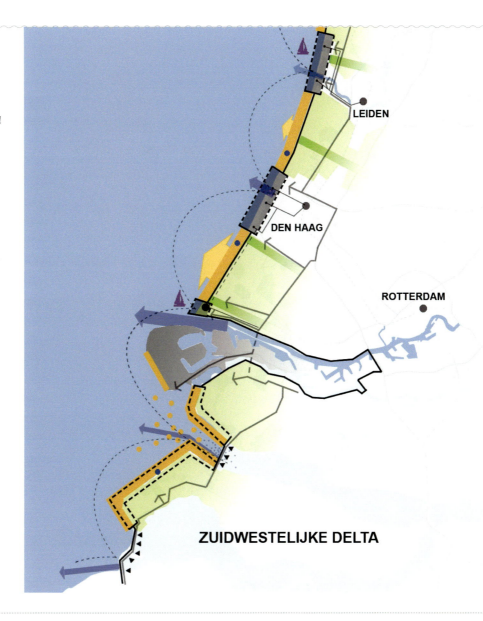

1.10 – 2013 – Scenario for the South-West Delta

The South-West Delta is one of nine subprogrammes making up the national Delta Programme. In addition to the processes geared to taking what were referred to as Delta Decisions, a design studio carried out research-by-design studies to explore the added value of coastal management interventions for other functions and interests. In 2013, landscape architects Bosch Slabbers presented four scenarios based on the rate of climate change and various development pressures.

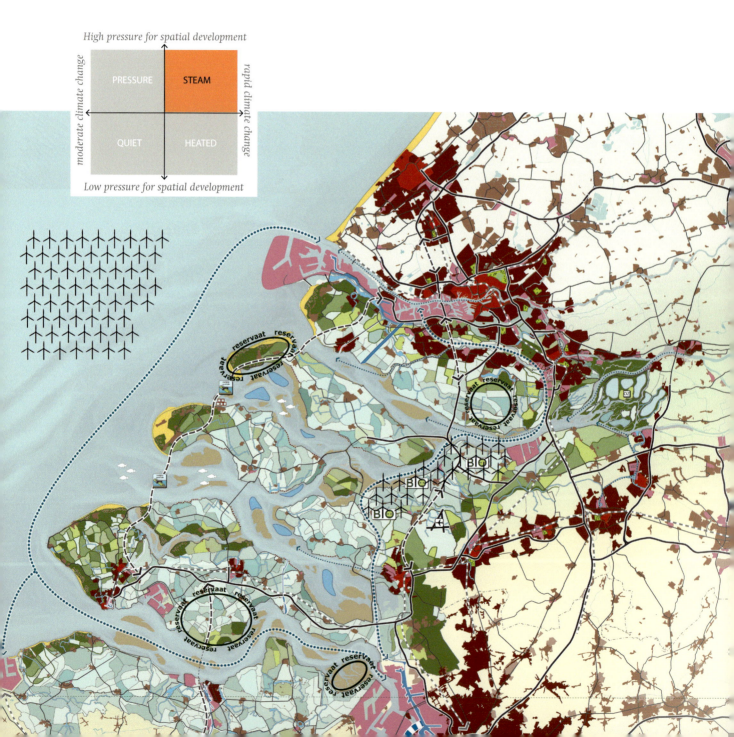

With its alternating wide and narrow rows of dunes, the characteristic structure of the Zuid-Holland coast determines the nature of the regional challenge. The seaside resorts lie sandwiched between wide rows of dunes. Anyone driving from The Hague or Leiden towards the sea will not notice that the coast is nearing until quite late – apart from on sunny days, when this will be apparent from the busy traffic. The wide strip of dunes could provide walkers and cyclists with an experience of nature and the landscape that is rare in an urban region, but at the moment the area is too fragmented. The various functions (sea defence, nature conservation, drinking water resource) have resulted in a segmentation of the dune area. Public access is limited to demarcated areas and a handful of longitudinal routes.

If the coastal zone is to fully realise its significance for urban society, it seems that improvement is needed in two areas: access to the dunes and the quality of the routes toward the coast. Both objectives are included in the strategic agenda for the Zuid-Holland coast (see Figure 1.9). This has to happen without compromising the vulnerable values. Public alarm at permanent building on and behind the beach has already led to the Coastal Pact (*Kustpact, 2017*). As a result, the province tightened its spatial policy by introducing zones

where recreational building is permitted on certain conditions and zones where it must remain quiet. The establishment of the Hollandse Duinen National Park, an initiative by the Dunea drinking water company, is a significant next step in this direction. Recent upgrades of public transport to Scheveningen and the Hook of Holland also fit in with this picture.

Regional design is characterised by permanent visioning and cannot always be placed within a cycle of vision, elaboration, implementation and evaluation. The current situation will give rise to new regional development agendas, structured by new regional design. In the 1990s, the regional designs for the coast set out to open doors and minds and reveal new opportunities through the designs for a Coastal Location. When it became apparent that there was no public support for this, but that the coast did have weak links that urgently needed to be strengthened, regional design contributed by creating connections between various values and approaches. This was a precondition for arriving at integrated solutions at the local level. It now appears that the main need is for an exploratory and graphic type of regional design that shows how the significance of the coast for the living environment in Zuid-Holland can be increased in a responsible manner.

F2.1

URBAN

Urban Growth

2.1 – 1989 – Spatial concept for urbanisation: *Parkstad tussen Hof en Haven?* (Park City between Palace and Port?) *Design study by the province's planning department showing locations for the development of 50,000 homes in the area between Rotterdam, Delft, The Hague and Zoetermeer. The design method can be characterised as a layer approach avant la lettre. The construction of new homes is combined with the creation of a landscape park that reinforces the existing structure of green space and water. Industrial and office development is located along the network of motorways, and greenhouse horticulture in the east. A green wedge prevents the formation of a continuous block of greenhouses.*

During the course of the 20th century the Netherlands produced a number of renowned planners. The best known of these is probably the modernist Cornelis van Eesteren, chair of the CIAM (Congrès Internationaux d'Architecture Moderne) from 1930 to 1947. Others also planned urban extensions that have acquired a heritage status, such as Vreewijk and Pendrecht in Rotterdam-Zuid (designed by Marinus Granpré Molière and Lotte Stam-Beese respectively). The fact that they consist mainly of social housing did not preclude a high quality of design. The traffic-restricted 'home zones' (*woonerven*) from the 1970s and 1980s have also been influential internationally.

This tradition of housebuilding with a social dimension is grounded in the Netherlands Constitution, which states that it is a 'concern of the authorities to provide sufficient living accommodation.' In the 20th century housing corporations and municipal housing departments were mainstays of national government, not only in meeting its responsibility for providing sufficient housing, but also in its constant pursuit of concentrating new development in growth centres.

In the 1990s the government was again faced with the task of building hundreds of thousands of new homes, but now the cards were dealt differently. To meets its constitutional obligations, the government needed investment capital from the market. Moreover, the growing interdependencies between the housing and labour markets in the Southern Randstad made the usual practice of allocating housebuilding programmes across different cities and their agglomerations increasingly untenable.

__ Takeaways from this chapter

The number of people living in cities is increasing worldwide. The challenges of urban growth exceed the responsibilities and capacities of local governments. Regional design is useful for scaling up local growth plans to the regional level and an aid when arranging suitable forms of regional cooperation. The regional scale is where new planning concepts can be created to find a balance between suburban extensions and urban densification. The key takeaways from this chapter:

- Regional design is essential for taking an integrated approach to urban growth. Experiences from the 1990s and 2000s show that an integrated approach to mobility, economic development, green space and housing delivers robust area development concepts. At the same time, these have to meet the twin challenges of climate adaptation and the energy transition.
- Regional design is a laboratory for the development of new urban growth concepts. Urban growth is not a linear planning process; each generation builds on the ideas of its predecessors, the continually changing territory and new societal challenges.
- Regional design links regional growth agendas to territorial values. Place-making based on landscape qualities is just as important as building the required number of houses.
- Regional design can help create opportunities to combine public and private funding and find new ways to balance costs and benefits. It reveals the changes that need to be made in regional cooperation processes.

F2.2

1 _Between Palace and Port: A shot across the bows

More than 120,000 homes were needed for the Rotterdam and The Hague regions alone. The year was 1995, and the Randstad area was set for a new round of urban development. Central government and the two urban regions had concluded agreements known as 'covenants' about where and how the new housing was to be built, where the business estates were to be located, and what infrastructure was needed. The plan was to build some 50,000 new homes within existing urban areas and the remaining 70,000 in what would soon be known as VINEX neighbourhoods, named after the abbreviation for the *Vierde nota Extra*, the 1990 Supplement to the Fourth National Policy Document on Spatial Planning, that set out national policy for this housebuilding programme. These developments would change the urban landscape of the Southern Randstad (see Figures i.1 and 2.2)

Seventy thousand new homes is a lot in a country characterised by towns with populations somewhere between 50,000 and 100,000 inhabitants. A series of new residential neighbourhoods were built within the space of ten years. The Netherlands Environmental Assessment Agency later called these neighbourhoods icons of an era. It considered them successful as long as it was recognised that they were to be suburban rather than urban environments. But the pattern of development could have turned out very differently.

In 1989 the Province of Zuid-Holland presented a design study for the 'intermediate area' between Rotterdam, Delft, The Hague and Zoetermeer, an area just short of 100 km^2. In that design, the construction of 50,000 new homes included the creation of a landscape park that was to reinforce the existing structure of green space and water. This design study was named *Parkstad tussen Hof en Haven?* (Park City between Palace and Port?). The question mark is an indication that this was a radical design that broke away from the planning conventions of the time. The developments were not neatly allocated to each of the city-regions of The Hague and Rotterdam, but were to be shared by both; it was not a plan for sites on the edges of each city but in between them; it was not suburban, but a pattern of alternating urban and green neighbourhoods in a park-like environment served by a metro system (see Figure 2.1).

A brief introduction to housing planning in the Netherlands

Housing planning in the Netherlands is a marriage between quantitative planning for housing programmes and spatial planning focused on urban development concepts such as the compact city – a concept that has long been widely embraced in Dutch planning. This tradition of planned housing development has resulted in substantial but controlled urban growth in the Randstad since the Second World War (see Figure i.1a,b). Dutch planning culture was, and still is, characterised by striving for consensus about the direction of spatial development, a consensus between municipal, provincial and national government, the three constitutional levels of government in the Netherlands. In addition, municipalities generally work together in regions – a scale between province and municipality – which basically work as negotiation arenas. National government maintains a fairly strict division of ministerial responsibilities for housing, infrastructure, nature, etc. and until the early 2000s national spatial planning policy was aimed at integrating these compartmentalised interests, with differing success over the years. During the 2000s this responsibility for integration was effectively decentralised to the provinces and municipalities.

Municipalities have the lead role in making integral land use plans that accommodate urban development or protect areas from development, especially since the 2008 Spatial Planning Act. They work closely together with real estate developers on development plans and during the 2000s acquired land themselves, mainly for housing development. The provinces operate a system of checks and balances on local plans at the regional level through spatial policies, negotiation and regulations for land use plans. Although national and provincial government have the legal tools to overrule municipal plans and impose their own decisions, planning culture dictates that this power is used with restraint. Regional and local housing programmes are generally the result of multilevel coordination and negotiation, a non-linear process in which local plan development, regional housing programmes and regional spatial plans are prepared in an interactive step-by-step process.

The 1990s were an exceptional period for Dutch housing planning. The large housing programme that became known as the VINEX programme was backed by substantial national subsidies allocated to municipalities via the provinces or via regions for each batch of housing completed. National government played a significant role in deciding the locations for urban expansion, based on compact city principles. Public-private partnerships became the norm for developing brownfield sites and urban expansion plans, and complicated contracts were introduced to make sure there was enough funding for public amenities, public transport, roads and green space.

Shaping Holland - Urban growth 57

2.2 – 1997 – New Map of the Netherlands

The New Map of the Netherlands (1997) was a comprehensive map of planned developments and changes of land use in the Netherlands. It presented an educated guess at what a map of the Netherlands in 2020 would look like, based on a trawl of plans from the drawing boards of various organisations, varying from plans for new residential areas (red), new business estates (orange) and nature reserves (green) to infrastructure, and even plans for water storage and wind farms. The professional knowledge organisation for spatial planning Nirov collated this information and produced the map.

In the late 1980s this intermediate area between the two cities was under considerable development pressure. The upcoming housebuilding programme loomed, building in the Green Heart was taboo and the Coastal Location (see Chapter 1) as a potential space for development was a long way off. In the The Hague region, locations were already being prepared to build new neighbourhoods as extensions to existing towns and cities. There were plans afoot for further residential building, infrastructure (including the high-speed rail link to Brussels and Paris and new links in the motorway network), greenhouse horticulture and urban green spaces. Provincial urban planners were concerned for an inextricable tangle of projects that would stifle the tremendous opportunities in this area, which were not restricted to the landscape and urban structure of the area itself; the cities in the South Wing (*Zuidvleugel*) of the Randstad were becoming so interconnected that they were forming a single urban area, and that intermediate area happened to be situated strategically in the networks between the cities.

2.3 – 1994 – Exploration of urbanisation possibilities between Delft and Zoetermeer after 2005
During the 1990s the need for a comprehensive exploration of the potential for urban development in the intermediate area remained. This design proposal is one of the options developed by the province, based on early conceptions of regional transit-oriented development (see Chapter 5).

In Park City between Palace and Port? the province explored the possibilities for integrated development. The design was determined by regional structures, with the ecological structure and the landscape at its core. Lakes, ponds and a mix of peat meadow and woodland areas provided a park-like green structure, which was to lend the new urban area a strong identity of its own. New housing was then planned along the network of a regional rail network connecting the public transport networks of the four surrounding cities.

It was unusual for the province to come up with such an integrated regional design, and ignoring the usual approach to planning was almost unheard of. As far back as the Second World War, national urban development policy had focused on pooling growth, and now there was suddenly a proposal for residential neighbourhoods at an urban density, but set in a park-like environment. This went too far for central government, although the initiative did receive some support at the administrative level. In the 1990 VINEX policy document the government stuck to its own policy of compact cities, or in other words, urbanisation in or directly adjacent to existing cities.

2 _VINEX in practice

In the VINEX policy document, the government divided the housing construction programmes between the major urban regions and designated the main locations for new construction. In many cases, these bordered on an existing city, although there was often the barrier of a motorway to overcome. Central government provided subsidies for land costs, soil remediation and infrastructure. This package of measures was set down in agreements with the metropolitan regions, called 'covenants'. The provinces were the main negotiating partners only for the growth of the smaller towns and cities, which put the *Parkstad* concept out of reach. The provincial government assented to this without too much protest because they appreciated the decisive action taken by Hans Alders, the planning and housing minister, to resolve the housing shortage.

By 2005, 80,000 homes had been built in the urban expansion districts of The Hague and Rotterdam – 10,000 more than agreed in 1995. A substantial number of these were built in the intermediate area between the cities; new neighbourhoods in Delft and Zoetermeer were considered to be for the The Hague region, while Rotterdam's

'You cannot achieve cohesion at the regional level when no one feels responsible.'

Marcel Wijermans, landscape architect at the City of The Hague, previously at the Ministry of Housing, Spatial Planning and the Environment (VROM)

development focused on expanding horticulture-based villages north of its urban core area. As a result, the two regions grew towards each other. In one place the distance between the built-up areas of the two regions is just 100 metres. In accordance with the traditional division of roles, the province attended to the green space outside the urban area, which was a somewhat thankless task. The only remnant of the dreamt-of park landscape of *Parkstad* was a green connecting strip meandering between the new housing in the two urban regions: the Green-Blue Streamer (see Chapter 3). The regional rail network remained limited to conversion of the local railway line between Rotterdam and The Hague to light rail, as a result of which only the VINEX neighbour-hoods in the direct vicinity got a rail connection to both regions (see Chapter 5).

The time was not yet ripe for *Parkstad*, and the design remained embryonic. It was drawn up within a year, which was too quick for municipalities and other stakeholders to take the idea on board and incorporate their own ambitions into it. Soon after the *Parkstad* design study was published, all the attention shifted to the VINEX policy document and so the concept was not taken any further and

did not get the chance to prove its worth. The need for new urbanisation concepts did not disappear with the VINEX, however, and the province kept its eye on the opportunities in the area between Rotterdam, The Hague, Zoetermeer and Delft (see Figure 2.3).

3 _A different language

While developers prepared sites for new construction, the professional world continued to study the development potential of the area. One tried and tested means was the open design competition. Zuid-Holland participated in two competitions. Together with the Ministry of Housing, Spatial Planning and the Environment (VROM) and Nirov, the professional knowledge organisation for spatial planning, a competition entitled *Schakelen & Schakeren* (link, shift and diversify) was organised in 1993, challenging urban planners and landscape architects to come up with a development concept for intermediate areas in general, and that between Rotterdam, Delft, The Hague and Zoetermeer in particular. The outskirts of the Green Heart were the subject of the fourth Eo Wijers competition in 1994, a recurring Dutch competition for regional design. This edition was

'At the time of the Inside Randstad Holland competition, regional design was still geared towards supply and research, a kind of laboratory. Things are very different now. Nowadays, regional demand is central, as well as the commissioning bodies who have to define and shape this demand. Things are closer to implementation, with design as a factory, as it were.'

Ronald Löhr, Plein13 Consultancy, former secretary of the Eo Wijers Foundation

entitled 'Inside Randstad Holland'. The competition formula made it possible to step back from the daily reality of policy and implementation: entrants were free to come up with entirely new solutions.

Entirely new concepts were indeed put forward, both by the five winners of *Schakelen & Schakeren* (see Figure 2.4) and in submissions to the 'Inside Randstad Holland' Eo Wijers competition (see Figure 2.5). Some are enthusiastic and aim to appeal, while others, in contrast, seem intended to shock – saying this is the effect of large-scale urbanisation. These exercises helped to show that the customary spatial planning principles did not have to be slavishly followed, and that a new era perhaps called for a new approach. However, the distance from daily practice was also a barrier to translating them into feasible proposals. The winning entries attracted interest from within the profession, but made little connection with the realities of government. Twenty years later, the results of the competitions have not left any recognisable trace in the developments on the ground.

Around the same time, in 1994, the province conducted its own studies into opportunities for spatial development in the South Wing which were not limited to urbanisation. The public

authorities had other concerns. Construction of the VINEX neighbourhoods was progressing, but the cities in the South Wing were not faring so well. In the policy statement for the future entitled 'More Elbow Room for the South Wing' (*Meer armslag voor de Zuidvleugel*) the province talked of 'relative impoverishment' in some respects, 'whether we are talking about deterioration of nature and the landscape, a decline in some agricultural sectors, the increasing housing shortage, the loss of job opportunities, the increasing inaccessibility of the cities or the decrease in the quality of life in general.'

The single core city and its region as a measure of spatial development no longer matched the realities of social life. The province saw society and economy developing within a larger network of urban regions, which required strategic visioning at the level of the provincial territory (see Figures 2.6 and 2.7).

The province adopted a two-pronged strategy. In the short term, attention was focused on creating favourable conditions for the new VINEX neighbourhoods. For the longer term, the province set its sights on the South Wing as a network, spatially and therefore also administratively. That

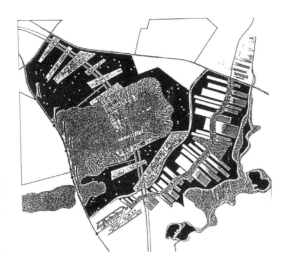

2.4a – *Integrated design for the intermediate area*

2.4 – 1993 – Winner of the Schakelen & Schakeren competition

The intermediate area between The Hague, Rotterdam and new town Zoetermeer was the subject of a competition entitled Schakelen & Schakeren held by Nirov, the Province of Zuid-Holland and the Ministry of Housing, Spatial Planning and the Environment (VROM). The competition was a way of taking the development of the Parkstad concept a stage further. The winning plan offers a range of solutions for the demand for new homes outside the city. At the same time, it addresses issues such as connections with public transport and closed waste and water systems. A precursor to the 'layer approach', the plan is based on two layers: primary (soils and water systems) and occupation. The occupation layer was further elaborated in four spatial solutions.

 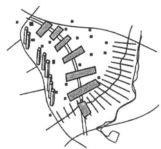

2.4b – *Subsoil layer and occupation layer*

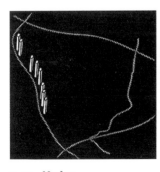 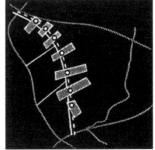 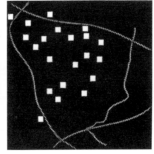 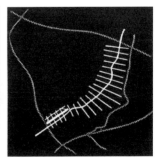

2.4c – **Nodes**
Living at the nodes is intended for mobile people who experience the Netherlands as a single metropolis.

2.4d – **A String of Beads**
Existing settlements and new 'beads' are strung along a dual cable of rail and road in the rhythm of the stations. The beads contain the public services and facilities for the entire area.

2.4e – **The Clusters**
These are autonomous, idyllic little neighbourhoods in contact with nature. Variation in the primary layer creates a variety of residential environments.

2.4f – **The Greenhouse Strip**
The greenhouses are relocated to the southern fringe and environmentally sustainable. Their lighting forms a beacon for planes landing at the new airport.

2.5 – 1995 – Winner of the 'Inside Randstad Holland' Eo Wijers competition: Ladder Metropolis (VHP urban planners and landscape architects)

To accommodate 50,000 homes in the west flank of the Green Heart area, a linear urban development about 25 km wide was proposed, with a second line of infrastructure parallel to the A4. The concept was accompanied by detailed landscape typologies. It was also intended as a warning. 'Do we really want this?' The answer was 'No'. Urbanisation of the landscape on this scale was never seriously considered.

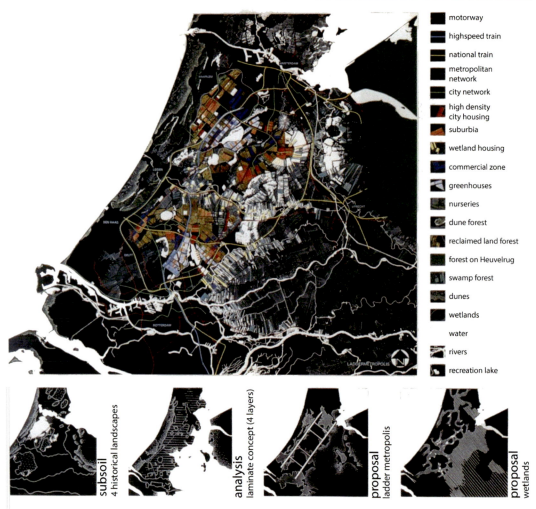

2.5a – *The Green Heart re-envisioned as a Ladder Metropolis*

Shaping Holland - Urban growth 63

2.5b – **The implications of the Ladder Metropolis for the regional landscape north of Rotterdam.** *This includes the Zuidplaspolder, an area that was later identified in spatial policy as a potential site for large-scale urban development.*

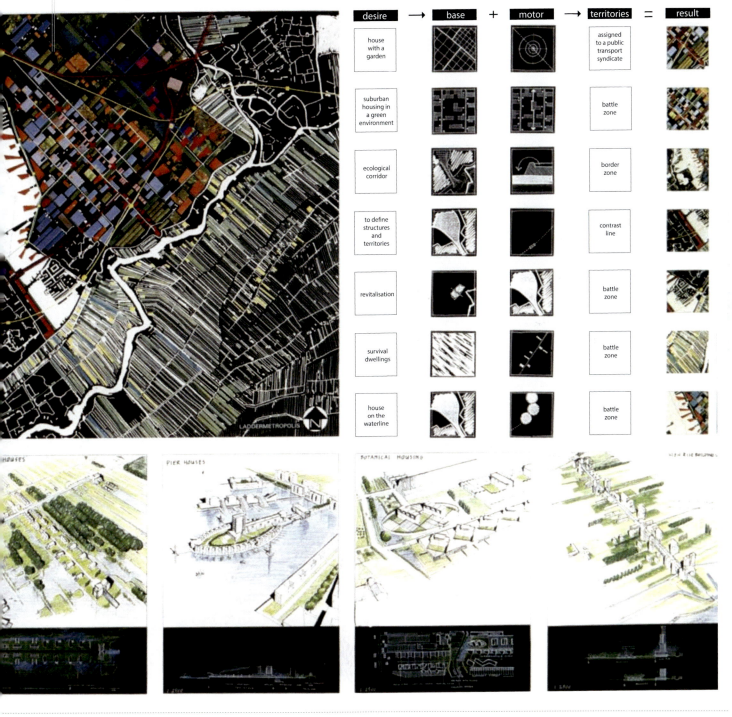

2.6 – 2002 – North Wing and South Wing: different urban systems

In 2002, the chief government architect set up a design studio called Deltametropolis to reconceptualise the Randstad area through design. Three urban design practices set to work. This drawing by design firm OMA breaks down the structure of the urban area into in three regional structures: Amsterdam as the central city in a region, the Oude Rijn river zone as a linear urban system, and the South Wing as a network city.

2.7 – 1994 – More Elbow Room for the South Wing: integrated regional strategy and development of the layers approach (see next page)

As a step towards structural cooperation between the province and municipalities, the province published the policy document 'More Elbow Room for the South Wing' (Meer armslag voor de Zuidvleugel). The spatial concept was highly schematic, leaving much room for interpretation and elaboration of the details. This is one of the earlier examples in which the layer approach was applied to regional design. Since then this approach has been widely adopted in Dutch regional design practice. The vision proceeds from the 'Foundation' of ecology and environment, the 'Network' of economy and mobility, and the 'Tapestry' of homes and urban facilities. The series shown here constructs the schematic strategic vision from five basic schemes arising from these layers.

Shaping Holland - Urban growth   65

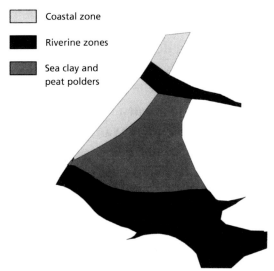

2.7a - *South Wing substratum*

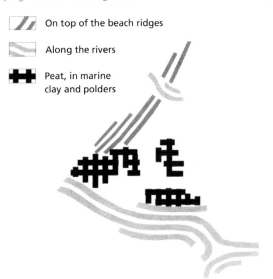

2.7b - *Present urban pattern*

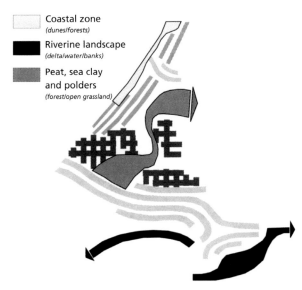

2.7c - *Nature and landscape structures*

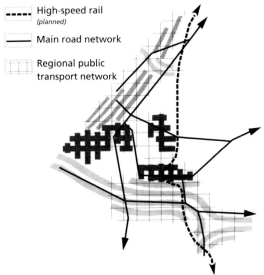

2.7d - *The network of connections*

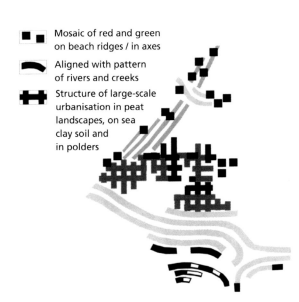

2.7f - *Room for further urbanisation*

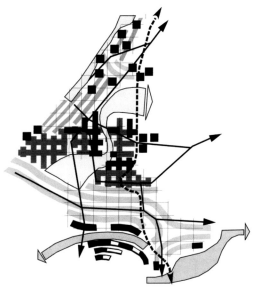

2.7g - *Strategic vision for the South Wing*

'Many regional designs get stuck at that one regional level and are killed by their own perfection. So the trick is to think, design, draw and organise across all scales.'

Ejsmund Hinborch, urban designer and landscape expert at the Province of Zuid-Holland

created the space for a process in which parties worked together for this new future. And this in turn meant a different style of designing from the topographically rather detailed sketches of the *Parkstad* study and the design competitions, one that is more abstract and more concerned with showing connections than with presenting solutions. 'More Elbow Room for the South Wing' did not propose projects, but rather collaboration. As the middle tier of government, the province took on the responsibility for coordinating this cooperative effort.

Together with the five municipal partnerships and Rotterdam and The Hague, the province set up the South Wing Administrative Platform (*Bestuurlijk Platform Zuidvleugel*). In this forum the compact city concept became embedded in a different line of reasoning – one that was about systems and structures, connections and distinctive qualities. Regional development projects were put on the agenda, such as the *Stedenbaan* transit-oriented development programme (see Chapter 5), horti-cultural complexes and the recreation programme *Groen in en om de stad* (Green space in and around the city). The partners collectively supported major projects for individual municipalities whenever these contributed to the international position

or quality of life in the region. This illustrates the administrative impatience of the time, when capital for area development was relatively easy to arrange. The sum of the projects constituted the future vision, not the other way around.

The urbanisation agenda was also back in the picture. In 2001 the government presented the successor to the VINEX policy document, the Fifth National Policy Document on Spatial Planning (*Vijfde nota ruimtelijke ordening*), which was adopted in a significantly altered form in 2006 as the National Spatial Strategy (*Nota Ruimte*). This led to a new housebuilding programme, of which a total of 165,000 new homes were allocated to the South Wing in addition to the homes to be replaced in the areas under redevelopment (the 'restructuring neighbourhoods'). Priority was given to brownfield development, at both national and regional level. The South Wing Administrative Platform focused primarily on transit-oriented development. However, the Platform determined that there was also a need for living environments that could not be provided within existing urban areas, but 'in a rural setting, in harmony with nature, landscape and water.' By 2004 the province had embraced such a dual strategy of densification and expansion in its Provincial Spatial Structural

Shaping Holland - Urban growth   67

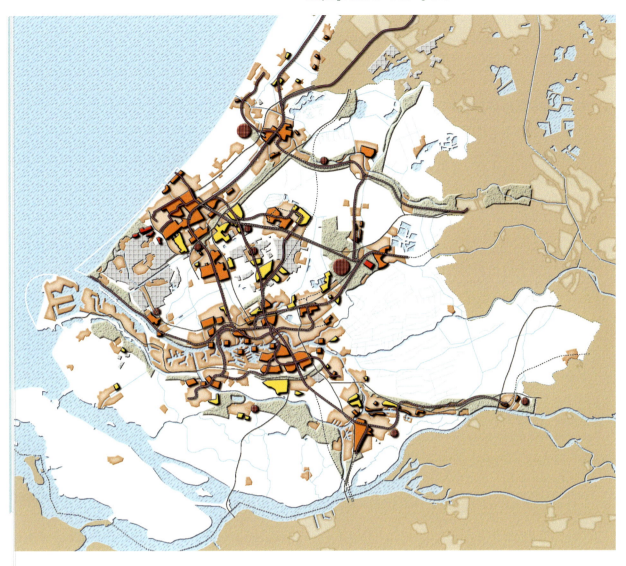

 Current urban expansion plans (VINEX)

 Urban redevelopment agenda

 South Wing public transport network: *supporting urban densification*

 New location for urban expansion

 Search areas for urban expansion

 Transformation and linking zones

2.8 – 2004 – Provincial policy for densification and urban expansion

In 2004 the province embraced a dual strategy of densification and expansion in its Provincial Spatial Structural Vision, the formal planning policy for its territory. A search area approach was used to lay a policy basis for large-scale urban expansion projects, such as the Valkenburg and Zuidplaspolder locations.

'Structure plans offer a framework for accommodating long-term spatial developments more flexibly. They are not supposed to give the impression that it is clear what will happen in the coming decades.'

Frank van Pelt, former programme manager at the Province of Zuid-Holland

Vision (*Provinciale Ruimtelijke Structuurvisie*, see Figure 2.8). A search area approach was used to lay a policy basis for post-VINEX large-scale urban expansion projects, such as the Zuidplaspolder location.

4 _Dilemmas in the Zuidplaspolder

In the Fifth National Policy Document on Spatial Planning and the National Spatial Strategy, the national government embraced the concept of the network city (or urban network), initially at the level of the Randstad and later for the South Wing and North Wing, which opened up the prospect of a different type of urban expansion. In the Fifth National Policy Document, the government opened up the possibility for new housing in the Rotterdam–Zoetermeer–Gouda triangle, north of Rotterdam, mainly projected in the Zuidplaspolder. In 1998, that option was brought forward during an area-based exploration by the South Wing Administrative Platform. It would be possible to create a green living environment not possible within the existing urban area, but for which there was high demand in the region. The government declared that it would be prepared to formally remove this area from the Green Heart, provided that 'a design study to be drawn up by the region can show that

a general improvement in spatial quality is possible in combination with the new development.' The design task was therefore explicitly allocated to the region (see Figure 2.9). Government policy dictated that to bring about an improvement in quality, sufficient attention had to be paid to the development of a green structure – and to rainwater retention capacity, because the building in the Zuidplaspolder has one major disadvantage: it is one of the lowest-lying areas in the Netherlands.

The province chaired a steering committee in which no fewer than twenty-three parties were represented. The lessons of the *Parkstad* study had been learnt: in order to operate effectively in large-scale urban development programmes, more was needed than just a design. From the outset, the provincial government opted for intensive collaboration and an active role. That active role even went so far that the province took risks investing in the acquisition of land for housing development. In the VINEX period, municipalities were still the only public bodies that purchased land for housebuilding.

This type of broadly based and intensive collaboration has an impact on design style. By definition, design is an investigative process.

F2.3

All the partners in the area need to be involved and to be given the opportunity to contribute their own ideas and insights, and to have them tested. They can then converge towards solutions, which they can jointly accept and promote at the end of the process. The layer approach offered an objective point of departure for this process. This analysis and design method emerged in the 1990s with the principle of sustainable spatial development. The basic idea is that the landscape comprises three layers: the primary layer or sub-surface, including water systems and nature; the transport network; and the occupation layer. The primary layer has a slow rate of development and sets the conditions for the layers above it. In turn, the transport network sets the conditions for the occupation layer, particularly urban land uses. In a low-lying landscape such as the Zuidplaspolder, this layer approach is relevant because the groundwater level is relatively high and surplus rainwater has nowhere to go.

The design work for the Zuidplaspolder pursued the participatory process with the *Gebiedsatlas*, an atlas compiled with the aid of a large number of 'knowledge sessions' in the area. In this atlas, the three landscape layers were mapped and described as objectively as possible. This defined the scope for development, the margins of what was possible. In this phase, design was more about acquiring and sharing knowledge than about shaping the future use of the area. At this stage, a public land bank was also established, in which the provincial government, the City of Rotterdam and the five municipalities in the area at that time participated. The first steps were thus taken towards a truly coherent and integrated development. That was important because, in a process with so many parties, the tendency to allocate each party their 'fair share' is never far away and seldom leads to a satisfactory result in terms of the spatial configuration of the development.

The political pressure for site development was high, so planning had to be quick. The initial, collective regional design study was succeeded by the Interregional Structural Vision (*interregionale structuurvisie*), a formal planning document, which was adopted within a year after the *Gebiedsatlas*. The analysis was elaborated into a spatial development vision, with the layer approach remaining key. Relatively high-lying zones were considered for greenhouse horticulture and densely built-up areas, while nature and water predominated in the lowest-lying zones. Parcelling proceeded in accordance with the historical orthogonal

2.9 – 2003 – Spatial concept for the Zuidplaspolder and urbanisation variants
The spatial concept for the Zuidplaspolder is based on the layers approach. The low-lying polder dips down to its lowest point in the south-east, which is almost seven metres below sea level. The central green strip is shown as a kind of plantation landscape, while there is abundant space in the south-eastern corner for marshy areas, where any building should be sparse. The idea was that the scale of the development would be determined by the capacity of the landscape. Within these principles, various options were available for development. The policy documents were based on the Interregional Structural Vision and the Intermunicipal Structure Plan.

landscape pattern. Urban areas were assigned the greatest density around the new train and metro stations.

The design work walked a line between regional and urban design. On the one hand, the process required a conceptual intermediate stage, the design being a voyage of discovery in which all twenty-three parties had to be included. On the other hand, the design ventured into uncharted territory. This was inherent to the nature of the task and to the spatial context: a country living concept that was still unknown to the region and which would not support high densities in every location. The lowest-lying areas of marshy habitats could contain a small amount of building. The middle zone could become a kind of plantation landscape that would gradually transform from an agricultural to an urban environment. To breathe life into this abstract and unknown concept, the designers also produced potential plot layouts and cross-sections. Not least because of pressure of time, something happened that should have been avoided: the regional design gave the impression that the province had imposed detailed designs at the local level, and not everyone felt that their contribution had been taken seriously.

The obligatory next step was to convert the urban and landscape design concept into land uses and planning regulations in a regional spatial plan and an intermunicipal structure plan (*intergemeentelijke structuurplan*), which has a formal legal status. Although the essence of the design was maintained, the subtlety was lost from view. That was not necessarily a problem. After all, the province had put itself in a position, together with the partners in the area development, to maintain control over implementation – in stark contrast to the arrangements in the VINEX covenants. Funding was already in place for all the investments in green space, and for the first elaboration area, the *Rode Waterparel* (Red Water Pearl) in the plantation area, the province, with its partners, was in control of the development process, even though the land was owned by private developers.

History cannot teach us to what extent this approach enabled the province to take the regional design forward in a direct line to implementation as the line was brutally severed by the financial crisis of 2008. That crisis was a sudden trend break that no-one was prepared for. The Zuidplaspolder was no exception and developments took a different turn.

F2.4

Tentative building took place from the existing villages to the edges of the plan area. By the 2020s, after the financial crisis of the 2010s subsided, a substantial proportion of the planned housing development was still on the agenda for the long term. However, new metro lines and stations have been taken off the programme for the time being, and nature development has stagnated. In 2012, national government unexpectedly scrapped virtually all funding for nature and landscape, including for the Zuidplaspolder.

As a consequence of the faltering housing development, the province suffered substantial losses in terms of land value. Designs were then made for alternative development strategies based on the new conditions. The layer approach remains key, but investments in water and nature have been considerably reduced and housing construction is now limited to the village and country styles that by definition cannot be built within the existing urban areas. The land bank still existed in 2019, but the joint implementing organisation had been discontinued, and by 2020 the province only had a role in the development in the capacity of landowner. Administratively, the traditional relationships between province and municipality have been restored. The initiative for the building of housing and employment areas lies with the municipalities, within the frameworks set by the province, while the province is responsible for creating the conditions for urban growth by providing larger-scale infrastructure and green space outside the cities. However, with new urban development programmes on the horizon, the Zuidplaspolder might conceivably be back in the spotlight again.

5 _From laboratory to factory and back

The past crisis tends to colour the current design agenda. Adaptivity is now a key word: designs must be able to accommodate economic fluctuations without compromising their essential quality. Even a development that is abandoned half way through must have quality. The crisis has thrown the value of small-scale urbanisation strategies into sharper relief, while reconsideration of locations for large urban extensions has increased the desire to build on sites within the existing urban area. Strong cities are vital for the new economy, which is based on knowledge and innovation. The regional spatial strategy therefore focuses on strengthening the core axis of the larger region through densification (see Figure 2.10). The target

'The urbanisation agenda is no longer about building neighbour-hoods, but creating cities, improving the urban economy and reducing long-term unemployment, which is still growing in the South Wing. This calls for a regional agenda onto which local politicians and officials can pin their preferences.'

Gielijn Blom, urban designer at the Province of Zuid-Holland

for the proportion of planned new homes to be built within the existing urban area still stands at 80% (Figure 2.11). The remaining out-of-town housebuilding programme also has to be a qualitative addition to the housing market, even more so than in 2000 when the Zuidplaspolder was first put on the agenda. As a rule, open landscapes are no longer sacrificed for the creation of living environments that can also be created within cities or which are already abundant. However, this policy intention is severely tested by the fact that property developers and municipalities have acquired greenfield land holdings.

The context for new development in the wake of the 2008 credit crisis is different from that following the building crisis of the 1980s. Working in public and public-private coalitions is now standard practice and regional cooperation has settled into a new, informal mould. The search for a new urbanisation strategy is a joint effort by national, provincial and local government in which quality is more important than quantity. Urban development must contribute towards a vibrant polynuclear metropolitan region. The municipalities realise that they do not all need to have a wide range of residential and working environments in an urbanised region

such as the Southern Randstad and that this metropolitan network actually gives them the opportunity to develop their own particular qualities and identities.

In recent decades, regional design has been a laboratory for new urbanisation concepts. Results trickle through into practice slowly. Much research work is conducted in the context of the MIRT, the Multi-Year Programme for Infrastructure, Spatial Planning and Transport, in which central government and the region coordinate their investments in spatial development and mobility infrastructure (see Text Box in Chapter 4). However, an investment programme does not automatically lead to a broadly supported integrated urbanisation concept, although this is clearly needed. No laboratory-type research that has to negotiate a tortuous route to reach the boardroom tables is required, but something closer to practice. The design challenge for the 2020s is to bring together the innovations of the MIRT studies and the former South Wing Administrative Platform into a coherent concept that will stand the province of Zuid-Holland in good stead for years to come.

A single central theme runs through a quarter of a century of regional design for urban expansion

'It is quite unusual for regional design, with its long-term orientation, and politics, with its short-term cycles, to come together. Major policy challenges such as brownfield housing development and the energy transition make this more likely. As designers, we have to make sure that we do not miss out on that momentum.'

Walter de Vries, planner at the City of Rotterdam, formerly at the Province of Zuid-Holland

by the Province of Zuid-Holland: the search for alternatives for the regional urbanisation model that has coloured national spatial planning since the post-war reconstruction. The province was looking for alternative concepts that were more devoted to differentiation and quality than production figures, and based more on green and water-rich environments than proximity to a city. Since the experience with the *Parkstad* design study, it also looked for other forms of commissioning practice and for administrative coalitions that know how to take an integrated approach to real estate, infrastructure and green areas. The decentralisation of the Dutch spatial planning system that came into effect in 2011 recognised the role of the province. From being a coordinating and supervising intermediate tier of government, the province became officially responsible for urbanisation strategy and landscape quality. That creates opportunities, but also imposes obligations.

However, you cannot change a system in a day. Even legislative changes and major government policy documents only impact daily practice slowly, unless backed by substantial funding. Within the province itself there was considerable debate as to the path that should be followed. But even

if agreement can be reached on the direction development should take, and the initiative does indeed lie with the province, real change is still a long way off, as the crisis that thwarted the planning for the Zuidplaspolder development shows. The other large regional urbanisation study, *Parkstad*, was a victim of the political forces behind the VINEX programme – but even without the VINEX covenants, that concept still had a long way to go before anything could be built.

2.10 – 2013 – Zuid-Holland urban development axis

The policy narrative of the urbanised area of Zuid-Holland centres on two main spatial structures: the North–South as an axis of urbanisation, and West–East as a logistical-industrial system (see Chapter 6). This 2013 drawing visualises the North–South axis, including the 'knowledge axis', as a graphic representation of policy for the Provincial Spatial Structural Vision.

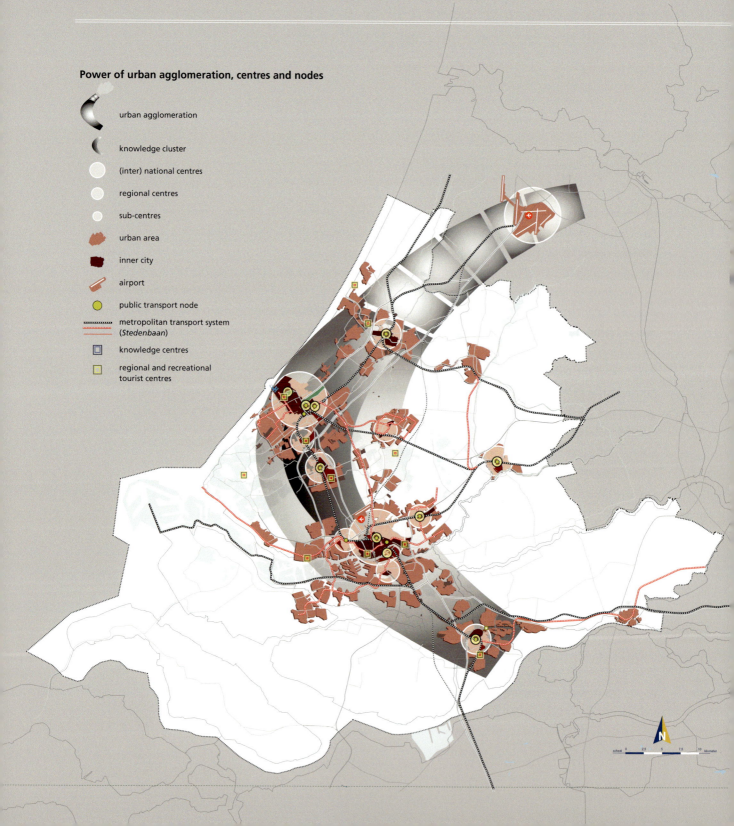

2.11 – 2014 – Densification opportunities in the South Wing as seen by the Deltametropolis Association

In studies, policy and strategy, there has been a continuous search for a balance between the desire for compact development on brownfield sites and the need to find space for urban expansion. By around 2013, the financial crisis had ended and inner urban development was back on the administrative and political agenda. Various parties produced studies in an attempt to demonstrate that the existing urban fabric offers far more possibilities for densification than is generally thought. This map is the result of a study by the Deltametropolis Association in cooperation with the Board of Government Advisors on architecture and the built and rural environment.

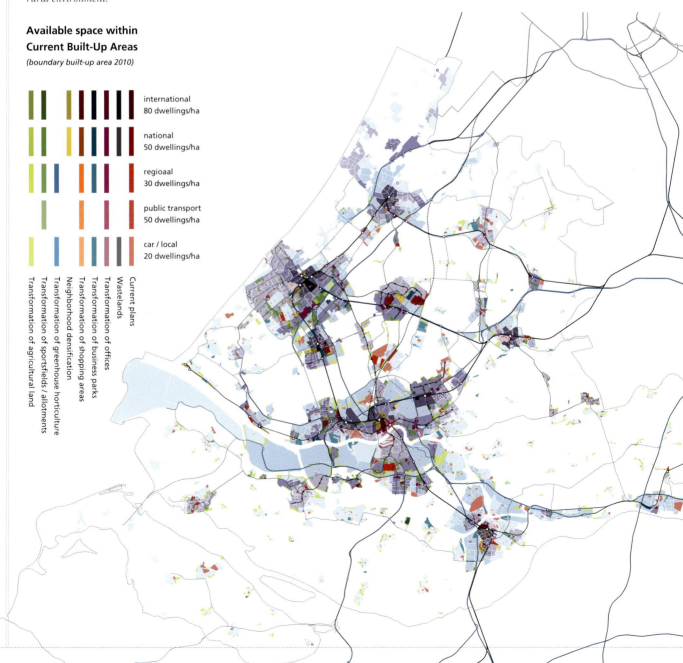

Available space within Current Built-Up Areas
(boundary built-up area 2010)

international 80 dwellings/ha
national 50 dwellings/ha
regioaal 30 dwellings/ha
public transport 50 dwellings/ha
car / local 20 dwellings/ha

Current plans
Wastelands
Transformation of offices
Transformation of business parks
Transformation of shopping areas
Neighborhood densification
Transformation of greenhouse horticulture
Transformation of sportsfields / allotments
Transformation of agricultural land

DSCAPE
3

Landscape

The people of Zuid-Holland love their landscape. The green pastures stretching into the distance, the marram grass swaying in the dunes, the rivers winding lazily through the low-lying polders – all have been widely lauded, written about, painted and photographed. The people of the province are also mostly aware of the fact that there is little in this landscape that can be called truly natural. The area was originally an impenetrable swamp where the rivers changed course at will. The land is habitable because of the polders, which were first created in the Middle Ages. Dikes were built around an area of land and excess water pumped into a ring canal to turn the marsh into workable farmland.

For a long time the landscape and spatial planning were entirely separate worlds. With the adoption of the first urban development policy, planning embraced the goal of keeping rural areas open. But as the use and design of these spaces was the responsibility of other government agencies, new housing estates were often built with their backs to the open countryside. The residents may have been able to look out from their homes across the open countryside, but they were not allowed in it. Moreover, agriculture was made more efficient at the expense of the attractiveness of the landscape.

Over the past twenty-five years the distance between town and country has been reduced and the landscape has become a significant factor in the urban living environment as an expression of regional identity. Globalisation has given this cultural value new relevance – made it something for people to hold on to. Nevertheless, a tradition of 'living apart together' cannot be turned into a truly integrated approach in a day.

F3.3

__ Takeaways from this chapter

Rapid urban growth raises issues concerning the liveability of neighbourhoods. In the face of climate change and with growing interest in health, the provision of well-designed green space and water features (Figure 3.1) in urban regions is becoming increasingly urgent. The transition to sustainable food supply will lead to changing landscapes in and around urban regions across the world. In that respect, the Netherlands is unique: the polynuclear structure of the Randstad means that the open landscape is never very far away. At the same time, every square metre has been touched by human hand, nowhere is nature untamed. In this chapter we show how the landscape can become a relevant aspect of urban development programmes; in fact, it is frequently treated as an urban concept and included as part of the urban space. This chapter contains the following messages:

- Regional design, even in an urban context, starts with the soil and underlying strata. Teasing out the various 'layers' in the landscape helps to draw attention to issues of regional cohesion, ecological capital and the relation between the nature of the soil or subsurface and spatial development.
- Regional design can help stakeholders to assemble relevant landscape values in appealing and shared spatial development visions. Besides the functional values of the landscape, such as for agricultural use, there are cultural, heritage, ecological and amenity values. The landscape is not an empty space ready to be filled in, but a public good.
- Regional design puts the landscape in the picture as a valuable component of the urban region as a counterweight to dominant economic activities such as housebuilding. Regional design takes the new tasks on the regional agenda, such as energy generation, the greening of agriculture and climate adaptation, and translates them into thought-provoking visualisations of the future landscape that provide springboards for political debate.

Shaping Holland - Landscape

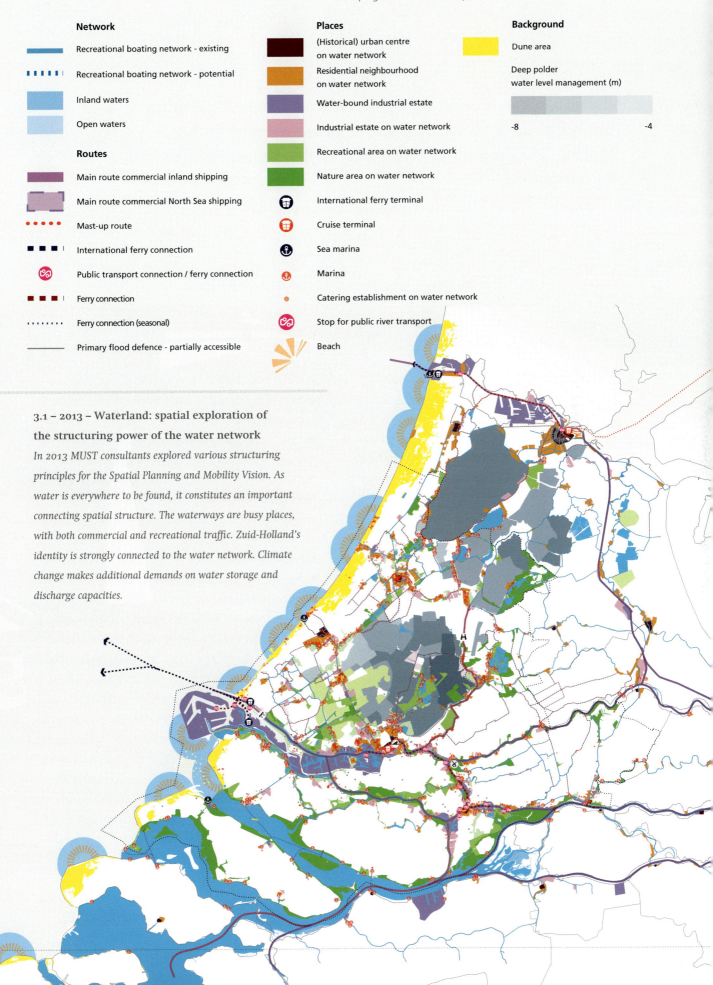

3.1 – 2013 – Waterland: spatial exploration of the structuring power of the water network

In 2013 MUST consultants explored various structuring principles for the Spatial Planning and Mobility Vision. As water is everywhere to be found, it constitutes an important connecting spatial structure. The waterways are busy places, with both commercial and recreational traffic. Zuid-Holland's identity is strongly connected to the water network. Climate change makes additional demands on water storage and discharge capacities.

'Buffer zones were political dogmas. It was a counter-narrative. You had to leave them well alone. A lot went wrong in the province of Zuid-Holland because the buffer zones were neglected for a long time.'

Wim Keijsers, landscape architect at Nieuwe Gracht, previously at the Province of Zuid-Holland

1 _Varying values

Major river deltas are impressive landscapes where land and water are perpetually in motion, creating ideal circumstances for a rich and varied natural environment. At the same time, river deltas world-wide are ideal locations for urbanisation and economic development. People are attracted to the fertile soils and the opportunities for trade and employment in the ports. This is as true in the province of Zuid-Holland as elsewhere. The Rhine-Meuse delta has always been one of the most densely populated areas in what is now Dutch territory, but which was settled long ago by the Romans, who built fortifications there on their northern border. Archaeological remnants from this time can still be found at various sites in the province.

The landscape qualities and economic potential of deltas are often at odds with each other, and the landscape usually comes off worse. This is also true for Zuid-Holland, particularly in the 1960s and 1970s when the port, cities and greenhouse horticulture were growing rapidly. Back then the ecological and cultural significance we now attribute to the landscape carried little weight. Today, the province has 3.6 million inhabitants

and the use of urban and industrial space has grown phenomenally. The towns and villages on the islands and in the eastern part of Zuid-Holland are still set in open landscapes, but in the most densely urbanised zone between Dordrecht via Rotterdam and The Hague to Leiden, the roles have been reversed: enclosed open landscapes now offer oases of calm within an urban field.

Open landscape is becoming scarcer and therefore more valuable. As urban development encroaches further into the landscape, increasing attention is paid to preserving and enhancing the landscape through the development of multifunctional cultural landscapes, landscape zones and landscape parks. Formerly the domain of farmers, the landscape is increasingly in the service of the city. The main aim of landscape policy and design over the past twenty-five years has been to create suitable conditions for urban development and urban life, based on the realisation that large green spaces are essential for liveability. Efforts have been directed mostly at landscapes that were under urban or industrial pressure, while relatively remote rural areas were given less attention.

In that quarter century the assessment of landscape value has changed considerably. Landscape is a

Shaping Holland - Landscape 83

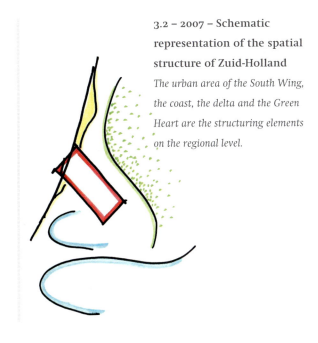

3.2 – 2007 – Schematic representation of the spatial structure of Zuid-Holland
The urban area of the South Wing, the coast, the delta and the Green Heart are the structuring elements on the regional level.

3.3 – 2004 – Main spatial structure of the Randstad landscape
The landscape structure of the Randstad consists of two sizeable landscape areas – the Green Heart and the Delta – with smaller-scale landscapes sandwiched between the urban areas. A restrictive building policy for the Green Heart and the Delta means that cities can only expand inwards, surrounding the remaining open areas of the landscape.

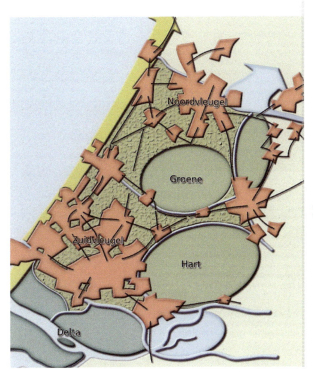

broad term. It has been interpreted and defined in different ways involving as many different issues and values, from climate change and identity, leisure time and food production to preservation and transformation. Priorities have changed, and so have design strategies. The landscape that has evolved contains traces of all those strategies. This happened against the background of an ever present underlying current, less visible than the surface current of urbanisation, that responds to the three major characteristic landscape types in the province: delta, coast and peat – three types of landscape that are not easily moulded and shaped; each presents its own unique set of conditions and opportunities and possesses its own inherent values (see Figures 3.2 and 3.3). These landscapes first appeared explicitly on the policy map as a physical basis for provincial spatial policy in the 2004 Provincial Spatial Structural Vision (see Figure 3.4).

2 _Counterweight to the city

Post-war spatial planning was aimed at constraining urbanisation. For half a century, until 2011, the national government designated rural areas where no urban expansion was permitted. While the Green Heart is probably the most well-known example, it is predated by green buffer zones

3.4 – 2004 – Landscape: quality zoning as a spatial strategy in Zuid-Holland

Identifying different landscape units through spatial analysis is the basis for different spatial strategies for landscape protection and development. Larger landscape units are in need of protection to retain their wide, open character. The smaller units with specific landscape qualities are under relatively more pressure from urban development or recreational use. The challenge here is revival for recreational use and protection from encroaching development. The third category is the fragmented landscapes, which need new landscape identities and offer additional possibilities for development. This map aimed to introduce a transformation zone strategy for this last category.

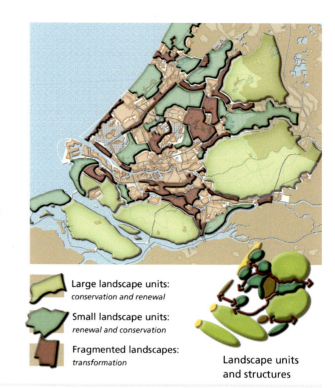

Large landscape units: *conservation and renewal*
Small landscape units: *renewal and conservation*
Fragmented landscapes: *transformation*

Landscape units and structures

between urban areas to prevent them from merging. The national government designated three such buffer zones in the province of Zuid-Holland (see Figure 3.5)

Initially, planning protection was sufficient for the open areas. Landscape quality was not a major consideration. The use and layout of the landscape was determined by agricultural land consolidation and landscape improvement schemes. This changed in 1985 with the advent of the implementation programme for the Randstad Green Structure (*Randstadgroenstructuur*). As a condition for continuing the restrictive urban development policy, government funding was made available for acquiring green belts and laying out amenity areas and other areas of green space with significance for the city. The urban population had to be able to escape to quieter green areas, and the landscape had to be structured for this purpose to fend off the continuous threat of large chunks being sacrificed as building land for the city.

The buffer zone of Midden-Delfland, between the Rotterdam and The Hague regions, was in many respects a forerunner of the new approach, regionally and nationally. The original reclamation of the area can still be seen in the characteristic water-rich peat meadow landscape of strip parcelling with rows of long, straight drainage ditches (see Figure 3.9a). Narrow polder roads are lined with pollarded willows and farms are located on sandy creek ridges. To withstand the pressure for development from the port, greenhouse horticulture and the cities, a Landscape Reconstruction Act was adopted by national government in 1977 for this particular area. The Act made it possible to redevelop the landscape as a whole, a different approach from traditional agricultural reparcelling schemes. It was in force until 2009. After 1985, as part of a wider regional policy integrating regional and local green structures, the province initiated the planting of woodland in part of the buffer zone to enhance its qualities as recreational area near the city. The typical open qualities that are so highly valued nowadays, however, were partially lost. During the 1990s a new round of investments followed, linked to the extension of the A4 motorway through this landscape (see Chapter 4). Step-by-step, the redevelopment of Midden-Delfland became integrated into a wider narrative on regional structures for nature and recreation (see Figures 3.6 and 3.7).

'Concepts like buffer zones and the Randstad Green Structure were backed by legal and financial instruments. That was necessary, because otherwise you could come up with great plans, but that's all they would be.'

Guus van Steenbergen, former programme manager at the Province of Zuid-Holland

The traditional division of responsibilities is that the municipalities build the neighbourhoods and parks, while the provinces develop the recreational areas outside the city. These are robust green spaces which are capable of resisting the pressure of urban development and enhance the quality of city living. Recent projects show that this division of roles still applies. In 2016 the Bentwoud forest was completed, planted on 800 hectares of open agricultural land near to the 1970s new town Zoetermeer to enhance its value as a recreational area.

Over the years, these types of green projects have become more multifunctional and more successfully embedded in integrated designs for urban areas. The first plan to come up with such a project was also the most radical. In that plan, *Parkstad tussen Hof en Haven?* (Park City between Palace and Port?; see Chapter 2), the province set out a new urban development concept for the urban network that was emerging in the Rotterdam–The Hague region. In this concept, green spaces outside the city were not so much seen as an amenity for which land should be reserved, but rather as a supporting framework for new development alongside infrastructure. Agricultural use was to remain a defining feature, while ecological and recreational qualities could add value to these

areas. This green structure connected the peat meadow areas of the Green Heart to Midden-Delfland (see Figure 3.8a).

The existing landscape was the basis: the transition between peatlands and polders, and ribbons of buildings. The designers concluded that this in itself offered insufficient quality for an attractive environment for establishing housing and businesses, so they proposed to add a number of landscape elements. The most structurally significant of these was the series of linked bodies of water. The plan assigned functional, morphological and symbolic meanings to the landscape which were at least as important as the spatial-structural significance that prevailed in the 1970s and 1980s. The *Parkstad* concept for landscape development was a complete landscape design, attractive and multifunctional, and with a wide range of intended uses (see Figure 3.8a–e).

However, the VINEX housebuilding programme (see Chapter 2) stifled the *Parkstad* urbanisation concept and with it the landscape concept. The intermediate area between The Hague and Rotterdam was relegated to a buffer zone. Nevertheless, the subsequent design studies of the early 1990s showed that, for the province and

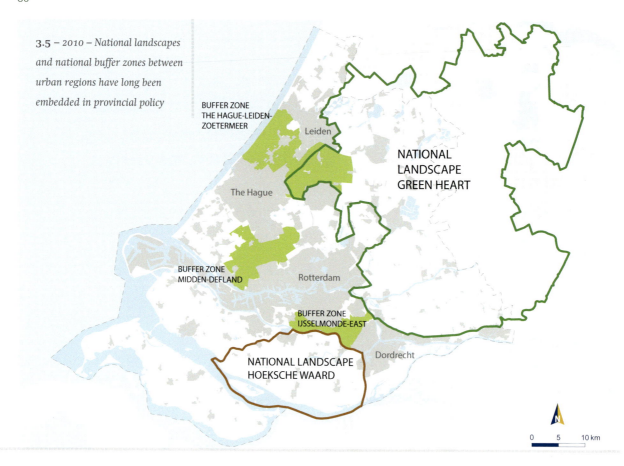

3.5 – 2010 – *National landscapes and national buffer zones between urban regions have long been embedded in provincial policy*

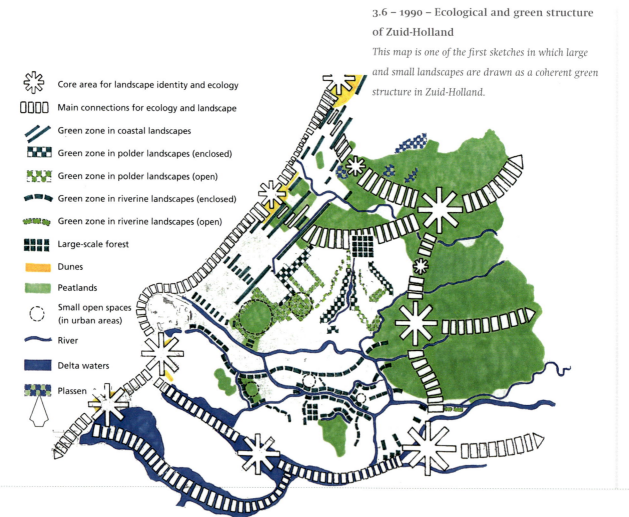

3.6 – 1990 – *Ecological and green structure of Zuid-Holland*

This map is one of the first sketches in which large and small landscapes are drawn as a coherent green structure in Zuid-Holland.

Shaping Holland - Landscape   87

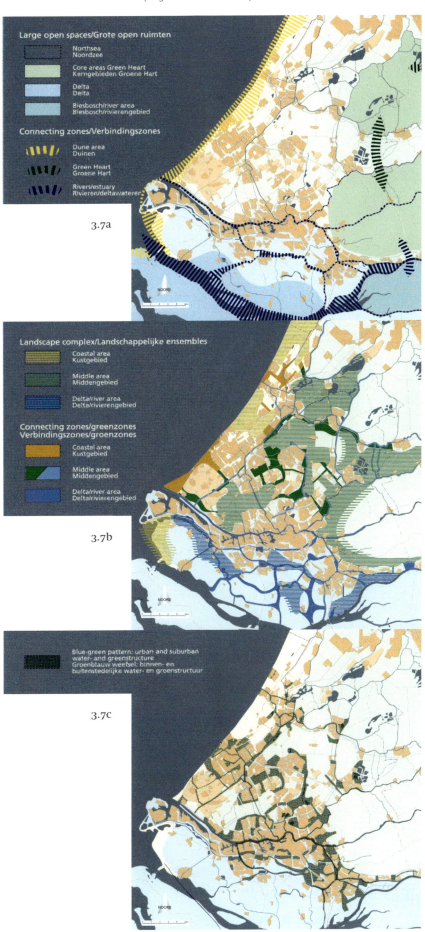

3.7 – 1999 – Green-blue
frameworks in the South
Wing: international, national,
regional and urban
*This series of maps was probably
the first to distinguish between
landscape structures with
significance at various scales.
It created a narrative of stacked
ownership of the landscape framework for Zuid-Holland, funding
and division of responsibilities
between authorities.*

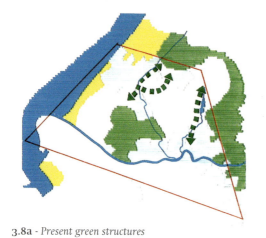

3.8a - *Present green structures*

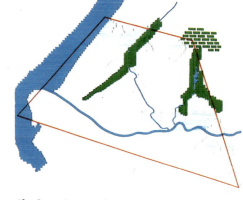

3.8b - *Large interventions …*

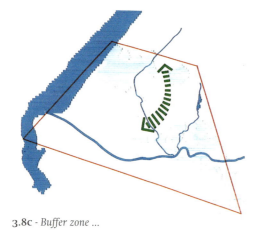

3.8c - *Buffer zone …*

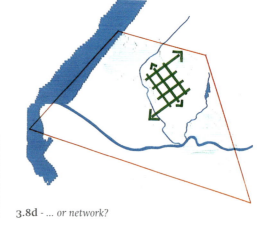

3.8d - *… or network?*

3.8e - *Compilation: the green framework of Parkstad*

3.8 – 1989 – Building blocks for the green framework of Parkstad

In their study for a green framework for Parkstad, designers experimented with the articulation of the landscape fragments. Ultimately, a concept was chosen that served as many objectives as possible by responding to the structure of the landscape, the new constellation of city and countryside, the recreational component and the ecological structure.

'The Green-Blue Streamer was based on a regional vision. It was a concept rather than a plan. It was implemented in separate little pieces, to the detriment of its overall connectivity. Working across different scales is not an automatic process.'

Tony van der Meulen, former Green-Blue Streamer programme manager at the Province of Zuid-Holland

for the cities of Rotterdam and The Hague, this intermediate area was to be more than just another green add-on to the cities, but rather a framework for development (see Figure 3.9a–c). In the best tradition of buffer zones, a green belt was needed to prevent the two urban regions from growing together. However, it would have to do this without the protection afforded by formal designation as a buffer zone: the government buffer zones that existed within Zuid-Holland were all designated between 1958 and 1976. The planning rationale had been reversed. Keeping the urban regions apart was not a goal in itself; it was now all about keeping the surrounding landscapes together. The peatland complex in Midden-Delfland and the Green Heart and the zones connecting them were assigned the status of a regional investment project under the moniker of a 'Green-Blue Streamer' (*Groenblauwe Slinger*) (see Figure 3.10a–e).

Again, in line with the tradition of the Midden-Delfland Reconstruction Act, the green space strategy was all about piecemeal landscape transformation projects building up to a bigger picture. This time, however, the regional landscape concept felt much more like an artificial concept, a desk exercise, and did not receive the same

level of recognition as Midden-Delfland. Urban development ultimately determined the location of the Green-Blue Streamer, not the landscape or geomorphological basis; the name itself betrays the lack of a topographical reference. That was at least part of this reason why a VINEX neighbourhood and a provincial road were allowed to occupy space that had been marked out for the Green-Blue Streamer zone. At the narrowest point, the built-up areas of The Hague and Rotterdam are a mere hundred metres apart. There was a consistent line from concept to implementation: the current strip embodies the green space highlighted on the first vision maps of the South Wing. However, this counterweight to the urban onslaught of VINEX neighbourhoods was not an easy win.

3 _Layers in the landscape

Partly due to the work on the *Parkstad* project, there had been a fundamental shift in thinking about landscape within the province. Landscape represented an intrinsic value that went beyond idyllic recreational areas or the rational patterns of agricultural land. The Green Heart was no longer just a sparsely built area in the Randstad area, but was now a landscape in its own right, with peatlands and reclaimed lakes, criss-crossed

3.9a – 1990 – Underlying structure: strip parcelling, reclaimed lake parcelling and creek structure

This influential drawing by the urban planner Frits Palmboom shows how the original parcelling pattern can be used as a foundation for urban development in the area between The Hague and Rotterdam.

3.9b – 1990 – Relationship between landscape and urban development

The landscape patterns explored by Palmboom in 1990 were used as an underlying structure for the new VINEX neighbourhoods between Rotterdam and The Hague.

by rivers and their clay deposits. A restrictive building policy alone would not be enough to safeguard the area from urbanisation – neither the villages, which needed some degree of growth to remain viable, nor the landscape. The peat was oxidising due to the low groundwater level needed for livestock farming, reducing the thickness of the peat layer and threatening its very future. Dependency on the global market made the future of agriculture uncertain. Groundwater was salinising. Biodiversity was decreasing: the meadow bird populations in particular were struggling to survive.

It was becoming increasingly clear that solutions for the Green Heart also needed to come from urban society, and that meant that the Green Heart was frequently the subject of regional design (see Figure 3.11a–e). Sometimes its relationship to the Randstad area was central and designing focused on accessibility, connections and gradations of recreational use, particularly on the periphery of the Green Heart. At other times the landscape itself was the centre of attention: the fraught issue of water levels and land use, the frictions between agriculture, nature and recreation, and between planning protection and the vitality of the villages.

3.9c – 1994 – Green framework for urban development between Delft and Zoetermeer

In 1994 the province explored the possibilities for urban development between Delft and Zoetermeer. Designing took a comprehensive perspective in which green areas formed a 'countermould' to urban developments (see Figure 2.3).

Regional design did not limit itself to the larger concept of the Green Heart, but also paid attention to integrated area development at the periphery (Figure 3.12). The designs gave direction to small-scale interventions and planning policy, as well as larger-scale restructuring of the landscape. Integrated peat meadow programmes were set up in a few rural areas, where the province collaborated with farms, nature conservation organisations and other regional players on future forms of agriculture, new nature, combined farming and recreation, and improving water quality.

The landscape was no longer a more or less coincidental result of land use in a rural area, and it did not have to be attractive only to urban visitors. Landscape structures provided continuity in areas that were in transition, a welcome development in the rapidly changing province of Zuid-Holland, but one that was hard won. Landscape architects in particular had been searching for years for a basis for a more sustainable spatial development, and it eventually came from a renewed awareness that the landscape was the result of a system, or rather, a system of interacting systems. Nature policy gained a spatial component in the form of the national ecological network, consisting of natural areas, nature development areas and connecting zones, the purpose of which was to stop the decline in biodiversity. The natural water system was reclaiming a larger slice of the green area again. The first consequences of climate change were starting to become apparent and simply pumping away all excess water was clearly not a sensible option any longer. The illusion of complete control was disappearing, but how much room for natural systems was there in the intensively used environment of Zuid-Holland?

Regional planning in the Netherlands gradually adopted the layer approach. The bottom or primary layer consists of the underlying soil and water systems, the nature and properties of which determine the possible uses of the land. The next layer consists of the infrastructure. The land uses themselves constitute the top layer and are derived from the other two layers. This planning approach could generate the conditions for sustainable regional development. Universities, landscape architects, the National Spatial Planning Agency (*Rijksplanologische Dienst*) and the Province of Zuid-Holland all worked with this method. The design study for *Parkstad* had already been conducted using this principle, as had a series of agenda-setting vision maps for the South Wing (see the final chapter; Figure iii.5a–c).

3.10a – 1990 – Landscape structure as basis

3.10 – The Green-Blue Streamer

The Green-Blue Streamer is an elongated area stretching southwards from Alphen aan den Rijn in sweeping curves between Leiden and Zoetermeer to Midden-Delfland. It consists of five connected sub-areas. This is a watery green area of 200 km² of recreational and ecological significance for over two million inhabitants. Open, natural and recreational spaces close to residential and employment areas are essential location factors for residents and businesses, especially with the realisation of VINEX-neighbourhoods (red on the maps). The Green-Blue Streamer is vital for the economic potential of the South Wing of the Randstad.

Shaping Holland - Landscape 93

3.10b – *2001 – Green-Blue Streamer as part of green-blue framework for the Randstad*

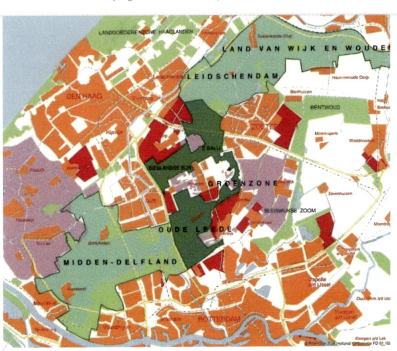

3.10c – *2001 – Transformation and adaptation areas as a spatial strategy for the Green-Blue Streamer*

3.10d – *2004 – Progress made with implementation of the Green-Blue Streamer in 2004*

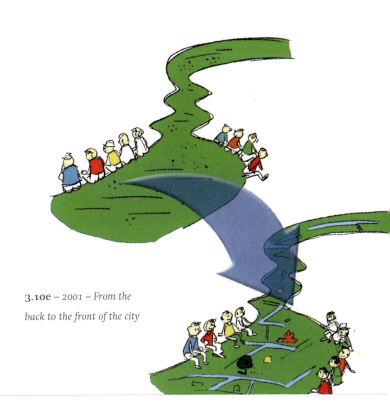

3.10e – *2001 – From the back to the front of the city*

3.11a – 2000 – Quality zoning for the Green Heart

This map made it clear that the Green Heart is not a single clearly defined area but is actually made up of various different types of landscape, which continue into the urban areas.

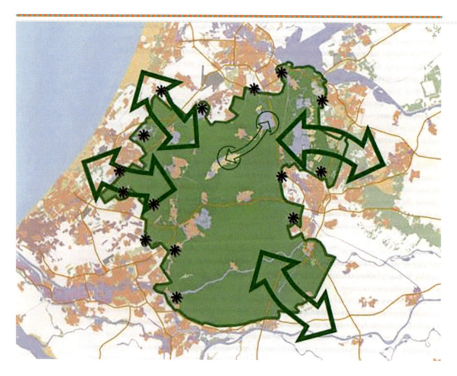

3.11b – 2000 – Green Heart: boundaries, diversity of peripheral zones and quality zoning

The boundaries of the Green Heart protecting it from urban development have been the subject of debate for decades. The introduction of a quality-oriented approach led to a rationale based on the actual identity of the area. The focus of policy shifted to the periphery and the transitional zones with urban areas.

Shaping Holland - Landscape   95

'Green Line'

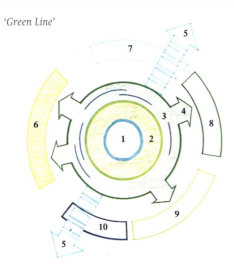

1. central zone Green Heart
2. peat meadow core
3. transition zone
4. corridor
5. blue arrow
6. coast and dune zone
7. waterland
8. Utrecht Hill Ridge
9. River Land and around
10. Delta

3.11c – 1990 – Green Heart: a green narrative for the Randstad

An early exercise at the Randstad level came from the Randstad Spatial Planning Consultative Group (Randstad Overleg Ruimtelijke Ordening), an early collaborative forum of the Randstad provinces. The frameworks and solutions for the green structure were a precursor to thinking about the Deltametropolis and its green-blue framework. The important discovery in the 1997 design vision was that the Green Heart is not a single homogeneous unit. The area-based agenda for tackling the problems of the peripheral zone are not limited to the periphery, but reach to the core of the Green Heart. Following development by the three provinces, the 2000 policy map was included in the government's National Spatial Strategy.

3.11e – 2003 – From Randstad to Deltametropolis – Ambitions for 2030

The introduction of the Deltametropolis concept created an opportunity to integrate the green-blue concept of the Green Heart into the urban concept of the Randstad, with a key role for the layer approach. This raised the level of conceptual development and cooperation between provinces and city-regions to that of the Randstad as a whole.

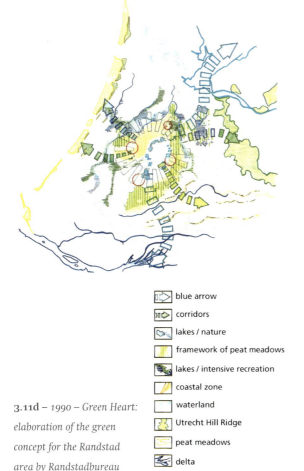

- blue arrow
- corridors
- lakes / nature
- framework of peat meadows
- lakes / intensive recreation
- coastal zone
- waterland
- Utrecht Hill Ridge
- peat meadows
- delta

3.11d – 1990 – Green Heart: elaboration of the green concept for the Randstad area by Randstadbureau

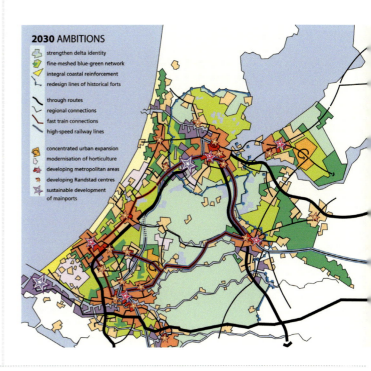

Legend

 regional park Merwede

 north-south spatial connection

 recreative node

 newly planned business parks

 Triangle Sliedrecht

 optimisation business parks

 wind energy: preferred location

 strategic spaces 'the Eye' and 'Papland'

 lightrail stops Merwede Lingelijn

 transform business parks into residential areas

 potential waterbus stop

current waterbus stop

Shaping Holland - Landscape   97

 planned and/or in progress residential location

 new planned residential location under influence area stop Merwede-Lingelijn

 existing industrial areas

 waterbus stop daily / summer and weekends

 'The Window'

 Green Spine

3.12 – 2009 – Map of the Merwede zone transformation vision (Transformatievisie Merwedezone)

The Merwede zone consists of a ribbon of settlements between the Merwede river and the parallel infrastructure bundle, each one a product of the economic possibilities afforded by the river. The transformation vision aims for quality improvements at the regional level and to establish better connections, including those between town and country. Urban development takes place along the Merwede-Linge railway line. To the north of the infrastructure, the aim is greater integration of agriculture, nature and recreation. The programme also provides for improvements in water quality and additional space for water retention. Within the structure of development as it has grown over time, there is little scope for the water system to steer land use to any significant extent. The vision is a result of close cooperation between the province, the water authority and the municipalities. The urban development concept included in the transformation vision never became part of the area vision.

3.13 – 2014 – Spatial Quality Map of the province of Zuid-Holland

The Spatial Quality Map (Ruimtelijke Kwaliteitskaart) gained official planning status when it was included in the 2014 provincial Spatial Planning and Mobility Vision (Visie Ruimte en Mobiliteit). On the map, the three large landscape units of peat, delta and coast are clearly distinguishable. Spatial quality is thus interpreted at every scale, from landscape units to individual plots. This map was the first formal policy basis for evaluating the spatial quality of local initiatives against regional public interests. Detailed descriptions for specific areas, called area profiles, were derived from this map.

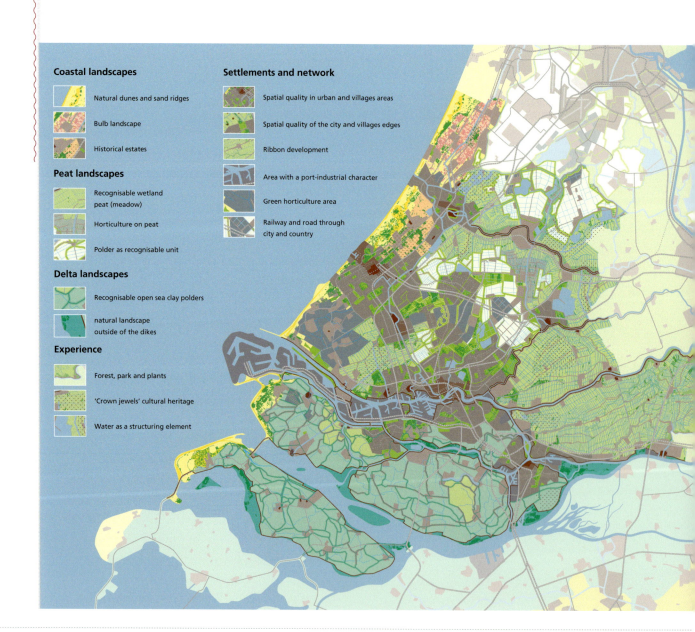

'Once the results of a regional design have been included in a plan, the underlying ideas tend to be sidelined. Then it's all about the land use, and the background against which it was determined is forgotten.'

Isolde Somsen, landscape architect at the Province of Zuid-Holland

Although this would be a logical point of departure for a watery delta potentially rich in natural habitats, for decades the urban and agricultural structure had developed independently of the water system. The urbanisation process followed different laws, which could not be changed just like that. This layer approach was valuable within the open areas that were to be developed, certainly where there were both urban and green programmes. In such situations, it provided a solid basis for sound and sustainable design which was sufficiently objective to get the backing of all relevant parties.

In short, urbanisation continued to be the main driver of provincial landscape design. The subject of much of this design work was the peat meadow landscape of the South Wing and Green Heart, particularly where urban pressures were greatest. Less attention was given to the coastal zone, with its protected dune areas, and the delta landscape was somewhat neglected over the years. However, landscape quality was being eroded almost everywhere by encroaching building, agricultural expansion or a deterioration in the quality of the soil, air and water. At the same time, public awareness of the value of the landscape was growing.

4 _Carrier of identity

Between 1990 and 2010 the professional world took the layer approach further, while at the same time the 'cluttering' of the landscape became a major concern in society and a heated debate arose, in Zuid-Holland as well as elsewhere in the country. People saw industrial estates and greenhouse horticulture complexes springing up which were devoid of any architectural ambition; numerous small housing estates were built alongside the large VINEX neighbourhoods; isolated wind turbines, farm buildings, holiday homes and other structures had little impact individually, but put together they were ruining the landscape in the eyes of many people.

Initially, many provinces responded to this concern by assessing the value of the landscapes. The term 'cluttering' reflected people's perception of the landscape and their idea of beauty. But what exactly constitutes this beauty, and how subjective is it as a concept? Buildings that are dropped in a landscape without any relation to it tend to be seen as ugly and untidy, but who can say whether a building relates to its surroundings?

3.14 – 2012 – Area profile for Goeree-Overflakkee (water layer)

The seventeen area profiles of landscape regions in Zuid-Holland contain a series of digital maps, each digital layer focusing on a single aspect. This map illustrates the aspect water as a structuring element for Goeree-Overflakkee. Here we see, for example, the last remaining medieval creeks and creek beds, the drainage ditches for the agricultural polders and the historical harbours of Middelharnis with its harbour canal.

'The province can make a difference outside the city, where there are major planning and landscape challenges – such as energy and the climate. The province makes a quality map and area profiles, but these don't generate good future visions.'

Abe Veenstra, former provincial advisor for spatial quality

Cultural history provided a solution. The national government's work on the Belvedere programme on cultural history and spatial development also sparked off thinking at the provincial level. 'Beautiful' was an elusive term in the context of design and policy, so 'indigenous' (*gebiedseigen*) was adopted as a workable alternative. The Province of Zuid-Holland examined maps of the heritage framework in search of landscape characteristics that had developed over centuries and still exist – such as reclamation patterns, water engineering structures, architectural styles, archaeological expectations and traces of previous land uses. These are distinguishing features of a landscape which lend it its character and are therefore valuable. It follows that these characteristics should be maintained or at least remain recognisable when new developments are introduced, whether large or small. The amenity value of the landscape was now based on identification rather than beauty. If people could continue to identify with their environment in spite of new developments, they would not feel alienated or experience the landscape as becoming cluttered.

From 2011, the province pursued this regional approach, with a Spatial Quality Map for the whole province (Figure 3.13) and more detailed elaborations of specific landscape units called 'area profiles'. The same system was used as for the heritage framework. Together with municipalities, water authorities and social partners, the province meticulously analysed landscapes in terms of their distinctive qualities (see, for example, Figure 3.14). This resulted in an overview of distinctive landscape elements and characteristics that were to be taken into account in policymaking and projects. The seventeen area profiles were typical design exercises. The work of a designer involves identifying determining structures and objects, but compared to other designs, little attention was paid to the future – no projects or land use claims came out of them, and neither was it possible to remove existing landscape clutter. The province never implemented structural, area-based clean-up programmes based on a design typology and backed by a budget. The only planned landscape clean-up was the systematic removal of scattered horticultural greenhouses. The area profiles were not supposed to present a vision, but provide a common basis for spatial quality in the province.

Although this inventory approach takes a different perspective from the layer approach, the two approaches complement each other. Characteristic landscape patterns and elements follow almost

Urban functions

- residential and industrial areas
- motorway
- railway

Green functions

- forest, recreation area, urban green spaces
- dunes
- water
- marshlands, lands outside the dikes
- open pasture areas, main function agriculture
- open pasture area, agriculture with great scenic, recreational and ecological values
- open arable and horticultural areas, main function agriculture
- open arable and horticultural areas with great scenic, recreational and ecological values
- greenhouse horticulture area

Landscape, recreational and ecological cohesion

- coherence between forest and recreational areas
- coherence between dune areas
- coherence between water and wetlands
- coherence between pasture areas
- concentration of major scenic recreational and ecological values

Randstadgroenstructuur

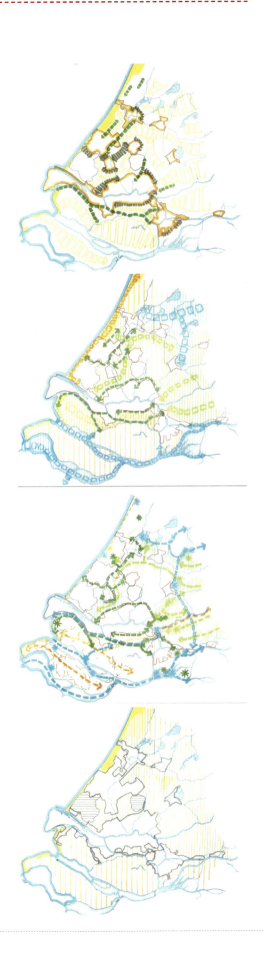

3.15 – 1988 – The Randstad Green Structure in Zuid-Holland in 2000

In the late 1980s, the Randstad Green Structure (Randstad Groenstructuur) set out a vision for 2000 of an urban area permeated by green spaces. This layer planning concept consisting of various green structures, each with its own relationship to the urban environment, has remained more or less intact over the years.

F3.4

automatically from the natural soil and water conditions, not from the post-war housing developments or agricultural rationalisation. The spatial quality policy covered all the landscapes of Zuid-Holland, including those less in the urban shadow or unaffected by urban development. By emphasising amenity value, the area profiles filled another gap. The theory of spatial quality breaks it down into the three components of use value, future value and amenity value. Whereas the use value of the landscape had been given full attention from the time of the agricultural land consolidation schemes, the layer approach put the emphasis on sustainable regional development (and therefore on future value), and now the area profiles brought amenity value into the picture.

Over the past quarter of a century the landscape has become increasingly important. Initially, the landscape was a necessary counterpoise to the city, its openness being its key quality; now it forms the starting point for regional developments and spatial policy. But although quality policy is firmly embedded in planning policy and legislation, it remains vulnerable in practice. Neither the area profiles nor the analyses of layers of the landscape lead directly to projects or programmes.

They are driven by an entirely different set of forces. Urbanisation follows its own laws, as became apparent during the construction of the VINEX neighbourhoods. The same goes for other claims on land with a major impact on the landscape: the energy transition, flood protection, agricultural restructuring, etc. All these agendas have their own constituencies, interests and preferences that are not always easily reconciled with the landscape context. Area profiles work mainly on the local scale and municipalities make use of them when assessing small-scale developments to preventing further landscape clutter.

5 _Public interest

Counterpoise, system, carrier of identity – the significance given to the landscape shifted considerably, but more in relation to context than over time. It represented different values depending on the development agenda. Even the very definition of what landscape is may have varied – is it just the appearance of a rural area, as the dictionary suggests, or more to do with the combination and integration of all the functions of an area? And what about the collective memory it represents, either visibly or beneath the surface?

'Landscape and the public interest are bedfellows, but the public interest is in danger of being lost from view. Fewer and fewer people think in spatial terms, but society is moving forward and nine out of ten interests have a spatial dimension. So get drawing, give the landscape a face, and get it into the public consciousness!'

Ejsmund Hinborch, urban planner/landscape planner at the Province of Zuid-Holland

All the values, meanings and definitions have one common denominator: the landscape represents a public interest, which obliges government authorities to act. As landscapes are units and structures at the regional level, in the decentralised spatial planning system since 2011 this responsibility lies only with the provinces.

Landscape policy and design, however, are never completely independent, but are driven by other forces, and in the case of Zuid-Holland this has often been urban expansion. Sometimes the landscape is to function as a backdrop for residential neighbourhoods or urban regions, elsewhere it must provide recreational spaces. In the near future the driver for landscape transformation might be health or energy, or landscape as a factor in the business climate of the South Wing. The interpretation of the landscape and the assessment of its value will always depend on the driving force behind landscape change.

Over the past twenty-five years we have come to a pretty thorough understanding of the landscape of Zuid-Holland in all its facets and functioning (see Figure 3.15). Provincial plans for regional area development are based on the underlying landscape. The challenge for the coming period

is to ensure that the landscape is a structural part of spatial plans and designs – not as a mere underlay, but as a basis for design that integrates new development and existing values.

The theoretical foundation has been laid, but practice still lags behind, and there is often a gulf between policy and spending. National government used to fund landscape policy, such as the Randstad Green Structure and the national ecological network, but these resources are no longer available. The parties that now 'make' the landscape often have different motivations. For them, landscape quality is at best an extra, and at worst an obligation to avoid if at all possible. Moreover, national government funds were limited to clearly defined area categories, but now spatial quality policy covers the entire territory of the province and it is recognised that every landscape has its own specific values.

The provincial government now faces the task of developing a landscape-inclusive system of planning and development. To meet the current challenges we need a new balance between safeguarding existing qualities and focusing on new qualities, between planning restrictions and incentives for a good visual quality. A crucial factor here is governance, or in other words, how investors and other players are approached and brought into the process. Landscape policy must reach many parties – from individual farmers, agricultural enterprises to Rijkswaterstaat, the government agency for environment, infrastructure and water management, and from land managers to wind energy companies. Committed citizens have come forward and become co-producers of the landscape design, as in the case of the plans for Buijtenland van Rhoon, a new nature and recreation area on the southern edge of Rotterdam (see Figure 3.16), where two farmer's daughters managed to mobilise broad support for maintaining the agricultural use of the area. All these parties will have to have an appropriate position within any new landscape-inclusive planning process.

In today's world it is public and private investors who actually change the landscape and shape its appearance, but there is only one player that can see the bigger picture and can call itself the 'problem owner' and representative of society as a whole, and that is the province. It is the province's responsibility, and that means that the province needs to remain alert and active in the fulfilment of this role.

Nature

Shaping Holland - Landscape 107

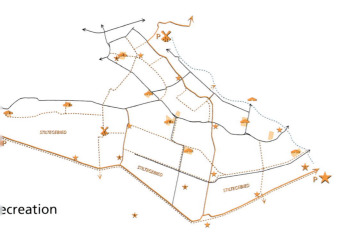

3.16 – 2018 – Spatial vision for Buijtenland van Rhoon

The spatial vision for landscape development in this open landscape just south of Rotterdam was the result of an intensive process initiated by and involving many local stakeholders. Nature development in this area was the result of negotiations on the Maasvlakte 2 port extension (see Chapter 6). Initial government plans proposed marshy ecosystem and a rigorous restructuring of the landscape. In response to considerable local opposition, this new plan for Buijtenland van Rhoon was produced, with detailed guidelines for landscape restructuring in its legend.

108_._Interview_ The Civil Servant

The Civil Servant

San
Verschuuren

*Worked for the Province of Zuid-Holland
from 1976 to 2002*

Fi.1

We wanted to take the plunge and make a proposal that broke the boundaries. It was 1988 and central government had published the Fourth National Policy Document on Spatial Planning. The cities had to grow and urban regeneration alone was no longer enough. Studies were carried out to identify building locations, but in an uncoordinated way. The Rotterdam metro could be extended a bit; a tramline might be added in The Hague. This was all terribly frustrating for us as experts at the province, but no less so for provincial executive member Loudi Stolker. An urban planner herself, she was concerned about cluttering up the landscape between Rotterdam and The Hague. Greenhouses were being built and villages were expanding. It looked as if the area was going to be ugly and inefficient.

We were looking for coherence and diversity, which brings you logically to the regional level. The key to it lay in sharing information and exchanging ideas, not only between cities but also between experts. Before then, economists calculated how many square metres of business space were needed, traffic engineers calculated how many cars would be on the roads, and so on. We were given those figures to fill in the details on the regional planning map. That wouldn't do any more, and we were given a year to come up with something. We had support from the National Spatial Planning Agency in the person of Steef Buijs, who was very much in favour of our approach. At the professional level, we consulted with Rotterdam and The Hague – the executive councillors sat on a steering committee – and with Stolker as our guardian angel. This led to a design study called

110_._Interview_ The Civil Servant

Park City between Palace and Port. We showed how living environments, green space, infrastructure and economy all hang together. It's not an exaggeration to call that a breakthrough.

And then national government came up with the major housebuilding programme called VINEX. Rotterdam and The Hague turned their backs on us because they were attracted by generous national funding for building VINEX neighbourhoods. We met with opposition from the greenhouse horticulture sector, even though Rabobank, the main agricultural bank, had calculated that our proposal was more favourable economically. Against its better judgement, the Provincial Council brushed *Parkstad* aside. Ultimately, it was all about power and money, which is a great pity. I am still convinced that we were on the right track.

As a designer, it is vital to be close to the seat of power, because we can show the executive members how the province works. You can do that on a map in a research-by-design process. And you have to switch between scales. For example, we made designs at the level of the A4 motorway corridor and then looked at how this approach affected a river crossing or stretch of urban motorway. We were at the service of the provincial executive but not the political agenda, which tended to change quite a lot. We were a stable factor, and that was appreciated. The members of the provincial executive clearly respected our work and our professionalism. We got that by consistently thinking ahead – unlike politics, which is concerned with the day-to-day.

We introduced regional design to the province, but Zuid-Holland was not the only one to benefit from this. The National Spatial Planning Agency also started designing at the regional level. The Rijnmond region experimented as well. A new generation of designers arrived and they got in touch with each other. We all made designs for the Randstad area, and then for the Deltametropolis, but it was not very successful, however well intentioned. And we made little impression on the politicians. At that time the future was looking increasingly uncertain and spatial planning was losing its appeal.

When I started working for the City of Amsterdam in 2002 I found a whole team of urban planners and designers in the spatial planning department. At the time, 250 people worked there. That was quite unusual, because Rotterdam, The Hague and Utrecht had cut back on almost all designers to economise. Amsterdam benefited greatly from this department. We didn't really deal with topics such as the future of the Randstad; we were trying to make progress on the regional scale. At first, the city tried to do that at the political level, but that soon led to disagreements. After that, we started to work with colleagues in the region to find shared issues and at first kept the municipal executive at arm's length. They had to give us our freedom to do things in our own way.

Our basic principle was that the region belongs to all of us. A few government bodies attempted to map out the region together, in an unforced way and on the basis of equality. All the municipalities, whatever their size, contributed the same budget, and parties such as the Albert Heijn supermarket chain and Schiphol Airport also participated. Other countries are often amazed that such an informal approach can be successful. They all have dysfunctional regional governance models, and we don't even have a governance model – but it works. Obviously, there will always be friction, but that can be discussed and appropriate measures taken. When we were left with a surplus of office space, a committee was set up that was authorised to decide which offices had to go. The municipalities picked it up, with Amsterdam in the lead. We prioritised solutions, not conflicting interests.

The South Wing of the Randstad is a different situation, being governed by two totally different cities, The Hague and Rotterdam. The agenda for the South Wing Administrative Platform was dictated from above. Research and design were contracted out because there was insufficient faith in anyone within the government authorities. Amsterdam chose to keep these things in-house. Efforts were made to promote mutual understanding, for example by organising dinners and cycling tours.

The purely sectoral approach of the past has disappeared from the Netherlands, probably for ever. We are now making regional designs and regional agreements, but the field of regional design remains tenuous and difficult to maintain. You can't just take on regional designers straight from university. There is no specific course of study to become a regional designer, even though it's a demanding profession. In the 1990s we produced four postcards with designs for the South Wing, drawn by various people, showing four ways to depict the same area. This illustrated the choices facing a regional designer. What do you want to show, what message do you want to communicate, how are you going to draw it, and at what level of detail? If you put all the layers on top of each other, you'll see nothing. If you look at things separately, you'll see the complexity.

The Politician

Asje
van Dijk

*Member of the Zuid-Holland provincial
executive for the Christian Democratic
Party (CDA), 2003–2011*

There is inevitably an element of uncertainty in future-oriented studies, but strangely enough, if all the parties get together to develop one or more scenarios, and everyone has some degree of faith in the results, things will develop in that direction. People will adopt a different attitude, and that will be reflected in their behaviour.

One of the best examples from my time at the Province of Zuid-Holland is *Stedenbaan* (see Chapter 5). From the outset, we vowed to complete it by 2025 – or at least, most of it. It's a lot easier to talk about such a dot on the horizon than projects for the coming four years. In that case, it's often about winners and losers, but now, it was about the joint final picture. Municipalities could do their best to participate in the first projects, while knowing they wouldn't be involved in the second round. In the end, they all have their parts to play. Meanwhile, *Stedenbaan* has had a fundamental influence on thinking in Zuid-Holland about the relationship between mobility and urban development, and has even been incorporated into national government policy. That really felt like a victory.

Before I was appointed to the provincial executive, I was director at Van de Bunt, a consultancy for strategy, organisation and management. I was actively involved in change management and engaged in a variety of interactive projects. In my dissertation I had written about co-production, or co-creation as it is currently called. This means that people and organisations have to be connected to a change process that affects them. In those days, I had not yet had much experience with spatial development.

For instance, when I arrived at Zuid-Holland, I barely knew what a land use plan was. A member of staff approached me with a document entitled Provincial Spatial Structural Vision. He said I was to take a good look at it because I was supposed to formally adopt it. At a time like that, it is wise to realise that you are dealing with people who not only know what they are talking about, but also work at an integrative level – involving other disciplines. It was also very significant that stakeholders from outside the provincial government building had been able to make contributions. Those three factors convinced me that the product had to be sound.

Co-creation was also important for the success of the development plans for Zuidplaspolder, an agricultural polder near Rotterdam to be developed for housing and new nature (see Chapter 2). Everyone assured me that no other project in the province had reached the decision-making process so quickly. This was shortly before the crisis, but there was no way we could have predicted that. The main condition for this alacrity was that we were clear about the national and provincial expectations from the outset. The North Wing of the Randstad had a new town, Almere, and we had the Zuidplas-polder. That was the scene of the action. National government and the province were both clear on that.

Politicians will only give the go-ahead for such a project once it is clearly defined and there is public support for it, and that was the case. This became apparent during one of our information evenings in the region. The room was packed, even though Holland was playing in an international football match that same evening. One well-known critic launched a vitriolic attack, and received a forceful response from the floor. Our consultant, Riek Bakker, went and stood in front of the board with the map and enquired, 'How would you do it, then?' From that point on, there was no opposition. We put it to the vote whether Rotterdam should take care of its own housing. And what do you think happened? 75% said no, we also build for Rotterdam.

It was a matter of communication. We invested really heavily in that. For instance, we published a serial in the local papers, and organised essay and drawing competitions for schoolchildren. People were aware that they had influence on the plan, and that it was very serious and not a game. Moreover, people recognised that building offered guarantees for the provision of facilities, such as schools, churches and supermarkets. And we were also to develop no fewer than 600 hectares of nature. Rather than waiting until the housing was ready, we started right away, and that helped bolster our credibility.

There was no opposition from the municipalities, but there was some to be felt within the network of stakeholders as a whole. The chief government architect, MPs and experts from the water authorities felt that it was not acceptable to build in the lowest point of the Netherlands. But of course it is! We're the experts in water management, aren't we? And from the perspective of the urban network, the Zuidplaspolder is an excellent location. So let us look at the situation in a different way: what will it take to build there? Delft University of Technology showed that it was perfectly possible, as long as proper account was taken of high water levels – for instance, with high floor levels or floating houses. It could be a terrific new development.

As a politician I am a fan of visions. Negotiations about projects and the associated budgets are only possible if there is agreement on the underlying vision, because that's what lends political and democratic legitimacy. Without a vision on the Leiden–Katwijk Axis (see Chapter 4), I would not have been able to arrange funding for the Rijnland route, a new road between the coastal town of Katwijk and the A4 motorway. The right level of abstraction is crucial. If the precise route had been drawn straight away, I would not have succeeded.

As it was, I was able to formulate one essential rule for the cooperation in advance. To engage in the discussions you have to accept that the road is going to be built. Then you can talk about where and exactly how. One organisation that declared from the word go that it opposed everything got left out of the discussions. The risk was too great that they would misuse my information. Another agreed to the road, but opposed the route. I gave them people and information to work out their own variant. With hindsight, I think I could have equipped them better for this. If, in such a situation, you arrive at different but valuable and legitimate alternatives together, a democratic assessment can take place. With an approach like that we could have made the light rail connection from the Leiden region to the coast happen after all. I'm absolutely convinced of that.

Regional development is not only about negotiating; it's also about organising creativity. I liked to have 'wild ducks' flown in, outsiders who have a very different view of a project. For instance, we invited an English urban designer to a strategic conference about the Zuidplaspolder. He proposed building very high buildings at a density five or six times higher than we intended. That would leave 90% of the area open. So think gorgeous parks, nature, water … I could see what all those people in the room were thinking: hmm, a bit strange, but very nice. That was exhilarating! It is important to step outside purely rational thinking now and then.

The Director
Joost Schrijnen

Director of Spatial Planning and Mobility
at the Province of Zuid-Holland, 2002–2007

There is a massive need for fundamental research into the metropolitan development of the Randstad area. Alongside the traditional spatial planning agenda, new issues are emerging. The energy transition is just one example. It involves more than just installing wind turbines; it's about creating a whole new energy landscape. The same goes for climate adaptation, the circular economy and health. All these issues have a spatial and land use dimension. If this is neglected the urban and rural landscape will become increasingly fragmented.

Regional design as a discipline is set to grow rather than diminish in importance. We're missing out on opportunities because many people don't understand that. Building the Blankenburg tunnel, for example, is a massive mistake. This new motorway connection connecting the northern and southern banks of the Meuse is meant to benefit the port, but it will now become a paltry link just west of Rotterdam, between the A20 motorway leading to the beach and the A15 motorway leading to the Maasvlakte 2 port extension. It will never connect to the A4 motorway, even though that is the corridor between the mainports and the major cities of the Netherlands and Belgium. If the courage had been found to opt for a tunnel further towards the coast, at a stroke it would have brought The Hague closer to the port. The residential districts in the south-west of The Hague, where unemployment is high, could then have benefited from jobs in the port. Now that would be an incredibly interesting development deserving of the name of spatial planning.

I've had a couple of experiences with national government that illustrate how difficult this is. At the City of Rotterdam, I worked on structure plans for twenty to thirty years, and subsequently did the same at the province. We put a vision on the map, even though not all the projects we included had funding. Then we set up and decided on an implementation programme for the first five years. That's how to do it. Subsequently, I was responsible for the South-Western Delta subprogramme of the Delta Programme for flood risk management, freshwater supply and spatial adaptation to climate change. A spatial vision was needed for three major water bodies south of Rotterdam. That could only be a national vision, as the area is divided between three provinces and several municipalities and water authorities. That vision centres on the ideological statement that the water basins must be connected so that they would all be tidal. That was a considered long-term strategy statement. So what did the government's decision show? The structural vision was not seen as a planning decision which could form the basis for concrete projects, but rather as an issue for the MIRT (the Multi-Year Programme for Infrastructure, Spatial Planning and Transport, which allocates government expenditure). The Ministry of Finance requires that funding for all proposals is arranged in a formal plan under public law. This type of spatial vision is therefore reduced to a series of projects that fit within the step-by-step 'rules of the game' of the MIRT. The national government's spatial planning is thus thwarted by the MIRT.

Regional design can be used as part of a research process. That's a very fundamental concept. The problem is that people often regard a drawing

as a plan, whereas a written statement is regarded as a proposal that needs
to be discussed. That is because no-one dares to pick up a pencil. As a
consequence, some executive members fear visioning and some designers
have a tendency towards arrogance. Designers tend to think that they
should be left to their own devices.

As director at the province, I set up the South Wing Studio to create an
arena for free thinking on the formation of a metropolitan region. It was
of fundamental importance for me to be at the studio every Wednesday
morning to check up on the results. I felt responsible for the connection
with the provincial executive. I was continually checking whether the
thinking would match the policy environment and whether it opened up
avenues for influencing the policy environment. Regional design needs
such direction. There must be freedom for new ideas, but they must be
grounded, otherwise it will look very good but it won't work.

I discovered the specific expertise of regional design a long time ago at
design studios organised by the Deltametropolis Association with nationally
renowned urban designer Dirk Frieling. He brought together designers
from the Randstad provinces, the major cities and national government to
work jointly on designs for the Randstad area. This took place in Hotel New
York in Rotterdam. It became apparent that there were many contrasting
design styles. Municipal designers made rough sketches, extending the city
strategy to the region; central government designers worked on a highly
conceptual level; the quality of the provincial designers lay in their

knowledge of the entire topography, including water management, infrastructure and the accompanying typologies. Research-by-design on a regional scale is about connecting all those layers and, in the context of the Zuid-Holland area, transformability to the metropolitan reality. That's a fantastic task, but also a profession requiring the appropriate knowledge. A province needs that kind of expertise. Such knowledge is sometimes perceived differently – designers are seen to come up with pictures to fit the policy, or, in contrast, make it unnecessarily complicated. It takes a lot of hard work to keep making it clear what designers can contribute. In my time at the Province of Zuid-Holland, the South Wing Studio represented the solution to that problem.

At that time, major projects were underway in which provincial responsibility weighed heavily: the missing link in the A4 motorway between Delft and Schiedam, the Sand Engine to strengthen the coast south of The Hague, and large-scale greenfield housing development for the Rotterdam and The Hague regions in the Zuidplaspolder. The studio was able to put this in a metropolitan context. This also led to the *Stedenbaan* transport-oriented development concept (see Chapter 5). The studio was fantastic for me, and allowed me to give my role as director real meaning. We had the opportunity to come up with regional concepts and develop the metropolitan concept. Unfortunately, the synergy needed for this is now lacking. The current metropolitan region of Rotterdam–The Hague now has a more limited agenda than the urban regions of

The Hague and Rotterdam had at the time. A voluntary basis is not sufficient for good cooperation, particularly if many municipalities are unwilling.

Leadership in the South Wing is awkward due to the lack of centrality. There will always be competition in an administrative sense, so it is necessary to look for a way to accommodate this competition while leaving room for new discoveries, and that takes time. The same applies at the level of the four major cities. As director of the Urban Development Department in Rotterdam, I met every few months with the directors of the other three major cities and people from national government to talk about development of the Randstad area, mainly at the administrative level, but sometimes at the political level. That synergy has now also disappeared, which makes things very difficult indeed.

We need to increase the quality of the four big planning departments and their willingness to cooperate, while involving the provinces – and to overcome the eternal animosity between the major cities and the provinces. Our task now is to reassemble a network of people who understand that this design work at the regional level is necessary; people who come together to think about what the next step should be, and who look for new initiatives.

F4.1

- Delta - Green Heart
- Coast
- Sea ports - Amsterdam Airport Schiphol
- High-speed railway (passengers) - Betuwe freight railway
- Motorways A4 - A15 - A16

4.1 – 2004 – Zuid-Holland within the wider context

Together with the South Wing and large parts of the Green Heart, the province of Zuid-Holland constitutes an important part of the Randstad area. At the same time, the province is part of the Rhine-Scheldt Delta, the area surrounding the seaports of Rotterdam, Zeeland and Antwerp. Social, economic and administrative trends all point in the same direction: network creation on a larger scale. The map is from the 2004 Provincial Spatial Structural Vision for Zuid-Holland.

© Provincie Zuid-Holland
Cartografie FD 04.1390/4

Corridors

Dutch spatial planning has always had a rather ambivalent attitude towards the main road network. While planning policy has always discouraged use of the car in favour of the bicycle and public transport, investments are continually being made in expanding and improving the motorways. The reasons are always the same: queues on the motorways are an annoyance and a source of frustration to many, and they come at considerable economic cost. Investments in the road network are therefore usually made to resolve specific bottlenecks and keep traffic moving. This main road network is shared by regional, national and international traffic.

As a result of this ambivalent attitude, motorways are rarely viewed as economic development axes. The business community in particular tried to change this in the 1990s in the wake of the government's decision in 1988 to stimulate the growth of Amsterdam Airport Schiphol and the port of Rotterdam. International competitiveness was introduced as one of the objectives of spatial planning, a key success factor being the quality of the hinterland connections. Economic policy flirted with the idea of creating corridors of urban development along the main infrastructure, but again, this turned out to be politically taboo.

However, this did not prevent the Province of Zuid-Holland from carrying out a research-by-design study into the A4 corridor. The A4 motorway connects Amsterdam, The Hague and Rotterdam with Antwerp in Belgium (see Figure 4.1), passing Schiphol Airport and the Rotterdam port area on the way. The economic potential is unmistakeable, even without the unacceptable prospect of a long ribbon of industrial buildings along the motorway.

__ Takeaways from this chapter

Investments in international accessibility act as a catalyst for economic development. The positioning of urban regions in national and international networks is an important driver of investments in road infrastructure. Around 1990 the globalisation of the economy went up a gear. As the patterns of daily life began to play out more and more on a regional scale, the idea of the 'daily living environment' likewise expanded to become the 'daily urban system'. Competitiveness and a sense of belonging will both be important in future, even in geopolitically unstable times. Regional design can increase the economic and social return on investment in road infrastructure by concentrating economic and urban development around a limited number of hubs. In this chapter we illustrate the various ways in which regional design can do this.

- Regional design of infrastructure corridors is a useful tool for finding innovative models for the economic and spatial development of regions. The solutions that emerge are more future-proof and have greater economic potential than traffic engineering solutions, which are geared primarily to resolving traffic bottlenecks and infrastructure capacity problems.
- Regional design facilitates the preparation of integrated investment proposals for infrastructure, landscape, and economic and urban development. This leads to high-quality area plans.
- Regional design opens up avenues to break through deadlocked negotiation processes, devise solutions to specific issues and put them to the most appropriate party.
- Regional design can help parties to obtain a place at the negotiating table or create new arenas in which coalitions of public and private parties are encouraged to negotiate collective solutions.

'The A4 is the product of a series of decisions over many years to link together existing sections of road. We now ascribe to this composite road the significance of a corridor. Regional designs legitimised this choice for a corridor.'

Eric Luiten, landscape architect and author of AReA

1 _Regional design from Amsterdam to Antwerp

A 170 km line may seem an unusual subject for regional design, but in the 1990s the need arose. The A4 motorway between Amsterdam and the border at Antwerp connects a number of rapidly growing economic hubs – not only the big cities, but also knowledge-based, logistics and horticultural clusters. The road's capacity had to be increased and missing sections built – no mean feat in a densely populated area with vulnerable landscapes.

Where the responsibility lay for commissioning this new section of motorway was a complicated business. Until it reaches the national border, the A4 crosses four provincial and dozens of municipal borders. The road is maintained by national government, but planning powers for the surrounding land and underlying road network are divided between many other parties. Once a road has been built, it has all kinds of repercussions for the surrounding area: there will be economic pressure for development, traffic flows will change, and the road may present a barrier, affect environmental quality or disrupt local cohesion. For this type of infrastructural task it is particularly helpful to stand above and look beyond administrative

boundaries, which is one reason for taking a regional design approach. The approach to the A4 as a 'corridor' does just that and opens up the prospect of developing the infrastructure in harmony with surrounding land uses.

It is no coincidence that the first plan for the zone between Amsterdam and Antwerp came from a coalition of provinces and the business community, without the involvement of national government or the municipalities. The latter are the main causes of the stalemate that often bedevils the construction of new infrastructure: quality of life versus accessibility. The design dates from 2000 and was named AReA (Amsterdam, Rotterdam and Antwerp) (see Figure 4.2). It was unique for the time that public and private parties shared a spatial vision, which reflected the feeling of urgency. The need for fast and reliable road connections was great, but decision-making had become bogged down.

The main task that the makers of AReA seem to have set themselves was to overcome the discrepancy between quality of life and accessibility. The catchline was 'mobility, enterprise and environment on a higher level'. The design showed the connections between road infrastructure and the various seaports in the delta and with the railway

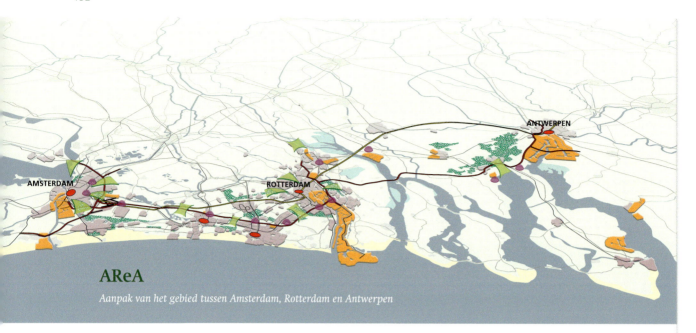

AReA
Aanpak van het gebied tussen Amsterdam, Rotterdam en Antwerpen

network. It showed where economic development was possible and where there were opportunities for strengthening urban areas and the landscape. Uncertainties regarding commissioning were accommodated using the formula of 'project envelopes'. The development programmes associated with the broadening or building of a section of motorway were grouped regionally and addressed to a body that could arrange for implementation. In Zuid-Holland, AReA presented six regional project envelopes for east–west urban axes and landscape sections across the north–south motorway corridor.

In taking this approach the authors of the design had made a fundamental choice to look for continuity in accessibility and circulation, on the functional level. The spatial design emphasised articulation of the urban and landscape differences rather than imposing uniformity.

The same conclusion was drawn from the second design exercise for the line as a whole, dating from the 2005–2007 period. The A4 is one of the four motorways for which an 'integral route design' was drawn up (see Figure 4.3), a national government initiative based on the conclusion that the motorway was a sizeable public space where many people

4.2 – 2000 – AReA: mobility, enterprise and environment on a higher level

According to the AReA study, the area between Amsterdam, Rotterdam and Antwerp constitutes a network of three mainports. The study was set up by the provincial governments of Noord-Holland, Zuid-Holland, Noord-Brabant and Zeeland, the employers' organisations VNO-NCW and AVBB (now Bouwend Nederland), and the ANWB motoring organisation. They advocated an integrated three-dimensional approach based on mobility, economic activity and green space. The A4 motorway is not posited as a central or connecting axis, although AReA did envision the road as an international through route, with exclusive lanes for long-distance traffic.

spend much of their time. The A4 was dubbed the 'Delta Route', a concept which was elaborated in a series of 'architectural specifications' and in the ambition to showcase the open landscape panoramas, urban infrastructure landscapes and the mainports as 'acceleration points' along the route. Due to the scale of the landscape in the Holland region and the polycentric structure of the Randstad, the urban, landscape and infrastructure backdrops come in quick succession. Moreover, the authors note that the road is often secondary to transverse relationships: field patterns, rivers, dikes, and even the new high-speed railway line and urban infrastructure (see Figures 4.3 to 4.5).

'Fitting roads into the landscape is a negative notion. I associate that with hiding or camouflaging. The key is to treat infrastructure projects like environmental or landscape projects. This increases the chances of getting a better quality design that will be embraced by residents and other stakeholders.'

Jan van der Grift, former Delta Route Project Manager for Rijkswaterstaat, currently at Bureau Plano

The national infrastructure and transport investment programme

Since the early 1990s, national investments in transport and infrastructure in the Netherlands have been bundled in the Multi-Year Programme for Infrastructure and Transport, an annex to the annual national budget. Decision on the projects to be included in this investment programme are made in close cooperation between regional government and national government in regional arenas such as the Southern Randstad. This is because the national and regional road and rail infrastructure are closely interconnected and the national motorway and rail infrastructure is used by local and regional traffic. It is also a natural product of the institutionalised planning culture of cooperation and consensus.

To come to decisions in such a multistakeholder setting, parties cooperate and make joint decisions based on an agreed set of 'rules of the game' which ensure that decision-making moves forward and that stakeholders are heard. The scope of decision-making was purely focused on traffic and infrastructure until 2008, when the scope of the programme was widened, in theory, to include a more area-based approach, with attention to spatial development in connection with infrastructure investments (see Figure 4.9a). At the same time, national spatial policy was looking for new bridging concepts to connect spatial policy and infrastructure policy (see Figure 4.9b).

The 2012 National Policy Strategy for Infrastructure and Spatial Planning (*Structuurvisie Infrastructuur en Ruimte*) integrated the national visions on spatial development and infrastructure, and since then national and regional governments have slowly been taking steps towards integrated investment programmes for infrastructure and spatial development. Infrastructure and transport considerations, such as traffic bottlenecks, remain the major motivation for national government, while considerations of spatial and economic development are brought to the table mainly by regional stakeholders. Deals on programme priorities and project investments for realisation are often made by all parties contributing budgets to a shared solution.

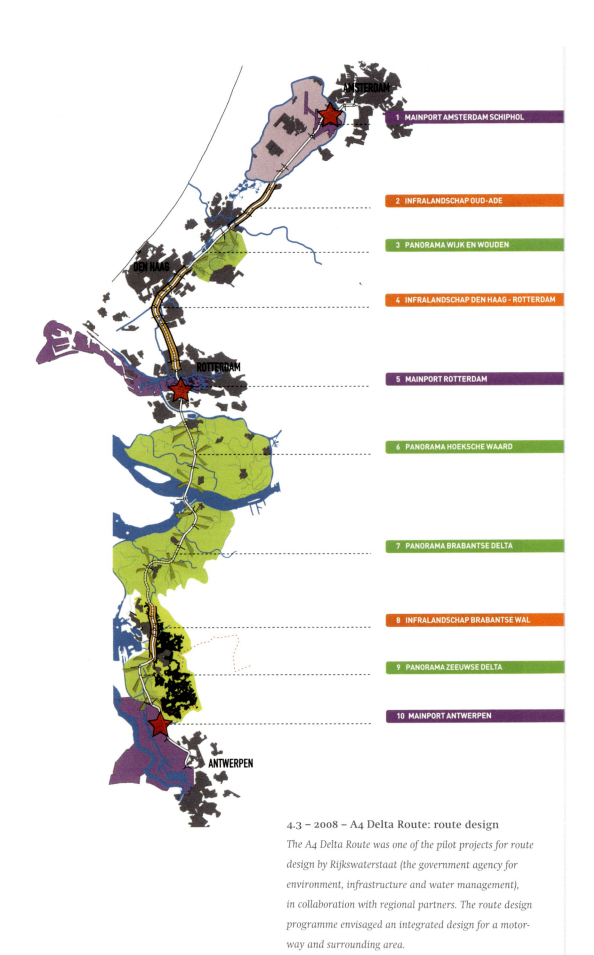

4.3 – 2008 – A4 Delta Route: route design

The A4 Delta Route was one of the pilot projects for route design by Rijkswaterstaat (the government agency for environment, infrastructure and water management), in collaboration with regional partners. The route design programme envisaged an integrated design for a motorway and surrounding area.

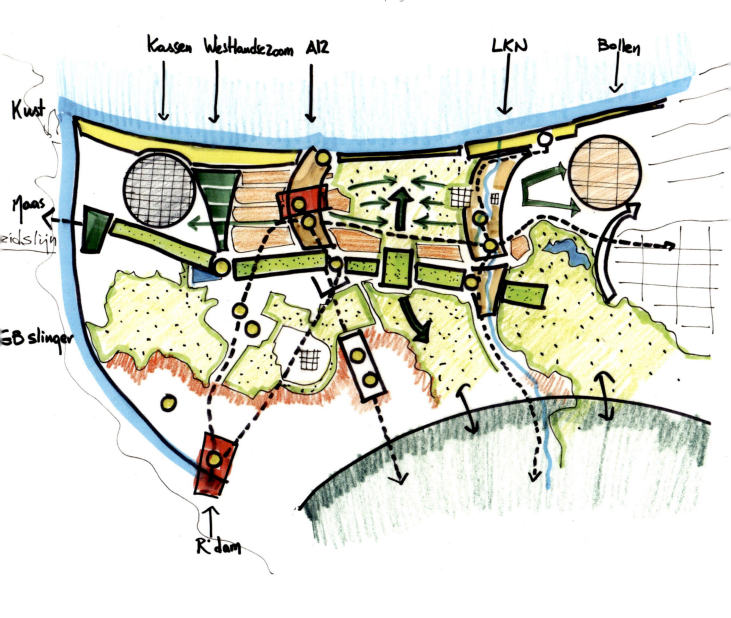

4.4 – 2003 – Transformation zone along the A4

This drawing was a building block in developing the strategic map for the formal 2003 provincial policy document 'West'. The drawing illustrates the design task for the A4 corridor as an integrated development programme including green spaces, urban development and infrastructure rather than a mere road-building project. This regional design is the root of what became the 'transformation zone' policy concept for this and other regions of Zuid-Holland.

4.5 – 2008 – Delta Route: strategy map for the area between Leiden and The Hague

In 2007, the route design for the A4 motorway was incorporated into three key or 'jewel' areas. One of these was the 'panorama' between Leiden and The Hague: the open landscape between the two cities. To further develop the panorama, meetings took place between Rijkswaterstaat and regional parties. Recreational and ecological networks cross the motorway and connect various inland landscape zones with the coastal dune landscape.

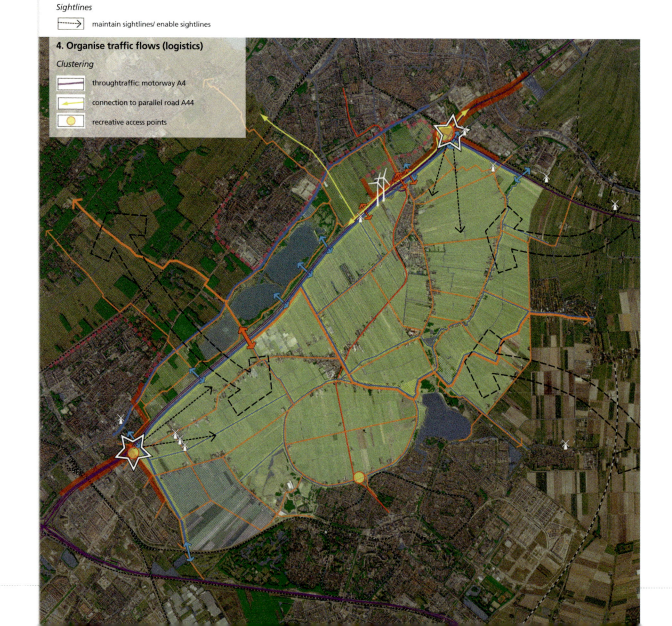

1. Reinforce major landscape zones
- Panorama Wijk en Wouden (Green Heart)
- Vlietzone
- Duivenvoorde corridor

2. Strengthen spatial relations
Ecological connections
- macro-gradient
- wet ecological connection
- green-blue network

Recreational spatial cross connections
- recreational network
- recreational connections

3. Staging the highway
Access Points
- access points

Contrasts
- emphasise city edges (contrast city - country)

Sightlines
- maintain sightlines/ enable sightlines

4. Organise traffic flows (logistics)
Clustering
- throughtraffic: motorway A4
- connection to parallel road A44
- recreative access points

F4.2

2 _Escaping from the dichotomy between city and countryside

National spatial planning in the Netherlands has evolved around a strict division between town and country, based on a policy of protecting the open countryside as much as possible from the effects of encroaching urban development. The AReA and the Delta Route designs can be understood as attempts to escape from this dichotomy. They posit infrastructure and not urbanisation as the driving force behind spatial development and built on the late 1990s discourse about corridors. That planning concept never made it to the stage of policy, precisely because of the fear, justified or not, that these infrastructure corridors would be filled with ribbon development – but it did leave a mark on policy.

The debate was vigorous in the South Wing of the Randstad, particularly among the partnership of municipalities, regions and the province working on the development of the urban axis in the province. The provincial government wanted to develop a concept that would do justice to both the corridor approach and the city/landscape divide. In 1998, it appointed a project team to develop such a concept based on a regional design approach. One result of this was a discussion framework on corridors, which divides the functioning of the A4 corridor (and with it, the design task) into five layers (see Figure 4.6):

1. Flow (centring on the transport clusters from and to the main ports)
2. Network (centring on the economic concentrations and large green spaces)
3. Hanger (centring on the structuring of and link to regional green spaces and urban systems)
4. Adhesion (centring on integration into an urban network)
5. Profile (centring on the traffic management organisation of the road)

In the AReA project the first three levels are clearly recognisable. The other two, adhesion and profile, were delegated to a suitable administrative level via the project envelopes. The plan can thus be seen as an attempt to structure the task. The Delta Route design did directly address the profile and adhesion levels, but in practice it was only applied sporadically. National government proved not to be the most consistent guardian of the plan, and regional parties felt that they

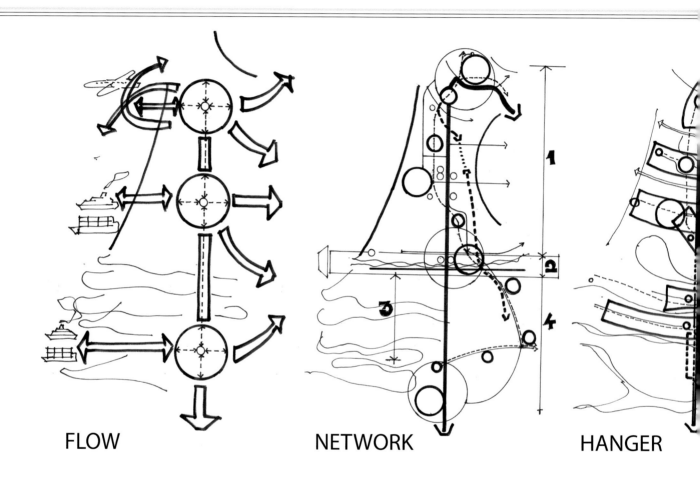

Shaping Holland - Corridors   139

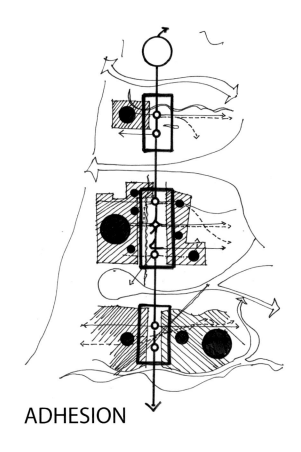

ADHESION

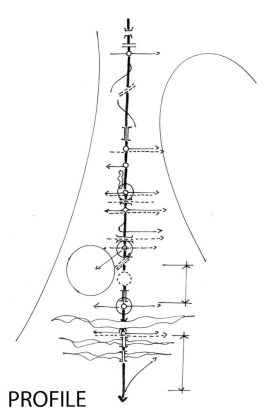

PROFILE

4.6 – 1999 – Five levels for comprehending designing the A4 corridor
Five levels for designing the A4 corridor, as defined by the provincial North–South Corridor project team in 1999. From left to right: flow, network, hanger, adhesion and profile.

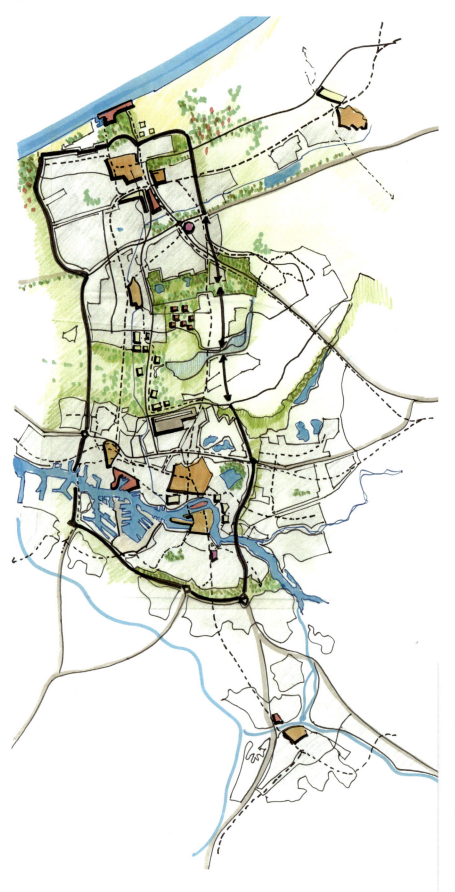

4.7a – 2008 – The Hague and Rotterdam Twin City

The concept of the Twin City shows how the cities of Rotterdam and The Hague could function more as a single entity. This 2008 map visualises the idea of a ring road for the twin city parallel to the RandstadRail network. To the right (north) the A13 motorway would be downgraded once the A4 connection between The Hague and Rotterdam was realised (to the left, south).

Shaping Holland - Corridors 141

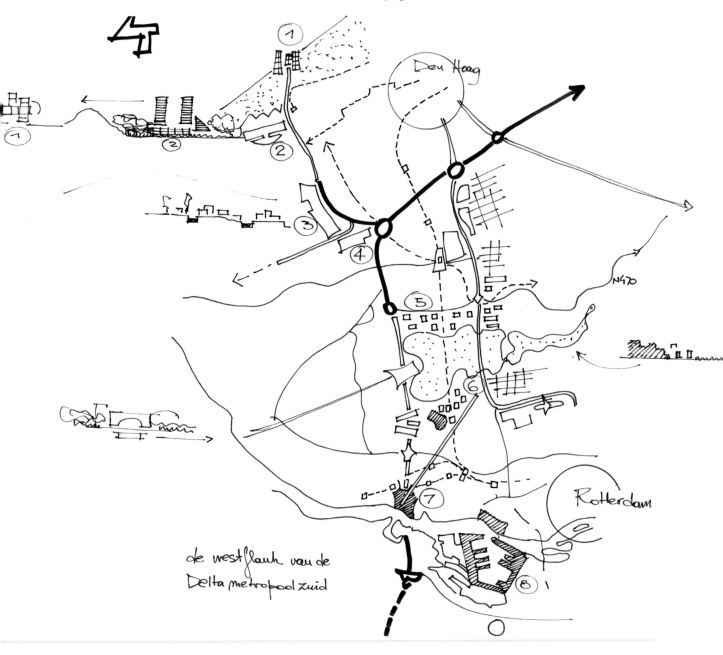

4.7b – 2004 – West flank of the South Wing: opportunities linked to the construction of A4 Delft–Schiedam section

This drawing was the basis for a regional economic study by Buck Consultants. Building the road below grade through Midden-Delfland offers new opportunities for the cities of The Hague and Rotterdam and the area between them. Expanding the daily urban system creates new possibilities for the labour market, real estate development and accessibility.

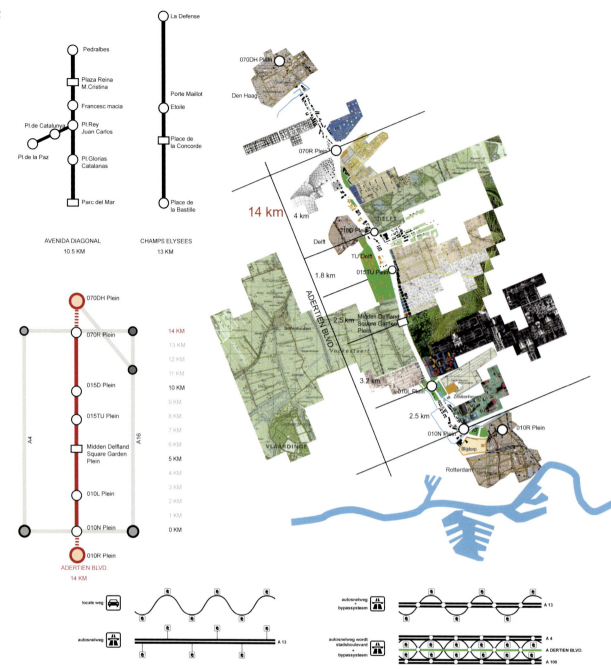

4.8 – 2002 – Deltametropolis design studio: elaboration for The Hague–Rotterdam A13 motorway, OMA 'ADERTIEN'

In 2002, the Ministry of Housing, Spatial Planning and the Environment requested the chief government architect to set up a Deltametropolis Design Studio. Three prominent architects (Teun Koolhaas, Dirk Sijmons and Rem Koolhaas) were asked to come up with a vision for a Deltametropolis. The OMA study (Rem Koolhaas) developed the concept of the A13 boulevard, downgrading the motorway to a connecting urban boulevard between Rotterdam, Delft and The Hague. This study was carried out in close collaboration with the municipalities and the provinces of Noord-Holland and Zuid-Holland.

'We finally managed to put the A4 Delft–Schiedam motorway on the map and scrape together the necessary funds because we were able to show the big picture. It was a cast-iron case, and I've told it hundreds of times.'

Hans Kleij, then Programme Director at the Province of Zuid-Holland for the Norder plan

were insufficiently consulted. The momentum behind Delta Route was running out of steam. Moreover, by 2005 preparatory work was already well underway for two precarious sections in Zuid-Holland – the city of Leiden and the historic landscape of Midden-Delfland. In Midden-Delfland in particular that was a historical breakthrough after a fifty-year planning history (see also Chapter 3). Regional design played a decisive role here.

3 _Road v open landscape: Out of the impasse

These days Rotterdam–The Hague can be seen as a twin-city region. This was not the case not so long ago. A series of investments in infrastructure and economic development as well as the trend towards more regional patterns of daily life made it necessary to expand the scale of urban planning policy beyond the borders of the core cities (see Figure 4.7a,b). Nowadays drivers have a choice of two routes between The Hague and Rotterdam: the A13 and A4 motorways. The different attractions of these two routes have been a regular topic of investigation (see Figures 4.7a,b, 4.8 and 5.5a,b). The A13 has a long history and takes a direct route between the two city centres. The A4 is the trunk road from Amsterdam to Antwerp and runs along

the edges of The Hague and Rotterdam. A recently built section of this road cuts through the heritage landscape of Midden-Delfland, a link in the motorway network that has been mentioned in national infrastructure plans since as early as 1959. The reason for this extremely long planning period was the major impact the road would have on the landscape. We have said more about designing with this landscape as a whole in Chapter 3.

From the 1970s growth turned out to be less vigorous than forecast and the damaging environmental impacts of road traffic have come increasingly to the fore. Many planned new roads were scrapped, but the plan for the A4 held its own in national policy as completing the international corridor from Amsterdam to Antwerp was still thought to be important for the economy. The new road could make use of the existing tunnel under the Meuse, while the A13 could not be widened because it was hemmed in on both sides by Rotterdam neighbourhoods.

By 2000, the seven-kilometre road section between the towns of Delft and Schiedam was still not under construction, even though it had been included in a series of transport structure plans. The problem was the vulnerable traditional peat meadow

4.9 – The A4 in national transport policies

The idea of an A4 corridor as a continuous connection between Amsterdam and Antwerp emerged in national transport policy in the 1970s. In previous years, as these maps show, the sections currently constituting the A4 had been accorded a different role in the expanding national road plans, which had as yet only been implemented to a very limited extent.

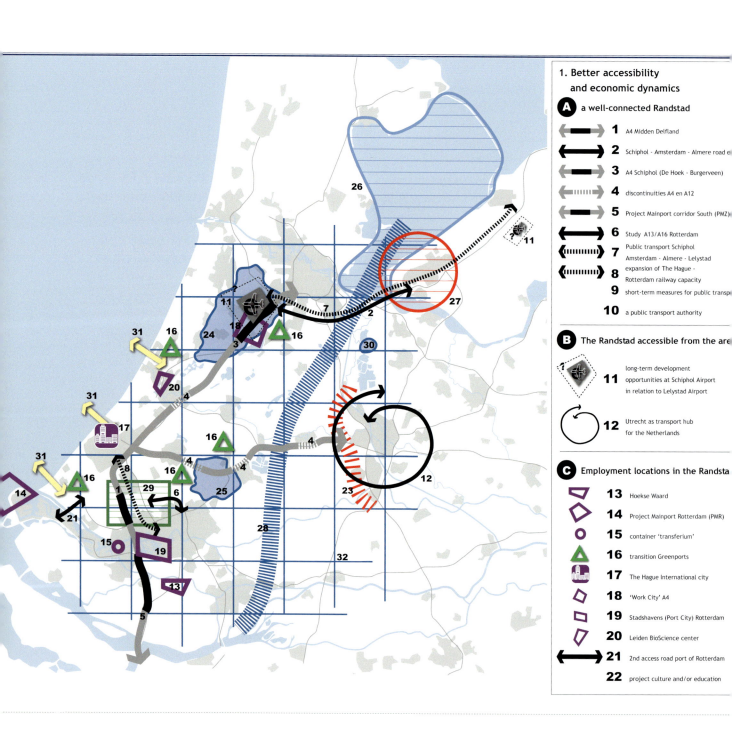

Shaping Holland - Corridors 145

4.9a – 2007 – Randstad Urgent programme: reinforcing the cohesion and competitive position of the Randstad area

The 2007 Randstad Urgent programme was a programme of major projects aimed at strengthening the internal cohesion and competitiveness of the Randstad region, in which the national government and the region cooperated closely. Many of the projects were connected to the A4 motorway, either directly or indirectly. The section of A4 motorway through Midden-Delfland is number 1 on the map.

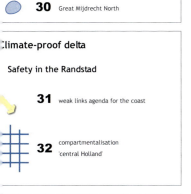

Attractive residential, working, and living environment

living in the Randstad

23 sustainable building in the region of Utrecht
24 Haarlemmermeer
25 Zuidplaspolder
26 agenda for the future IJmeer/Markermeer
27 jump in scale Almere

Recreation and beautiful areas in the Randstad

28 backbone for nature and recreation in the Green Heart, Water Axis
29 beautiful and vital Delfland
30 Great Mijdrecht North

Climate-proof delta

Safety in the Randstad

31 weak links agenda for the coast
32 compartmentalisation 'central Holland'

Long-term strategy

Robust approach looking to the future

33 Randstad Vision 2040

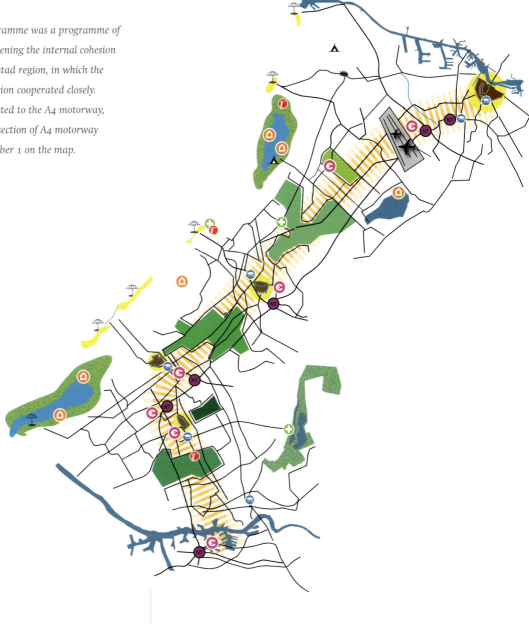

4.9b – 2008 – Coastal City scenario for Randstad 2040: development strategy

Randstad 2040 was a national government policy document on spatial planning published in 2008. In this scenario, the A4 motorway was an important backbone for the Randstad.

landscape of Midden-Delfland. Since 1965 this landscape had been a designated buffer zone separating the urban areas of Delft and Rotterdam. It was the only cultural landscape in the Netherlands with its own reconstruction act setting out the framework for development and land use in the area, backed by investments in agriculture, ecology and recreation (see also Chapter 3). The new section of the A4 motorway would cut right across this area, and over the years there had been vehement opposition to the road not only from residents and landscape lovers, but also from successive provincial executives.

But the pressure kept on increasing. Good-quality, reliable infrastructure had gained a permanent place in national spatial planning as a precondition for a strong international competitive position. The A4 was crucial to this as the main connection between two main hubs (the port of Rotterdam and Amsterdam Schiphol Airport) and three horticultural centres exporting fruit, vegetables, flowers and bulbs (see Figure 4.9a,b). The road connection between The Hague and Rotterdam emerged as a weak link in the spatial economic structure of the South Wing. Traffic queues on the A13 motorway, the old road, grew longer by the year and residents along the route in Rotterdam suffered increasingly from the poor air quality. A road-pricing policy to curb car traffic proved socially and politically unattainable and alternative improvements in the road connection between the urban regions of The Hague and Rotterdam drifted out of focus. The missing link was no longer only symbolised by the road number but also in the completion of the section of road between Rijswijk and Delft in 1999. This came to a sudden end at the Delft South exit, culminating in a big clover leaf at a viaduct over the A4 itself.

Regional design solved the problem. This was an era in which billions of euros were available for major new infrastructure projects and in which new ways to integrate infrastructure into the environment were being developed. Elsewhere in the Netherlands pioneering infrastructure projects were designed and built, in which motorways ran through urban areas hidden in 'hollow dikes' with a new park laid out on top. In this planning culture, provincial executive member Marnix Norder broke through the impasse for the A4 motorway with a plan for the integrated development of Delft–Schiedam (IODS). This plan provided for the construction of the A4 between Delft and Schiedam in a half-sunken tunnel so that it would be hardly noticeable in the landscape (see Figure 4.10),

4.10 – 2001 – Integrated development of Delft–Schiedam (IODS): Midden-Delfland region

Construction of the A4 motorway between Delft and Schiedam became possible thanks to a package of six interconnected projects which together constituted the cornerstones of the Norder plan and the ensuing IODS covenant, in which the government parties and civil society organisations involved concluded the agreements in 2006. The six projects are: a green-blue ribbon (comprising 100 hectares of new nature and the wildlife passages), clearing of isolated greenhouses, recreational routes, green farming (a new kind of agriculture), the Delft-Schiedam section of the A4 motorway, and urban development in Vlaardingen-Schiedam. This drawing aided the political breakthrough in 2001 by illustrating the minimal visual impact of a well-designed road embedded in the landscape.

4.11 – 2018 – Construction of the A4 motorway in time

The A4 motorway was never designed as a single complete route. It was designed in fragments from 1938 to 2015, each one a product of the conditions prevailing at that place and time. Construction of the last missing link south of Rotterdam still hangs in the balance.

as well as various measures and investments to enhance the landscape of Midden-Delfland. Agri-environmental management was given a boost, old isolated horticultural greenhouses were removed, and recreational access was improved. A 100-metre-wide 'eco-aqueduct' and wildlife overpasses over the A13 motorway and the Schie waterway provided ecological and recreational connections to the Green Heart. The cost amounted to €100 million per kilometre – in contrast to the government's estimate in the 1990s of the same amount for all seven kilometres in total.

The project's strength lay not in a compromise to keep all sides happy, but rather in the persuasiveness of a single integrated project which would actually lead to a better landscape. This also applied to the section of road in Schiedam along the border with neighbouring Vlaardingen, which had long faced opposition from the Schiedam municipal executive. The municipality argued that the A4 motorway should not be seen, heard or smelt. The solution was initially put forward by private parties, who showed what opportunities would arise if the two municipalities could grow together over the road. This was eventually included in the Norder plan in the form of a tunnel with an extension of the public urban space on top.

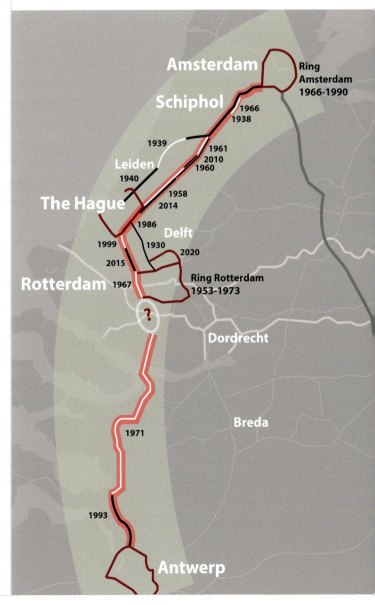

4.12a – Plank model

4.12 – 1996 – Design for bridging the A4

In this 1996 urban design study, the Province of Zuid-Holland aimed to remove the barrier effect of the A4 motorway and link the new VINEX neighbourhoods to The Hague. The Plank model was inspired by preliminary studies by Rem Koolhaas to identify sites for major new urban developments such as conference centres, stadiums and prisons.

4.12b – *A4 motorway overpass study*

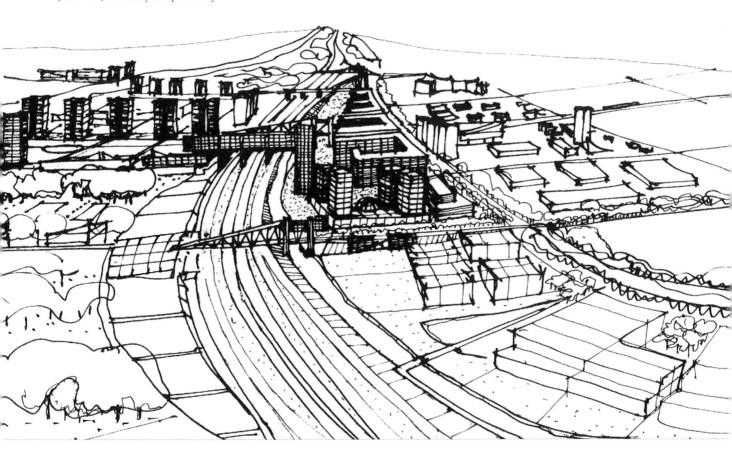

Conceptually, the Midden-Delfland approach is at the level of adhesion and hanger (see Figure 4.6), although 'adhesion points' and 'hanger hooks' were deliberately not sought along the road itself. The perception from the landscape is paramount. Road users only see the tunnel walls and have little inkling of the landscape above. The grounds for building the infrastructure are found at the levels of flow and network. The road profile itself is not a design objective. In the design for the Delta Route, the Rijswijk–Schiedam stretch was therefore included as part of the 'infrastructure landscape' between The Hague and Rotterdam, and not as a landscape panorama.

In itself there is much to be said for a corridor approach to an international trunk road such as the A4 motorway, with a varied staging of panoramic views over open cultural landscapes, stretches along city frontages and points of contact with the main ports and other economic hubs. People's perception of the surroundings gives the route an identity and reinforces awareness of the distance covered. However, the solution for Midden-Delfland shows that this approach also has its limits. A road can conceivably be incorporated into the landscape in an aesthetically pleasing way if it is designed as a whole and accompanied by a landscape plan. The A4, however, was never designed as a complete route between Amsterdam and Antwerp. It came about piece by piece, from one connection to the next, between 1938 and 2015, and under conditions determined by place and time (see Figure 4.11). To this day, one link to the south of Rotterdam is still missing, requiring a short detour. The unity of the line itself is purely traffic-based. This development history presents opportunities for regional design at the scale of individual urban and landscape sections.

4 _Design concepts for urban transformation

A corridor-based approach to a succession of motorway sections fits in with the Dutch planning tradition, with its deep-rooted principles of clustered urbanisation and open areas outside the cities. The planning task is then to regulate the economic pressure of development to make intensive use of suitable stretches of motorway and to look for interconnectivity with parts that are less or not at all built-up. In 1995 architect Rem Koolhaas's OMA firm came up with a visionary plan for the corridor at The Hague. A year later,

4.13 – 2010 – Artist's impression of A4 motorway entrance

This impression is an elaboration of the A4 zone as part of The Hague's Central Zone in a study by the City of The Hague. This study was conducted in 2010 within the framework of the city's structural vision.

the province had worked up proposals for overpasses between the suburb of Leidschendam and the residential neighbourhood of Leidschenveen, which was still under construction. The province elaborated area-specific, almost architectural designs to overcome the barrier effect of the A4 at the edge of The Hague, connecting it to the wider region (see Figure 4.12a,b). These studies were not followed up, partly because the building densities contrasted starkly with the suburban character of the surrounding neighbourhoods and partly because the priority of the City of The Hague was to consolidate the city centre rather than building on the edge of the city. At the same time, the east–west A12 motorway corridor, which penetrates deep into the city, developed as a business district with built-up covered sections, high-rise development and overpasses. In later years the City of The Hague revisited the visions for the area along the A4 motorway corridor, again looking for integrated solutions for urban development, water and green space, and local and regional infrastructure (see Figure 4.13).

The development of zones situated along the main infrastructure requires cooperation. Processes are needed in which urban and landscape design challenges are tackled step-by-step, leaving room for adaptation to plans along the way. In 2003, Zuid-Holland introduced the concept of 'transformation zones' as a framework for such processes (see Figure 4.4; see also Chapter 3 and Figure 3.4). These are zones in which many development agenda converge, urban and/or rural, often but not necessarily connected to infrastructure. Each transformation zone calls for its own governance arrangements and solutions for the integration of functions and qualities that cannot be transposed to other situations. Regional design contributes not only by presenting a vision for urban or rural interventions, but also by outlining the contours of the development programme in advance so that subsequent efforts deliver best-fit solutions.

One example along the A4 corridor is the Leiden region. Public opposition was not as strong as in Midden-Delfland, although the situation was more complex. The required increase in the capacity of the motorway would have direct consequences for regional development, but at the same time was also enabled in part by the associated urban development.

'Fitting the A4 into the landscape has been fairly successful, but no proper relationship was created with the urban surroundings. Urbanisation turned its back on the A4.'

Twan Verhoeven, traffic planner at the Province of Zuid-Holland

5 _Mutual dependencies in the Leiden region

The A4 motorway at Leiden is part of the The Hague–Schiphol stretch of road that was built around 1960. A new road was needed at the time because the old No. 4 national trunk road (currently the N44) could not be upgraded to a motorway. The new '4a motorway' was planned as part of a longer route and so unlike the earliest Dutch motorways did not run centre-to-centre, but rather at some distance past the urban areas. In the decades that followed a major traffic interchange developed near Leiden around new housing and industrial development, including a large Heineken brewery, to accommodate an increase in passenger and freight traffic and further growth of the bulb-growing sector in the region. Traffic from both the east and the west joined the motorway here. This infrastructure increasingly posed a barrier to the development of new housing in the Leiden region.

It was clear that these challenges impacted each other in complex ways and at various scales. The stakeholders requesting widening of the motor-way were the horticultural, logistics and other economic centres in the Randstad area. Responsibility for the profile of the road, traffic flow,

quality of life and safety lay with national government. The province was concerned about the impact of a widened road on the landscape and the provincial road network. The municipalities were looking for room for urban development and the development of green recreational areas. At one time there were so many ongoing projects and initiatives that in 2006 another regional design studio was started to pull them all together into a coherent package. Once again the outcome united the parties involved behind the wider narrative and gave new direction to the choices that had to be made (see Figure 4.14).

Regional design had also given direction to the search for a solution for the area east of the Leiden region, where the A4 passes the region, that was supported by all stakeholders. In 1999 a design study by the province showed what development possibilities would be opened up by an overpass over the A4. These opportunities were grouped together in four scenarios, ranging from at one extreme a clear-cut boundary with the protected landscape of the Green Heart to the east, and at the other extreme a business environment that could compete with Amsterdam and Schiphol Airport combined with a complete urban district on the other side of the A4.

Shaping Holland - Corridors   153

4.14 – 2006 – Leiden–Katwijk Axis: research-by-design

The Leiden–Katwijk Axis Design Studio (2006) conducted a research-by-design study into development opportunities in the Leiden region. This map shows the sizeable building programmes at the former Valkenburg airbase and the university (later named Bio Science Park). The proposed Rijnland road direct connection between the A4 and A44 motorways runs partly underground. The projected Rijn-Gouwe light rail line hugs the provincial road and the new residential areas are oriented towards the line. The results from the design studio formed the basis for formal adoption of the development in policy.

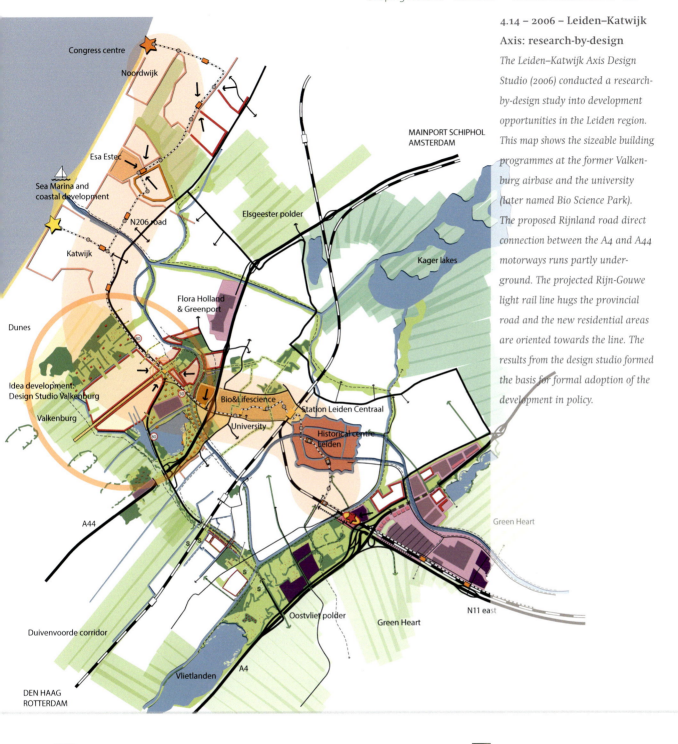

4.16 – 2005 – Masterplan and zoning for the Leiden-West interchange node

The Leiden-West interchange node was a partial elaboration of various studies into the development of the Leiden–Katwijk Axis. The idea of developing this node originated from a province-wide narrative on node development: integrated transport and spatial planning.

4.15 – 2001 – Planning map for the W4 project at Leiden

A co-production by national government, the province and the municipalities, the W4 Masterplan was supervised by a public-private partnership. In this map we can see the extended sunken section of the motorway, a number of residential and employment areas along the A4, the cross-connections, and the development of recreational green space in the Munniken polder as a gateway to the Green Heart.

Facilities

Social
SC   School, health
CE   Commercial education

Commercial
H   Restaurant / hotel/ leisure
SU   Supermarket
L   Mooring spot with catering
SP   Sports
T   Search location gas station

Architecture
A   Architectural accent

Current
U   University
M   Museum Naturalis

Area

++++   Municipal boundary

Project boundary node Leiden-West

Noise barrier A44

High-pressure gas pipeline

First row of buildings along the highway /
provincial road (high-visibility location)

*)   University grounds to be transferred
(to be further elaborated)

Road network

Car

Highway

Provincial road

Local road

Existing access to the area

Access to the area through indicative route

Access to the area depending on
the choice route for Rijnlandroute

Plan variants Rijnland route

Important avenues within project area

Existing avenues connected to the project area

P+R   Existing Park and Ride

P+R   New Park and Ride location depending on
the final route of Rijnlandroute

Cycling

Regional cycle route

Recreational route / Recreational connection

Location of a movable bridge over
the Oude Rijn for slow traffic

future recreational connection

Public transport

Stop RijnGouwe Line East- indicative preference
Steering group RijnGouweLijn (2003)

Route RijnGouwe Line East (from Gouda to Rijnfront-South):
indicative preference Steering group RijnGouwe Line (2003)
Route RijnGouwe Line West (from Valkenburg to Noordwijk
see footnote*)

Search area crossing RijnGouwe Line / Provincial road N206

Railway station

*) The decision-making around the RijnGouwe Line West is less
ambiguous. This part of the line is subject to Environmental
Impact Assessment (EIA). Decision-making about the route is
highly dependent on decision-making about the development of
the airfield.

Functions

Green / Recreation

Continuous zone with country estates

Oude Rijn Park N206: the ribbon

Oude Rijn Park: urban green space /
University Campus / sports facilities

Oude Rijn Park / Estate Rijnfront

Water / Recreation

Water Oude Rijn / Binnenrijn

Water Valkenburg Lake

Water axis estates - 't Duyfrak

Publicly accessible river bank

Residential Areas

Residential buildings between canals and avenues

Future residential areas
Voorschoterweg / Tjalmastrook

Residential buildings on islands in the Oude Rijn

Mixed-use areas for housing and employment

future locations Voorschoterweg /
Rijnfront Zuid-Zuid

Employment locations

University cluster / High-quality companies

future employment areas

Built-up area / urban centres

Leiden, Oegstgeest, Rijnsburg,
Valkenburg

Map detail Klei-Oost (south)

F4.3

The study led to the choice of a package consisting of a development zone along the A4, a longer than previously intended sunken section, development of a hub at the main access into to Leiden and green overpasses in the north and south. Here, too, a sunken A4 motorway was crucial. This ultimately took shape as a 1.5 km half-open tunnel, which included an aqueduct under the Oude Rijn river. This aqueduct is now visible from the road as a lowering of the tunnel roof. In 2002, the development model was elaborated in the W4 Masterplan (*Wonen, Water, Wegen, Werken* – housing, water, roads, work) (see Figure 4.15). As well as specifying the urban development solutions, the masterplan also contained arrangements for implementation. It formed the basis for a covenant with agreements on funding and commissioning of the various components. A development company headed by the private developer Bohemen was set up for the complex array of projects in the municipality of Leiderdorp. The revenue from land and real estate generated by this company enabled the municipality of Leiderdorp to pay its own contribution for the sunken section of the A4. These returns were essential, because this small municipality had to contribute close to €20 million.

Implementation of the W4 projects created opportunities to hook the wider region onto the 'hanger' of the A4. The Oude Rijn Zone in the east was designated as a transformation area, with investments in nature, new development and urban restructuring aligned with the Green Heart policy, the expected light rail connection via Leiden to the North Sea coast (the Rijn-Gouwe line) and the new eastbound N11 road. An initial exploratory design study was carried out on the west of the region, which resulted in further specification of two main options structured around the blue/green network and the regional infrastructure network: could the Rijn-Gouwe public transport line in this part of the region become a compact urban development axis or would the blue/green network determine the pattern of urban development with compact building only near the public transport stops? Should the projected westbound road connection (the Rijnland route) be part of the national trunk road network, or part of the regional infrastructure as a ring road around Leiden? These options were subsequently resolved in a design studio (see Figure 4.14) and constituted the basis for the formal regional spatial plan.

'The design studies on the A4 as part of the Randstad investigated the potential connections between the surrounding area and the motorway. It will be interesting to see whether ideas that were tested twenty years ago will be realised in the future, now that pressure continues to increase on the cities and roads.'

Gielijn Blom, urban planner at the Province of Zuid-Holland

Although an integrated masterplan was prepared for the west of Leiden (see Figure 4.16), the projects were not contractually or financially linked, as in the W4 project. It therefore proved impossible to combine the infrastructure, green space and urban development into a single programme, despite the connections between them. This led to delays in the implementation. After a great deal of political and public commotion, construction of the westbound Rijnland route finally started in March 2017, when most of the urban development projects were already well underway or had even been completed. The Rijn-Gouwe light rail line to the coast was finally cancelled. Meanwhile the two triple lanes of the A4 motorway were already proving insufficient, with this stretch regularly featuring in the national top five longest traffic queues in both directions. Although the stretch of sunken motorway was designed with additional lanes in mind, the underlying road network around Leiden was overburdened. In that respect, the regional design work for this area had not been convincing enough to drive through the integrated solutions that were ultimately needed.

6 _The organisational power of regional design

Twenty years of design on the A4 corridor have shown that its spatial structure and location do not lend themselves to developing a strong regional identity at the level of the line as a whole. The route from Amsterdam to Antwerp does not need a uniform identity. A design approach that expresses the differences in urban and rural sections is more in keeping with the Dutch planning culture and the history of the motorway.

Regional design was able to make the difference by organising and reframing the development agendas, both at the scale of the full 170 km and that of the individual sections through urban areas or open landscapes, where much of development pressure and activity patterns came together. By drawing in proposed developments and making connections, regional design contributed to setting up a new custom-made governance structure. It helped to resolve seeming contradictions and commit commissioning bodies to a shared development objective. The designs enabled them to implement their own projects in the knowledge that they would be part of a greater whole. This made it possible to tie the separate projects together, both physically and financially.

F4.4

These design interventions were important because the construction of large-scale infrastructure almost always involves political, administrative and social tensions, which regional design cannot always alleviate. However, regional design has proved a powerful means for broadening the perspective beyond the road itself and linking it into development opportunities for the landscape and the living environment. Good design can transcend the level of compromise or compensation and lay the foundation for a joint regional process that improves the quality of the environment in all respects.

Shaping Holland - Corridors 159

F5.1

5 REGIONAL-ORIENTED DEVELOPMENT

5.1 – 2005 – *Stedenbaan* as an integral urban development concept for Zuid-Holland
This drawing is the first illustration of the incipient metropolitan area. Urban development along the 'old line' makes it possible to create a coherent urban area.

Regional Transit-oriented Development

Dutch spatial planning has traditionally been strong on urbanisation and mobility policy. Urban growth had to be planned and contained, for one thing to prevent uncontrolled growth of car traffic, and new residential neighbourhoods were linked by tram, metro or rail connections to the centre of the city-region. This approach continued well into the 1990s. Each city built its own public transport network and there is no metro or light rail system for the whole of the Randstad. For longer distances there is only the national rail network, which is one of the most intensively used in Europe.

Around 2000, the Province of Zuid-Holland moved to a fully fledged policy of transit-oriented development at the regional scale: intensifying regional and national public transport networks, connecting the national rail network to the regional networks and envisioning a major programme of area-based urban development around new and existing stations. The regional spatial concept, the development programme derived from that and the collaboration between major players was called *Stedenbaan* – 'Cities Line'.

The *Stedenbaan* concept was motivated by the ambition to locate residential and employment sites within the boundaries of the existing urban area. The focus was squarely on station area developments. Homes, offices and public facilities had to be built where they were easily accessible by high-quality regional public transport services – which were few and far between. The step to transit-oriented development meant investment in light rail, but the financing model for real estate is completely different from that for infrastructure. Both sectors have their own logic. There was real risk that property developers would wait for passenger numbers to increase, whereas those additional passenger numbers were needed before public investments could be made in rail and station infrastructure. The essence of *Stedenbaan* was to package both types of investment in a single programme.

__ Takeaways from this chapter

Using public transport as a backbone for urban development is a proven strategy for sustainable growth. Various forms of transit-oriented development have been developed and put into practice in urban regions all over the world, often focusing on the area around the railway station itself or on investment in the physical rail infrastructure. A strong integrated approach is based on the knowledge that daily life involves trips on a regional scale. In this chapter we see what regional design can contribute to this approach.

- Regional design helps complex alliances of public and private parties to stay on course over a long period, even in times of political turmoil. At the scale of regional public transport systems there is often no metropolitan authority with the power to make decisions and carry them through. In this chapter we show various ways in which progress can still be made at the local and regional levels. Design studios can act as catalysts in these processes.
- Spatial design offers a new interpretation of the existing territory. For example, until the beginning of this century the whole system of public transport along the 'old' rail infrastructure in the Southern Randstad had never been graphically represented as a coherent urban area. Just drawing selected spatial structures, reinterpreting their contours and giving them new significance in relation to each other was found to be an act of design in itself.
- Regional design provides a platform for giving voice to common interests. Spatial concepts define the collective space for negotiation and visioning. They generate 'narratives' around which collective investments can be made by parties with different planning and investment time horizons.

> '*Who takes the train to hospital anyway? Ten years ago, that was the thinking. It was perfectly normal.*'
>
> *Paul Gerretsen, Deltametropolis Association and head of the South Wing Studio*

1 _Metropolitan transport system

The concept is attractively simple: build around railway stations to generate more passenger traffic while simultaneously increasing rail capacity to make it more attractive to build around stations. This is an efficient way to make progress towards the main objectives of urban development policy: strong cities, keeping car traffic in check and protecting the open countryside against development. In the 1990s national government had funded two new international railway lines: one for freight and one for passenger transport. This freed up capacity on the busiest lines of the national railway network within the Randstad. By 2005, the idea had grown into an urban growth agenda called *Stedenbaan* (Cities Line) – a transport-oriented development programme along 150 km of existing railway line between Leiden and Dordrecht. It had been calculated that 25,000 to 40,000 homes and a million square metres of office space could be built around main stations. Such numbers would allow the frequency of regional rail services to be increased to six local stopping trains per hour. This frequency rivals a metro train frequency, making it unnecessary for passengers to consult timetables – a fully fledged metropolitan light rail system. *Stedenbaan* was accommodated

as a programme within the South Wing Administrative Platform, the partnership of provinces and municipalities in the Southern Randstad.

The *Stedenbaan* programme was scheduled for completion in 2020, but the envisaged frequencies of rail services and square metres of new building space have not been fully realised. Nevertheless, much has been set in motion. The planning concept has undergone considerable development, particularly in the initial years. The apparently simple relationship between urban development and rail infrastructure has been refined and tightened up in many respects. The bigger stations have developed into central locations within cities and public transport has taken a qualitative leap forward. In contrast, the *Stedenbaan* programme itself was put on the back burner after the 2008 credit crisis. Like Sleeping Beauty, it was hesitantly kissed awake under a different name, and with another coalition, in 2018.

2 _Emerging network city

The *Stedenbaan* initiative was not the first to recognise the close link between urban development and public transport. Since the construction of Dutch new towns such as Zoetermeer near The Hague and Spijkenisse near Rotterdam in the 1970s, it has been recognised that good public transport connections are essential. The VINEX urban expansions of the 1990s are of a size that warrants high-quality public transport, but they often lack the necessary density for profitable operation. A recurrent problem with these large-scale housing developments was that proper public transport connections were not established until years after the first homes were completed. The transport companies and the transport ministry were responsible for the investments, but only started building and operating services when enough people were living in the new neighbourhood. By that time nearly all households owned one or two cars.

In the 1990s the national government operated a location policy for the construction of office space and facilities, which the provinces had to incorporate into their planning policy. Offices could only be built at 'A locations' – central locations near the main railways stations. Businesses that generated a lot of freight traffic and had a low density of staff per square metre were directed to 'C locations' along motorways. 'B locations' could be accessed both by car and public transport and were suitable for smaller offices and large-scale public facilities such as hospitals. This location policy did not apply to housebuilding.

The province launched the *Stedenbaan* concept on top of this with the aim of scaling up the urban system (see Figure 5.1). The daily urban system, the area within which people commute on a daily basis, was expanding and both passenger and commercial traffic between the Rotterdam and The Hague regions was increasing. It was also clear to the province that planning practice was not responding quickly enough as planning concepts such as the location policy and the compact city didn't provide an answer to these developments. Rotterdam and The Hague were both recognised as central cities with their own ring of suburbs. The cities each had their own VINEX neighbourhoods (see Chapter 2), with railway connections within their own urban regions. The orientation of public transport towards one city only is the main reason why VINEX neighbourhoods have effectively become car-dependent neighbourhoods.

The province attempted to break free of the entrenched city-regional approach, both regarding the pattern of urban development and the transport

5.2 – 1994 – Three models for rail infrastructure

These studies, made in the 1990s, for the public transport network in relation to urban development are based on urbanisation models for the area between Delft and Zoetermeer (see Chapter 2 and Figure 2.3). The options explored include the Delfy line between Delft and Ypenburg, the existing Hofplein railway line, the ZoRo line between Zoetermeer and Rotterdam, and various tram and bus connections.

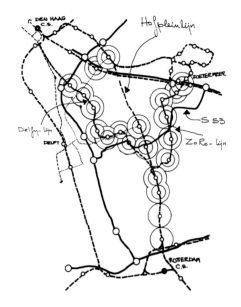

5.2a – Model M1

For this model the following infrastructure was chosen:

- Hofplein Line: The Hague-Rotterdam (via Pijnacker)
- Delfy Line: The Hague-Rotterdam (via Ypenburg/Delfgauw)
- ZoRo Line: Zoetermeer-Rotterdam (variant NS/4M, Voorafsche Polder)
- S53: Fast bus route

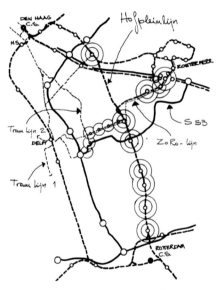

5.2b – Model M2

For this model the following infrastructure was chosen:

- Hofplein Line: The Hague-Rotterdam (via Pijnacker)
- ZoRo Line: Zoetermeer-Rotterdam (variant NS/4M, Voorafsche Polder)
- Tram Line 1: Ypenburg-Pijnacker Station (via Delfgauw)
- Tram Line 2: Delft Station-Pijnacker Station (via Delft University of Technology-Delft South)
- S53: Fast bus route

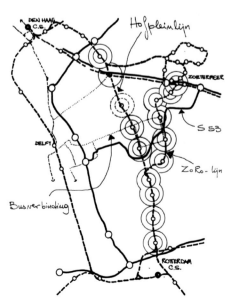

5.2c – Model M3

For this model the following infrastructure was chosen:

- Hofplein Line: The Hague-Rotterdam (via Pijnacker)
- ZoRo Line: Zoetermeer-Rotterdam (variant NS/4M, Voorafsche Polder)
- Bus connection: between Delft and Pijnacker
- S53: Fast bus route (variant south of new Pijnacker Station)

5.3 – 2003 – Walking distance to stations

Stedenbaan proposed a number of new stations to generate more room for development. Early on in the development of the Stedenbaan concept, proximity to stations was seen as a principle for urban development. Circles indicating walking distance to stations became symbolic of this transport-oriented development.

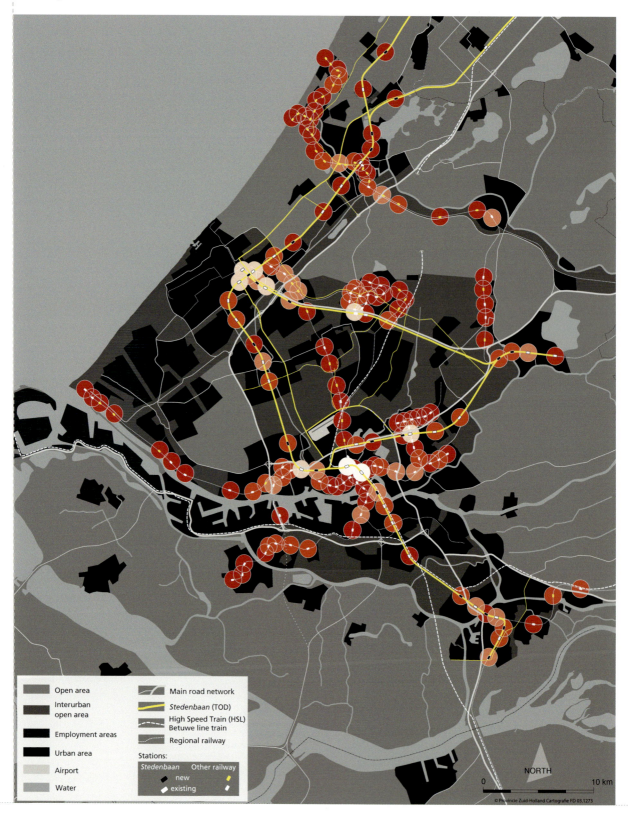

F5.3

networks. The South Wing of the Randstad was to start functioning as a single urban system and regional development had to keep pace with this to ensure a healthy future. This ambition was laid down in the 1994 policy statement for the future entitled 'More Elbow Room for the South Wing' (*Meer armslag voor de Zuidvleugel* – see Figure iii.5a–c), which already included a regional public transport network as a key aim: 'Urban systems increasingly operate on a scale that exceeds that of individual cities and agglomerations. We do not have a high-quality public transport system at this regional scale. To what extent is it possible to develop a high-quality and financially feasible interregional public transport network using parts of the NS (Dutch Railways) network and the city networks and by judiciously locating traffic-generating activities?' (see Figures 5.2a–c and 5.3).

Before the *Stedenbaan* programme, it was agreed that regional public transport should preferably be in the form of a light rail system. Relatively isolated lines serviced by local stopping trains would be prime candidates for conversion to light rail, especially the local lines in the area between Rotterdam and The Hague. In 1994, different integrated network options for these lines were explored (see Figure 5.2a–c). Eventually, the light rail option was chosen for development along former railway lines between The Hague and Zoetermeer and between The Hague and Rotterdam (the Hofplein line). This rail network, known as *RandstadRail*, has been integrated into the tramway network of The Hague and into the Rotterdam metro network.

It had been clear for some time that the success of these investments would partly depend on developments near the stations. *RandstadRail* was feasible thanks to the additional demand created by the construction of the adjoining VINEX neighbourhoods in both the Rotterdam and The Hague regions. In the areas surrounding other lines converted to light rail, since 2003 designated as 'transformation areas', the integrated area developments that would provide the required demand for transport were either in preparation or had already been started.

Large parts of the national railway network were unsuitable for conversion to light rail as they were used by both local trains and intercity trains. *Stedenbaan* was to resolve this problem and would become the backbone of the system. It would connect with all these light rail lines and pull them together to form a network (see Figures 5.3 and 5.4). It would

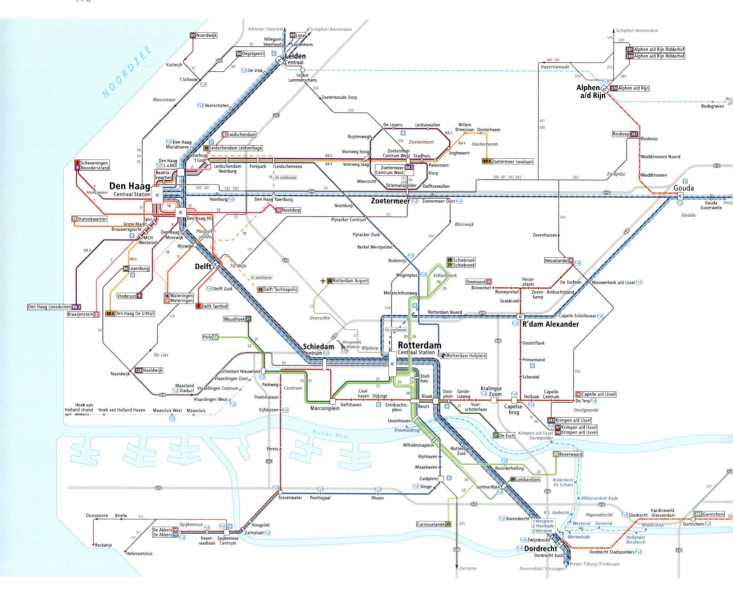

5.4 – 2007 – The South Wing public transport system as a metro map

The scope of **Stedenbaan** *has changed over the years. Initially focused on the 'old line', it later expanded to become a complete high-quality public transport network.*

also connect the main cities and towns of the Southern Randstad (see Figure 5.1). Even without a doubling of railway tracks, local trains with a frequency similar to the metro system could share the tracks with the remaining intercity trains. The space available for the urban development to be serviced by this increased frequency of rail services differed per station and the scoping of the areas destined for transformation and monitoring remained under discussion.

Realising the *Stedenbaan* concept depended heavily on good cooperation. Partners had to be able to rely on each other. Rail companies had to invest in infrastructure, stations and stock – all investments with a long turnaround time. It fell to the municipal authorities to organise implementation for each station. This not only involved real estate, but also public space, as it was clear from the outset that the areas surrounding stations had to be attractive places to live, work and spend time in. Municipal authorities had to trust that each would fulfil their own responsibilities, as the development of only a couple of station areas would not be sufficient to generate the necessary transport demand. This presented a task for the province as the coordinating intermediate tier of government and as the advocate of network creation in the Southern Randstad.

3 _*Stedenbaan* as regional design

As a transport system, *Stedenbaan* uses existing tracks and stations. Initially there were thirty-two stations, but by the start in 2005 a further fifteen new stations were envisaged. Thus far, however, only one of these, Sassenheim, has been built. Nevertheless, despite the limited changes on the regional map, *Stedenbaan* can be considered a successful example of regional design.

Simply naming the old railway as a spatial element that gives structure to the network city is an act of design in itself. Dating from around 2002, the first official drawings representing *Stedenbaan* were of a new infrastructural hierarchy for the South Wing, in which international and regional traffic were systematically separated: both for car traffic and rail traffic (see Figure 5.5). The A4 motorway corridor connecting Amsterdam, The Hague, Rotterdam and Antwerp (see Chapter 4) was intended for international road transport, freeing up the A13 motorway between Rotterdam and The Hague and the planned A13/A16 connection as

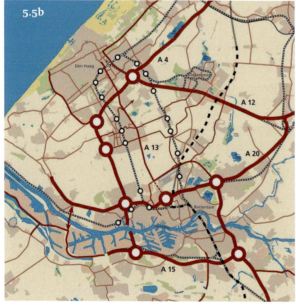

5.5 – 2002 – Separation of national and international road and rail traffic

Map 5.5a shows the situation in 2002. Map 5.5b shows the proposed separation of international and regional traffic. Two regional rail connections between Rotterdam and The Hague are the current RandstadRail and the Stedenbaan route along the 'old line'. This was a major step in the development of the Stedenbaan concept.

an additional ring road for Rotterdam for regional road transport. Similarly, the HSL high-speed rail link freed up capacity on the main rail network for regional rail services, opening up prospects of a frequency comparable to that of the *Randstad-Rail* network (which did not yet exist at the time).

As an urban development concept, *Stedenbaan* had a different logic. At the start of the project in 2005, studies were carried out into the feasibility of the new concept, one of which had an explicit design character: *Milieudifferentiatie langs de Stedenbaan* (Environmental differentiation along the Cities Line) by urban design firm Urban Unlimited and Utrecht University (see Figure 5.6). The title indicated the design task ahead. It is characteristic of network cities that they each have different qualities and supplement rather than compete with each other. The same goes for areas in and around stations, but in practice the researchers found that the developments in these areas tended be uniform, with the same types of apartments, offices, public facilities and local amenities. This uniformity had to be overcome, and there was every opportunity for that as the stations differed widely from each other in terms of surrounding land uses and their position in the network.

Shaping Holland - Regional transit-oriented development   173

5.6 – 2005 – Quality differentiation along *Stedenbaan*

This study into the opportunities for development around Stedenbaan stations was part of a programme entitled ReUrbA (Reconstruction of Urban Areas), which in turn was part of the EU Interreg IIIc programme. The map shows Stedenbaan hotspots for active youth on the left and for rehabilitating elderly people on the right.

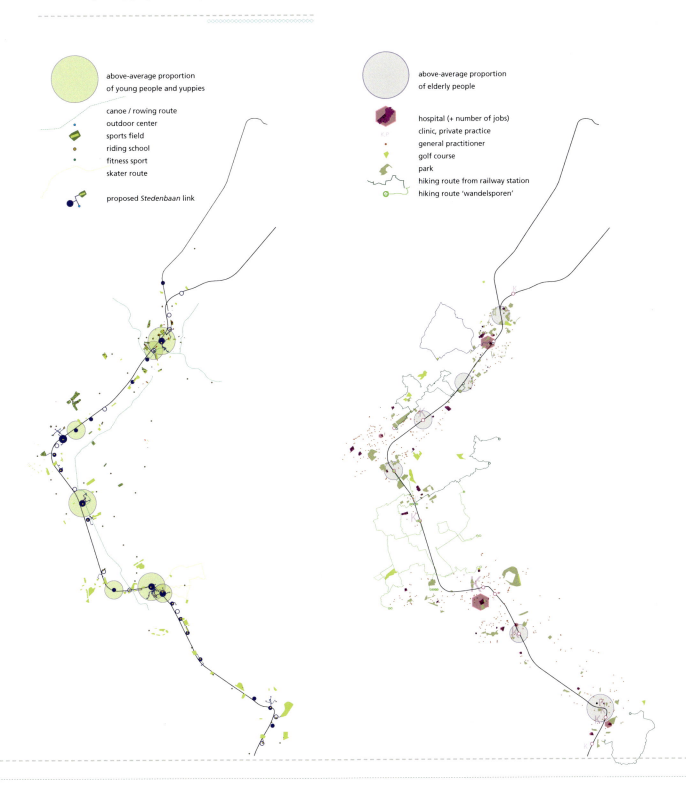

AGENDA PER STATION ON THE 'OLD LINE'
BASED ON STATION PROFILES

STATION
The focus of the Stedenbaan network is on the stations of the 'old line' and on linking stations into local road networks and light rail connections.

STATION PROFILE
The profile potential is based on the current situation and the ambitions that the municipality has for the station area.

RESIDENTIAL AREAS
The housing programme can be small or large depending on the rural or more urban context.

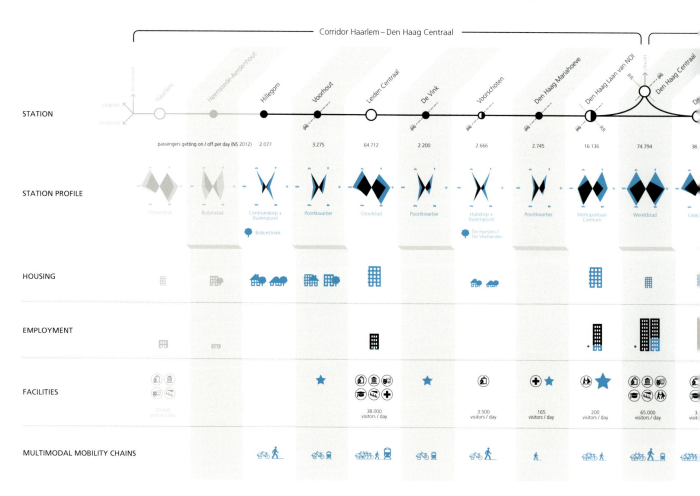

5.7a – 2013 – *Monitoring of development around stations along the old line based on their place values and node values within 1200 metres from the station*

Shaping Holland - Regional transit-oriented development   175

Publication Stedenbaan 2013

Research and composition by
Deltametropolis Association (VDM)
(adapted by the authors)

OYMENT LOCATIONS

f the office vacancy rate, transformation will have to
e, especially at stations that are not accessible by
transport modes. The mixed-use and multimodally
e locations are the most popular on the office market.

for transformation (based on station profiles)

t vacancy
+
on to other functions

vacant office space m²
source: Jones Lang LaSalle 2012

FACILITIES

Realisation of regional facilities shows the largest potential at multimodal stations (easily accessible by car and public transport). Development is required where there are no or relatively few facilities available.

Agenda for regional facilities

+ multimodally accessible
+ visitors per day <2.000*
+ multimodally accessible
+ visitors per day <2.000*
+ low current intensity

* visitors per day from regional facilities
multiple sources, processed by VDM

Existing regional facilities

retail
museum/day attraction
meeting-/conference centre
cinema
theater
hospital
MBO/ HBO/ University

source: LISA 2010

MOBILITY

Where the accessibility via public transport, slow traffic or car is insufficient, further development of the mobility system is required. Special attention is paid to the required number of bicycle parking facilities.

shortage of bicycle parking facilities
<500
500–1000
>1000 source: ProRail

Accessibility agenda
slow traffic   public transport   roads
smaller programme
large programme

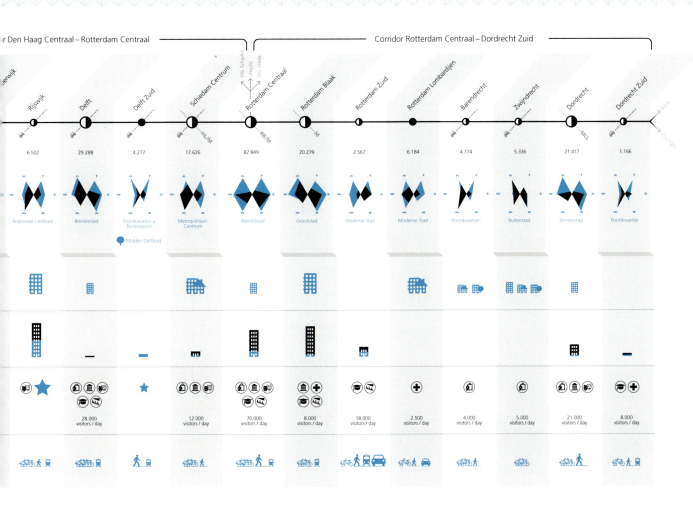

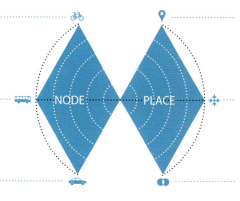

slow traffic
Available rental bicycle facilities, railway crossings and bicycle parking facilities, degree of fine-meshed network within 300 m

public transport
Availability, frequency and directions for public transport modalities

roads
Existence of motorways, motorway exits, regional roads and parking facilities

proximity
Intensity of use in the first 300 m in relation to the total

degree of intensity
Density of residents, employees and visitors per hectare (ha) within area of influence of the station

degree of mixed use
Ratio of inhabitants and employees per ha (100 x 100m)

5.8 – 2007 – Areas within the sphere of influence of *Stedenbaan* stations

This map is an initial exploration of what the areas within the sphere of influence of the Stedenbaan stations looked like, and thus the actual potential for transport-related development. Until this study, theoretical circles of 800 and 1,200 metres around stations were mostly used. The survey differentiated between the types of stations and how they were connected to the wider network and the urban region.

5.7b – 2013 – The butterfly model: picturing node value and place value

In the butterfly model of a station, one wing stands for the node value (determined by slow traffic, public transport and roads) and the other for the place value (determined by mixed use, intensity and the direct proximity of public transport-related forms of land use). Ideally, node and place values should be perfectly in balance with each other.

The researchers combined origin and destination profiles for all existing and potential new stations by asking who starts their journey there from home, and why people travel there as a destination. *Stedenbaan* can only achieve its ultimate goal if the origin and destination profiles of the stations differ sufficiently from each other. Regional public transport can then steer urban development and become a more realistic alternative to car travel. Densification at station areas is then no longer the ultimate goal; station development can also be about adding facilities or making improvements to routes and modalities of travel to and from the station. This logic of differentiation was maintained over the full duration of the programme and further operationalised in methods for monitoring development (see Figures 5.7a,b and 5.8).

Both this design exercise and the exploratory studies into the housing market and traffic effects generated promising results, and the province sensed it was on to something. *Stedenbaan* proved a feasible and effective programme for development into a network city at the level of the South Wing or Southern Randstad. The South Wing Administrative Platform, the partnership between the five regional organisations of

municipal authorities and the two major cities of Rotterdam and The Hague, put *Stedenbaan* on its own agenda as a strategic project. Dutch Railways had announced that its stopping trains (so-called Sprinters) would run every quarter of an hour from 2007 as a step towards the ten-minute frequency it had set as its ultimate goal. Two eastbound lines to Gouda were added. But *Stedenbaan* was still primarily an exercise in analysis and lobbying – no-one had committed themselves to actual realisation.

4 _Measuring is the key to knowledge

In late 2005, the South Wing Administrative Platform published a brochure entitled *Van idee naar programma* (From idea to programme). The province, the municipal partnerships and Dutch Railways signed a declaration of intent to implement the development programme. All the parties were to know, understand and act on their role, and they were supposed to understand and accept that their contribution was part of a larger whole, with objectives that transcended the local level. This applied in particular to the close to twenty municipalities which had one or more of the *Stedenbaan* stops. They had become involved with the process through their regional partnerships,

'One of the benefits of the South Wing Studio was that it lowered the threshold for municipal authorities to collaborate with the province. That has become much more commonplace since then.'

Francisco Colombo, urban planner at the Province of Zuid-Holland

that is to say indirectly. Pilot projects were being conducted in eight municipalities, but these were exploratory studies that did not yet necessarily require commitment. The municipalities examined how *Stedenbaan* could be implemented in each particular environment, mostly looking at whether a new station was feasible or desirable. Apart from local government, housing corporations and developers also needed to be involved, as they were expected to make the investments.

The division of responsibilities between the municipalities had not yet crystallised. The exploratory designs by Urban Unlimited and Utrecht University gave some direction, but not enough substance to serve as a basis for a multibillion programme like *Stedenbaan*. Although the investments were divided between a large number of parties, the programme as a whole would cost several billion euros. The regional design approach was again used to come up with a well-founded programme to capitalise on the differences between the stations – a programme, moreover, that would be comprehensible and acceptable to everyone: no impressionist panoramas, no inventive interconnections, but real, solid choices that could be monitored. The necessary design decision lay not

so much in the planning map as in the choice of the criteria that would structure the regional programme.

The South Wing Studio (*Atelier Zuidvleugel*) had already been set up on the initiative of Joost Schrijnen, director of spatial planning and mobility at the Province of Zuid-Holland. The studio consisted of an independent group of researchers who conducted research-by-design studies into how the Southern Randstad could develop into a network city, and what was needed to achieve that. This studio was given the design assignment.

The design method consisted of three steps. First, the research area was mapped out (see Figures 5.9 and 5.10): the transformation and expansion areas within a radius of 1,200 metres of each station that could become available between 2010 and 2020. Municipalities received, sometimes unexpectedly, a postcard showing developments already planned in the vicinity of their stations, with the request to confirm these or suggest alternatives. It was concluded that, based on development with average densities, the quantitative development programme was easily achievable. In the second step, the likelihood of success of the development was

5.9 – 2006 – Development potential around *Stedenbaan* **stations**
The South Wing Studio made an inventory of the development potential for homes, employment mixed uses, leading to a development concept for Stedenbaan *corridors.*

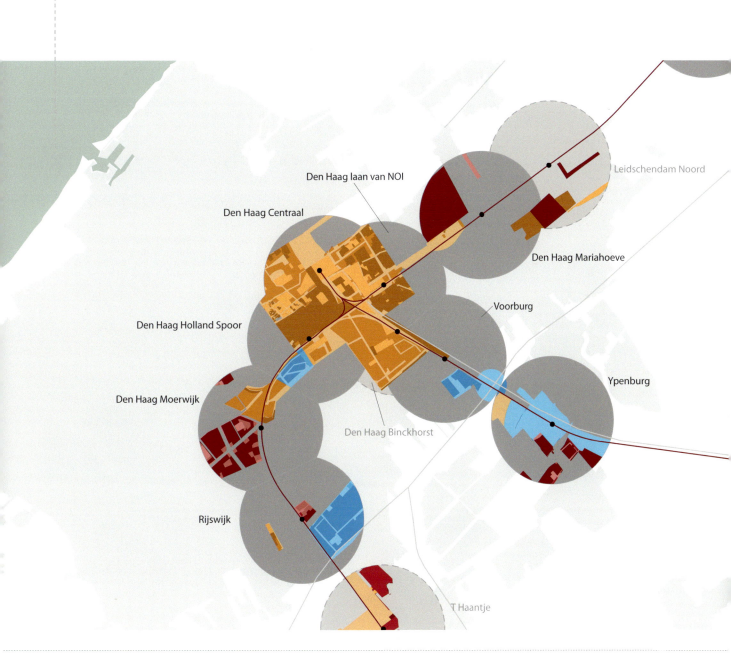

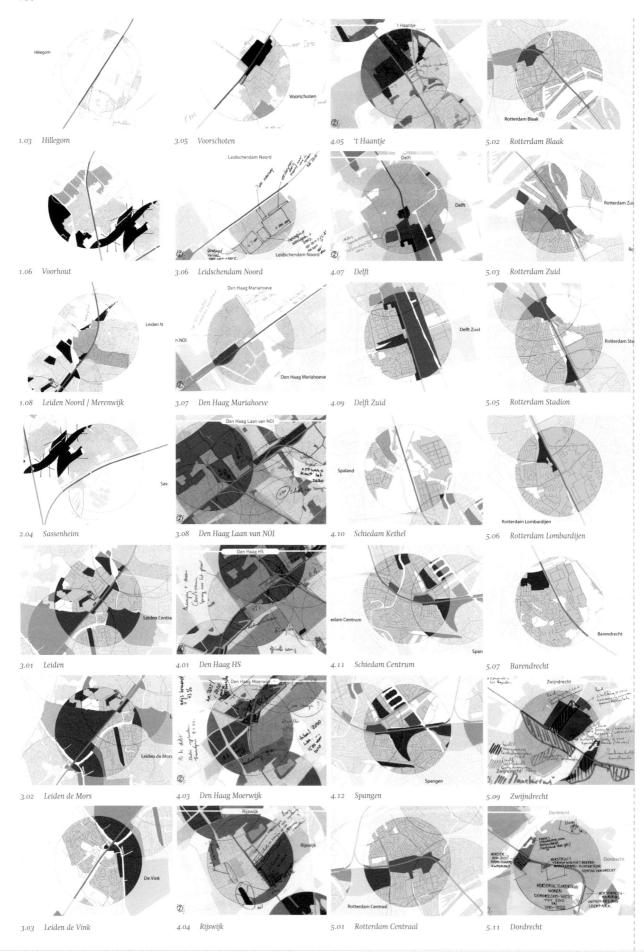

Shaping Holland - Regional transit-oriented development   181

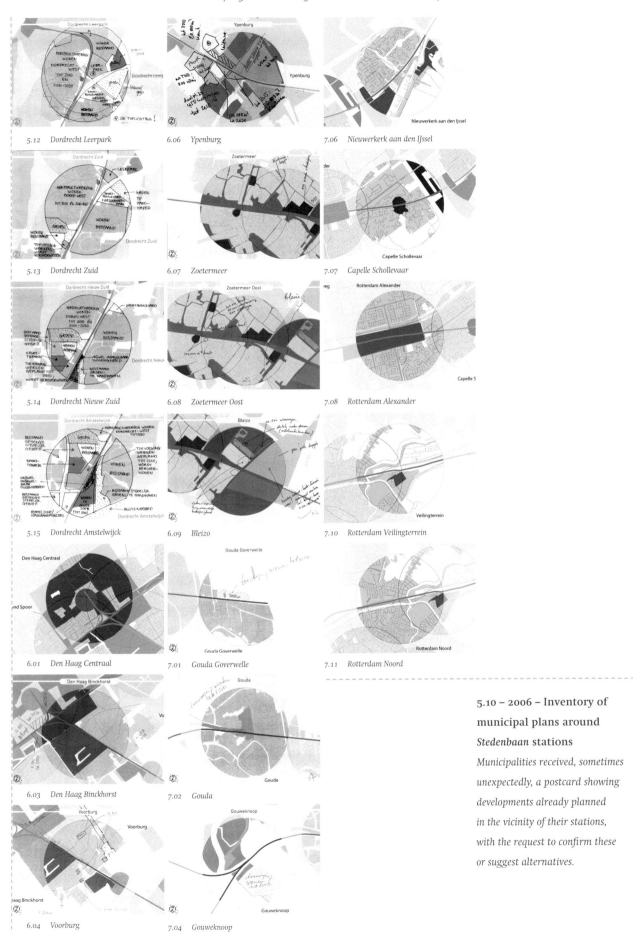

5.10 – 2006 – Inventory of municipal plans around *Stedenbaan* stations

Municipalities received, sometimes unexpectedly, a postcard showing developments already planned in the vicinity of their stations, with the request to confirm these or suggest alternatives.

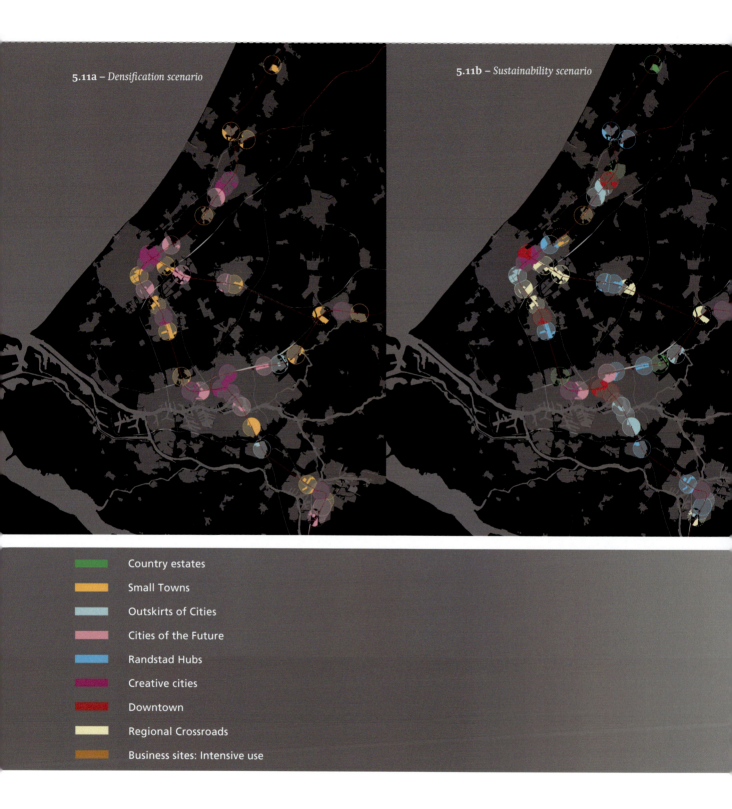

Shaping Holland - Regional transit-oriented development 183

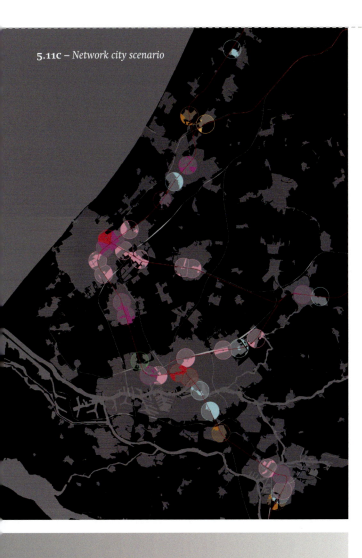

5.11c – *Network city scenario*

5.11 – 2006 – Three development scenarios for *Stedenbaan*

The South Wing Studio presented three scenarios showing how the joint development of the public transport network and the areas around the stations could contribute to different urban development visions: 'Urban densification', 'Sustainability' and 'Network city'.

'We worked intensively on the Stedenbaan *scenarios. How do locations change in relation to each other when you view them from the perspectives of sustainability, densification or the network city? That's something we did not do previously. You could call it a precursor to serious gaming.'*

Helmut Thöle, urban planner at the Province of Zuid-Holland and member of the South Wing Studio

closely examined. Here, the choice of criteria was crucial. The researchers defined four factors that determine the profile of a station. Two of these concerned the transport network, the position of the site in the public transport and road networks. The two others were about the spatial dimension: the residential and workforce densities and the degree of mixed use. The future potential of a station area are largely determined by these four factors. South Wing Studio presented nine combinations that occur along *Stedenbaan*, designated with names such as 'Randstad Hub' and 'Creative City'.

Each of these four determining factors are subject to change. Investments in the infrastructure or buildings can open up new opportunities for the future. That was the third step and the next design decision in the research. South Wing Studio showed how the prospects for the future change as sustainability, the network city or densification are consistently given priority, and the types of development programme needed to meet these priorities (see Figure 5.11). The result of the research project was not only three scenarios for the future but more importantly a rich database available to all *Stedenbaan* partners.

The regional design for *Stedenbaan* had far exceeded the conceptual level. With forty-seven existing and potential new stations, the study required considerable geographical precision.

For this exercise, the Studio contacted all the municipalities involved. This step was both logical and necessary, because *Stedenbaan* could not come about without the cooperation of the municipalities. However, the researchers encountered considerable opposition. They were advised to split the programme up into a number of railway lines because the relations between the stations would be clearer at that level. They were mistrustfully asked why the province was suddenly promoting urban densification – the fact that they were not acting on behalf of the province but a broad coalition of parties was not taken seriously. The larger municipalities had their own planning departments and spatial visions and had little interest in other development concepts. The plethora of facts and figures was overwhelming rather than convincing.

F5.4

5 _Local government

Regional design also led to the conclusion that there was a whole world to be gained – that of local government. Two executive members from the South Wing partners, the late Ronald Bandell, mayor of Dordrecht, and Asje van Dijk, provincial executive member, were particularly keen to advocate *Stedenbaan* to small and medium-sized municipalities. Those were the parties that would initially be needed.

But then, in 2008, the credit crisis hit. Real estate development programmes were shelved, and the station locations were no exception. Moreover, it appeared that public transport was growing anyway, even without an additional development programme. As a result of these developments, one of the anchors of *Stedenbaan* – the interaction between urban development and public transport – became less urgent.

In the background, there was uncertainty at a more fundamental level. Despite all the facts and figures that had been gathered in previous years, the willingness to invest remained shaky, also among private developers and corporations. The South Wing partners were all shying away from all-out commitment. They were behind *Stedenbaan*, but it remained an isolated programme that had insufficient influence on other spatial planning decisions. Municipalities set their own priorities, realising major projects elsewhere or extensive developments around stations. Examples of this are urban areas under redevelopment near the Moerwijk station of The Hague and around metro stations in Rotterdam-Zuid, which actually led to lower rather than higher densities. Large parking facilities were built near to central *Stedenbaan* locations, and the presence of a *Stedenbaan* station had no effect on the parking standards applied in housing projects.

The provincial government did not specifically oppose this. It had no tradition of planning for inner city densification and, partly for that reason, did not have the authority to enforce implementation of the programme – the *Stedenbaan* programme in its chosen form was sometimes experienced as a power grab. Finally, the South Wing Administrative Platform, which was the actual commissioning body of the programme, lost prestige. At the national level, the first Rutte government (2010–2012) imposed a rigid programme of deregulation aimed at smaller government and tidying up what was referred

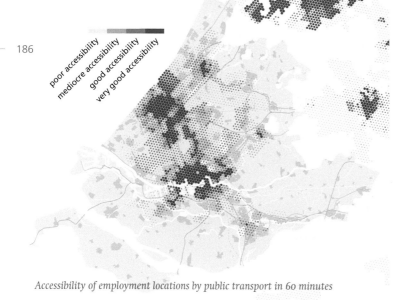

Accessibility of employment locations by public transport in 60 minutes

5.12 – 2011 – Isochrone map of public transport: accessibility of jobs by public transport within 60 minutes

A significant part of the thought processes surrounding Stedenbaan is to take a different look at accessibility. This map shows workplace accessibility from particular spots on the map. Darker colours indicate more jobs accessible within 60 minutes by public transport.

to as 'administrative spaghetti'. This put government partnerships under pressure and in 2017 the Platform was replaced by an informal network organisation for the Southern Randstad, which did not have its own office.

This course of affairs could easily have sounded the death knell for *Stedenbaan*, but the underlying rationale proved inescapable. Internationally, transit-oriented development, the coordinated development of transport networks and the areas served by public transport stops, was on the rise. The closest planning concept to this in the Netherlands was the *Stedenbaan* initiative. When the credit crisis put the brakes on building initiatives near stations, the South Wing Administrative Platform decided to prepare for the future after the crisis by carrying out research. In line with the database built by South Wing Studio, it decided to continuously monitor trends in mobility and urban development (e.g. see Figure 5.12). Since 2009, a *Stedenbaanmonitor* (Cities Line Monitor) has been published annually (see Figure 5.7). In 2011, the cooperation partners introduced an extension to *Stedenbaan* called *Stedenbaanplus* (Cities Line Plus), the plus referring to other metro and light rail lines and high-quality tram and bus connections included in the programme.

These initiatives kept *Stedenbaan* abreast of knowledge about transit-oriented development, providing a clearer picture of a station's position within mobility chains in which the train journey is just one link, and more accurate definitions of influence areas. The tremendous growth in bicycle traffic in particular continues to have an impact and bicycle parking facilities and bicycle sharing are now more prominent than in the early years of *Stedenbaan*.

6 _*Stedenbaan* returns

Stedenbaan is gathering a following. In 2013, the neighbouring province of Noord-Holland opted for an exercise similar to South Wing Studio, which included some of the same people. The perspective this time was more investigatory: there was no direct connection with a policy programme such as *Stedenbaan*, and the province was the only commissioning body – transport companies, for example, were only involved indirectly. And yet *Maak Plaats* (Make Space), as the study was called in Noord-Holland, took the thinking further. Here, the entire rail network was analysed, but coherence was sought at the level of nine corridors. The diagrams that represent the profile of the station have been refined into 'butterflies' (see

> *'The Environment and Planning Act will offer the Province an opportunity for a relaunch of the Stedenbaan concept: integral and based on societal challenges, but expanded to encompass quality at street level.'*
>
> *Jan Ploeger, programme manager at the Province of Zuid-Holland and former project manager at the Ministry of Transport, Public Works and Water Management*

Figure 5.7a,b), based on earlier academic work by Luca Bertolini at the University of Amsterdam. One wing stands for the node value (determined by slow traffic, public transport and roads) and the other for the place value (determined by mixed use, intensity and the direct proximity of public transport-related forms of land use). The basic principle behind this study is that the butterfly will only function properly if both wings are in balance.

The relationship between urban development and infrastructure remains topical and is increasingly urgent as building picks up again. Much new development should be concentrated in inner city locations. Urban development concepts are needed to guide this process and transit-oriented development can provide an answer, but this will have to go a step further than *Stedenbaan*, which was limited to the influence areas around stations. It had been insufficiently successful in this, partly because the influence of *Stedenbaan* did not extend to car traffic, for example in the form of lower parking standards for homes and businesses nearby stations. Full transit-oriented development permeates the entire territory of a region, which means that the opposite is also relevant: limited development outside the sphere of influence of a station.

With the current administrative structures, the initiative for such a steering development concept lies with the province. The Dutch government, which until recently had prime responsibility for this, has now shifted it firmly onto the shoulders of the provinces. A province cannot fulfil this role without having an influence on the strategies for inner city development. Ten or so years ago, this was still highly unusual. For that reason alone, the preparatory work for *Stedenbaan* has been particularly valuable.

The question, though, is what design repertory is needed. In the case of *Stedenbaan*, the designer was the engineer and it was all about optimisation. This can be made even more effective as availability of data increases and its use becomes more sophisticated. But it must be about more than that. Regional design has the potential to be a powerful integrative force. Design is capable of connecting regional goals with local values and ambitions, and has been shown capable of resolving challenges considered very difficult by locals and politicians to the satisfaction of all concerned. The power of regional design can be of help with this too. What is needed is a joint approach to developing railway station environments or working with development principles that allows sufficient scope for regional solutions by the local parties involved.

The battle for densification has not yet been won. The *Stedenbaan* programme began around 2005 in the expectation that it would be completed by 2020, but a transition like this means a change in structures and working practices that people are used to and organisations are built around. It affects the very fibres of the planning system. It will be at least twenty years before the focus can be fully concentrated on implementation. *Stedenbaan* will still not be complete even when stopping trains run every ten minutes and 40,000 homes and a million square metres of office space have been built. It will only be complete when executive members are called to account if they miss development opportunities around their stations and stubbornly continue to build where mobility depends on the car.

F5.5

Shaping Holland - Regional transit-oriented development 189

F6.1 BEYOND

THE PORT

6

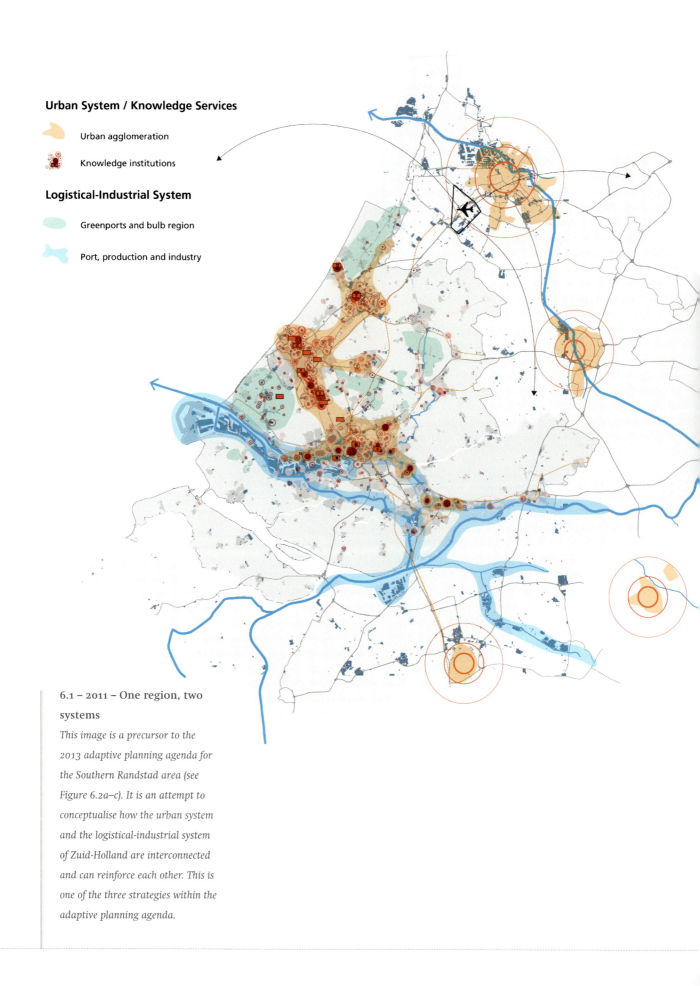

Urban System / Knowledge Services
- Urban agglomeration
- Knowledge institutions

Logistical-Industrial System
- Greenports and bulb region
- Port, production and industry

6.1 – 2011 – One region, two systems

This image is a precursor to the 2013 adaptive planning agenda for the Southern Randstad area (see Figure 6.2a–c). It is an attempt to conceptualise how the urban system and the logistical-industrial system of Zuid-Holland are interconnected and can reinforce each other. This is one of the three strategies within the adaptive planning agenda.

Beyond the Port

Every square metre of the Netherlands is carefully planned, right down to the areas of seemingly untouched nature. But that does not mean that every square metre has been designed. There are areas where neither architects nor landscape designers have left their mark – the industrial zones, where functionality is dominant. As long as such areas are extensive and mono-maniacal enough, they have a beauty of their own. Take the docklands of Rotterdam, for example. The petrochemical complexes, container terminals and enormous ships all add up to create a fascinating industrial environment. Almost next door, in a case of historical fortuity, is a 'glass city' where endless rows of horticultural greenhouses glisten in the sunlight. In this region a shared resource infrastructure is slowly developing, an example being the exchange of heat and CO_2 between industries and horticulture. Following the 'mainport' designation for the Port of Rotterdam and Amsterdam Schiphol Airport, the 'greenport' policy concept was introduced to bind together the port and regional logistics with the processing and trading hubs and the horticultural production complexes, and to project the image of a modernising agricultural sector with extremely high yields per hectare and servicing an international market: 'feeding and greening the megacities of the world.'

The Netherlands first emerged onto the world stage as a trading nation. The Dutch mercantile spirit drove the expansion of a small port city into Europe's largest maritime port complex, and it was the reason why the small-scale grape cultivation under glass in the Westland area grew into an enormous production and trading complex for fruit, vegetables and flowers. Carried forward on the wave of the globalisation, both complexes have gone through a period of unparalleled growth and were able to exploit each other's potential. Not only are many horticultural products exported via the port, but imported fruit and vegetables are now also processed and traded in the Westland complex.

Merchant and pastor are never far apart, as the Dutch saying goes. Industry, logistics and horticulture have been given room to grow, but the impacts on the environment and quality of life have never been lost from sight. The transition to clean energy and circular production processes now underway is putting these industrial complexes under the microscope again. Can regional design help to steer the transformation of the logistical-industrial system, including the horticultural sector, into a green and sustainable 21st century metropolitan region?

F6.2

__ Takeaways from this chapter

The world stands on the brink of several major transitions with far-reaching implications for globally operating economic clusters. The key global challenge facing industry and the food sector is making the switch to sustainable production processes. This chapter shows how design thinking can create the mental space needed to change course and explore new ideas. Principal players in Zuid-Holland are the greenhouse horticulture sector, which produces food and flowers for the international market, and the Rotterdam port area, an important hub in the energy system and for the transit and trade in bulk goods. Key points:

- Regional design can help to turn scenarios for unknown futures into conceivable, plausible and tangible spatial representations. Crucial to this design process is switching between scales, from global to local. This translates an abstract and unpalatable transition to a sustainable future into narratives about concrete infrastructure and development programmes. The relevant players can unite around these narratives and build a solid basis for the sustainability transition, such as a heat infrastructure.
- Regional design is not just about places and areas, but also about changing flows and networks, and designing interventions within these. This requires continual reinterpretation and visioning on different scales as circumstances change.
- Regional design helps to peel away the layers of complex problems, identify manageable subproblems and compile area-based strategies that can guide physical transformation and development.

'The age of the separation of functions was supposed to be over, but it is not. We're still doing it, but now at the scale of the Delta-metropolis.'

Marco van Steekelenburg, former project manager at Mainport-Greenport, Province of Zuid-Holland

1 _The province of Zuid-Holland expands

On 22 May 2013, Melanie Schultz van Haegen, the minister of infrastructure and the environment, waved the blue, white and red Charlie flag, the naval signal for 'Yes' to open Maasvlakte 2, the extension to the port that was reclaimed from the sea. 'Maasvlakte 2 opens our doors to the newest generation of container ships,' she said. 'The Netherlands now has plenty of space for state-of-the-art terminals. The port will grow by 20%, doubling the container handling capacity. Thousands of new jobs will be created.' On that day, not only the port but also the province of Zuid-Holland was officially 2,000 hectares bigger.

For the time being, this territorial gain concludes the port's westward expansion, which began in the 1970s. The port grew away from the city and towards the North Sea, a development driven by the enormous claim it makes on urban land and the impact it has on the living environment. Maasvlakte 2 continues this trend, making the port suitable for even bigger vessels (such as the MSC Oscar, which brought in 20,000 sea containers in

2015) and an even bigger offshore industry (such as the terminal for the assembly and embarkation of sea-bound wind turbines).

And yet, this port extension also signifies a turn-around, as the port opened itself up to other kinds of land use. This was born partly of necessity, as the Dutch Supreme Court had for years delayed its realisation because the ecological effects were insufficiently clear. In particular, the influence on the sea currents and concomitant effects were carefully investigated and incorporated into the design. The port complex itself, however, was also discovered to be a haven for nature. Between the industrial and logistics areas, seagulls, toads, orchids and many other types of plants and animals have been given their own habitats, and Scottish Highland cattle can be seen grazing right next to moored ocean vessels. And the city was welcome again, too. Maasvlakte 2 added a two-kilometre stretch of beach, an attractive information centre, routes for recreational traffic and carefully staged panoramas attracting tens of thousands of day-trippers a year. Systems that had been separated and pushed apart were gradually reconnecting (see Figures 6.1 and 6.2a–c).

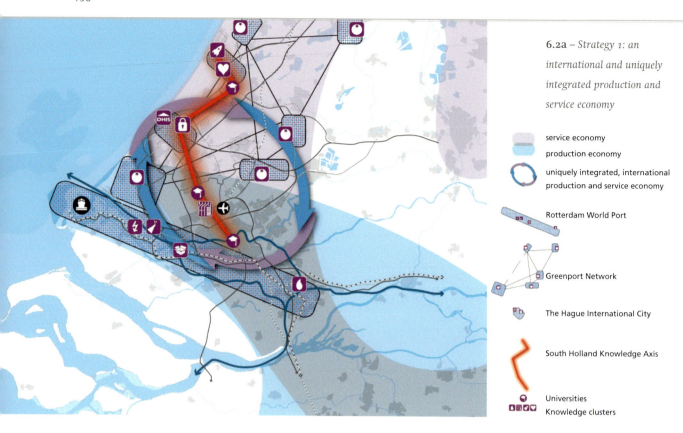

6.2a – *Strategy 1: an international and uniquely integrated production and service economy*

- service economy
- production economy
- uniquely integrated, international production and service economy
- Rotterdam World Port
- Greenport Network
- The Hague International City
- South Holland Knowledge Axis
- Universities
- Knowledge clusters

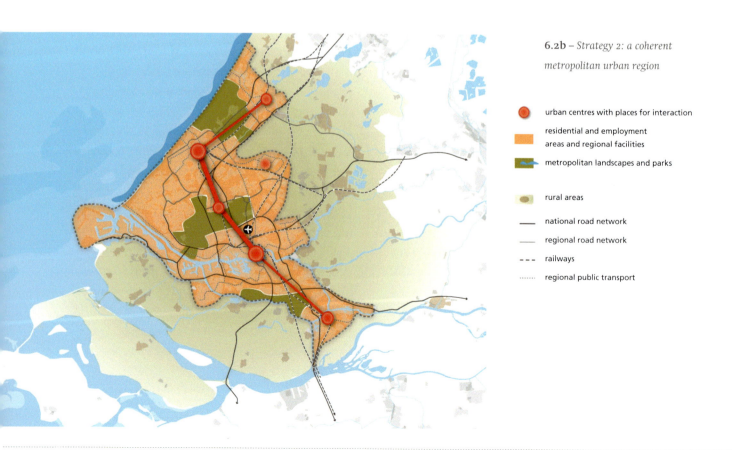

6.2b – *Strategy 2: a coherent metropolitan urban region*

- urban centres with places for interaction
- residential and employment areas and regional facilities
- metropolitan landscapes and parks
- rural areas
- national road network
- regional road network
- railways
- regional public transport

Shaping Holland - Beyond the port   197

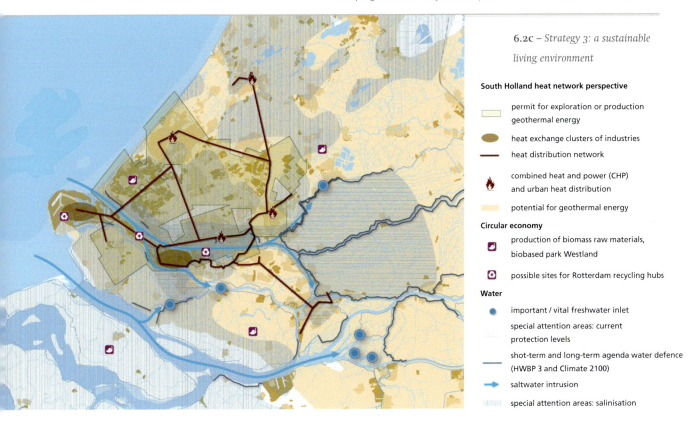

6.2c – *Strategy 3: a sustainable living environment*

South Holland heat network perspective

- permit for exploration or production geothermal energy
- heat exchange clusters of industries
- heat distribution network
- combined heat and power (CHP) and urban heat distribution
- potential for geothermal energy

Circular economy
- production of biomass raw materials, biobased park Westland
- possible sites for Rotterdam recycling hubs

Water
- important / vital freshwater inlet
- special attention areas: current protection levels
- shot-term and long-term agenda water defence (HWBP 3 and Climate 2100)
- saltwater intrusion
- special attention areas: salinisation

6.2 – 2013 – Collective strategies for the Southern Randstad 2040

The adaptive planning agenda for the Southern Randstad is both a product of negotiation as well as the context for negotiation between national government and regional government stakeholders about investment, projects and exploratory studies. It states a shared ambition with accompanying strategies and collective planning tasks with a view to 2040. The planning tasks are updated annually in close consultation with both the market and society. These three maps illustrate the key strategies in the adaptive planning agenda.

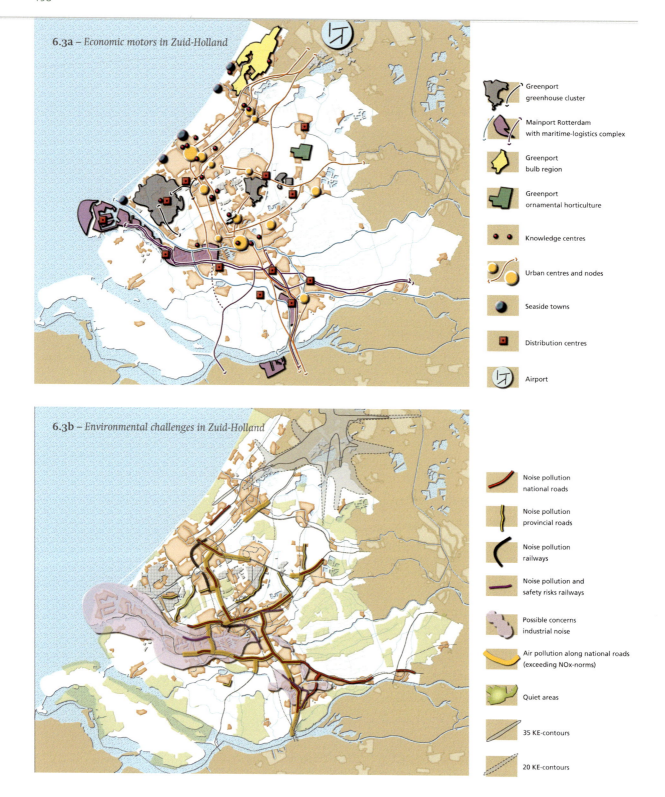

6.3 – 2004 – Provincial Spatial Structural Vision

The 2004 Provincial Spatial Structural Vision tackled the friction between economic development and the environment by identifying zones and pinch points. An economic distinction is made between service clusters, concentrated in the cities, and the extensive logistics clusters of the mainport and greenports.

'As a regional designer, you have to do in-depth research into network links and business processes. It's no longer enough just to plan for certain areas of land uses.'

Wil Zonneveld, Professor of Urban and Regional Planning, TU Delft

2 _Purple areas on the map

Although the province of Zuid-Holland had grown by 2,000 hectares, the province did not have a front-row seat at the opening of Maasvlakte 2. The seats of honour were reserved for national government and the Port of Rotterdam Authority as the main driving forces behind its planning and implementation. National government was in the front row because of its substantial funding of the two mainports, Amsterdam Airport Schiphol and the port of Rotterdam, which around 1990 had been allocated a leading role in strengthening the Netherlands' international competitive position. The privatised port authority took its position because it was responsible for the development and management of the Rotterdam port and industrial complex. As an intermediate tier of government, the Province of Zuid-Holland played a facilitating and oversight role. It was the province that made development of the port possible from a planning perspective and ensured that the agreed conditions were complied with.

This was in line with the province's position on the planning of local and regional business estates, which were seldom included as a part of area development projects. On the contrary: separation of functions and optimisation of the economic activities within the designated areas was the order of the day. The province was responsible for the match between supply and demand at the regional level and aimed at a balance, with liveability exemplified by a dual policy in its 2004 Provincial Spatial Structural Vision (see Figure 6.3a,b). Accessibility was seen as the most crucial business location criterion. A location policy in operation during the 1990s aimed to ensure that businesses were located where accessibility by various types of transport was suited to the mode and numbers of traffic movements they generated.

This is illustrated by the industrial zone planned for the north of the Hoeksche Waard, a rural area just south of Rotterdam. The port and industrial complex needed the space. It appeared as a purple area to the south of Rotterdam on the planning map of the Spatial Plan for the Rotterdam Region 2020 (*Ruimtelijk Plan Regio Rotterdam 2020)*, linked to the A29 motorway (see Figure 6.4). There was no other connection with the surroundings to speak of. The House of Representatives was not convinced and approved a motion designating the Hoeksche Waard a national landscape, which put paid to the plans for the industrial zone.

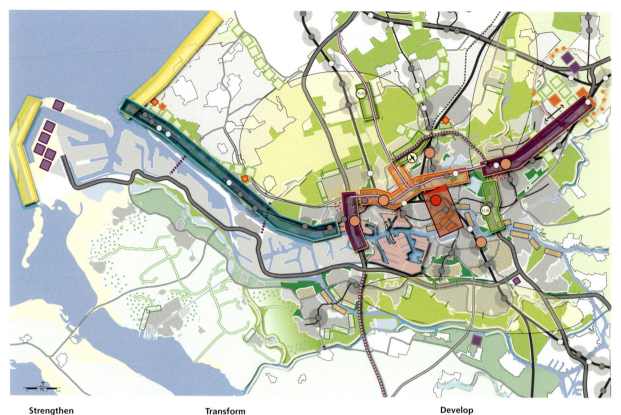

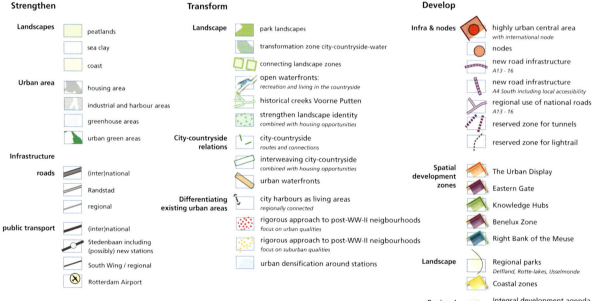

Figure 6.4 – 2005 – Strategy map for the Rotterdam Region 2020 (RR2020)

The 2005 Spatial Plan for the Rotterdam Region was groundbreaking in two ways. First, it was a cooperative policy project between the urban region and the province. Second, it pioneered policies focusing on spatial strategies rather than functional zoning. The map was contested by national government as the region proposed a search area for an industrial estate in the Hoeksche Waard to the south of Rotterdam, indicated by a purple dot. Functional zoning had trumped strategy for the time being.

6.5 – 2006 – Dual objective of the Mainport Rotterdam Project

This 2006 map shows details of the dual objective that the government attached to development of the mainport: economy and environment. The creation of Maasvlakte 2 involved compensation for loss of nature along the coast (indicated in dark blue). In addition, a range of projects were aimed at improving quality of life and economy in the Rotterdam region: intensification of industrial land use (red), environmental quality (grey) and compensation projects with the aim of realising new nature areas elsewhere. The result was a negotiated collection of planning and environmental measures without a regional design input. Among the many projects, the three regional parks of Rottemeren, IJsselmonde and Midden-Delfland, where a total of 750 hectares of green space was to be developed, are stand-out examples of the role that regional design played (see also Chapter 3 and Figure 3.14).

Regional Rotterdam Projects
- Intensify
- Environmental quality
- Projects for nature, recreation and spatial quaiity

Maasvlakte 2
- Maasvlakte 2
- Compensation dune areas Delfland
- Quiet areas all seasons
- Quiet areas winter season
- Seabed protection zone Voordelta

750 ha
- 750 hectare nature and recreation zone
- Green connection

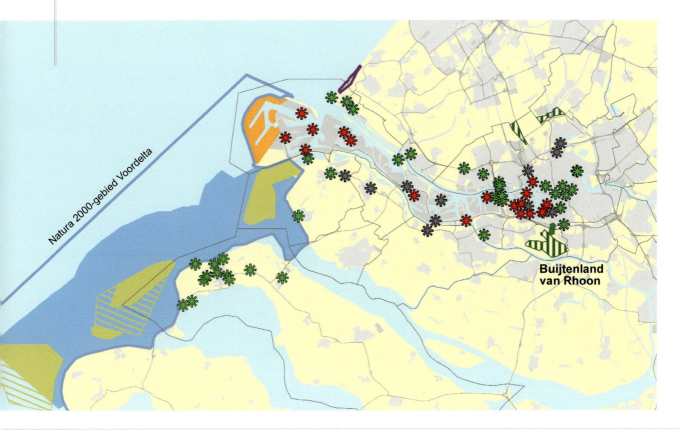

6.6a – *Metropolitan Zone in Zuid-Holland*

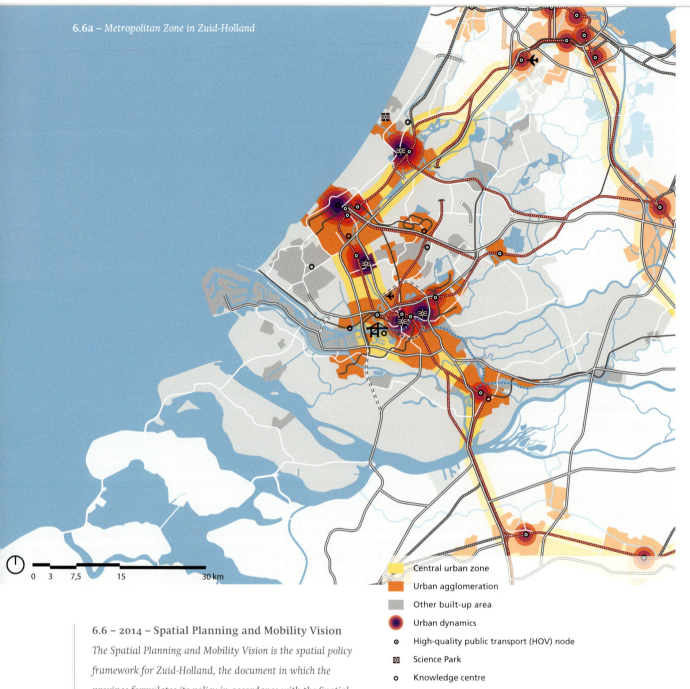

▬ (yellow)	Central urban zone
▬ (orange)	Urban agglomeration
▬ (grey)	Other built-up area
●	Urban dynamics
○	High-quality public transport (HOV) node
⌘	Science Park
○	Knowledge centre
✈	Airport
⚓	Mainport Rotterdam
▬▬	(Inter)national rail network (high-quality public transport)
▬▬	Regional rail network (high-quality public transport)
◁---▷	Missing link regional rail network
....	Regional public transport over water
▬▬	(Inter)national road network
═ ═ ═	Missing link (inter)national road network
▬▬	Regional road network
▭ ▭ ▭	Missing link regional road network
▬ (blue)	Water

6.6 – 2014 – Spatial Planning and Mobility Vision

The Spatial Planning and Mobility Vision is the spatial policy framework for Zuid-Holland, the document in which the province formulates its policy in accordance with the Spatial Planning Act. The map of the Logistical-Industrial System connects the five greenports (Westland, Oostland, Bollenstreek, Boskoop, and Aalsmeer in Noord-Holland) with the port and industry complex, the connections to the hinterland, transhipment points and urban centres. For the first time, the greenports are represented on a separate map from the agricultural centres. Comparison with the map of the Metropolitan Zone shows how the east–west-oriented system of mainport and greenports, located outside the cities, relates to the city-based north–south-oriented system of the knowledge and service economy.

Shaping Holland - Beyond the port 203

6.6b – *Logistical-Industrial System in Zuid-Holland*

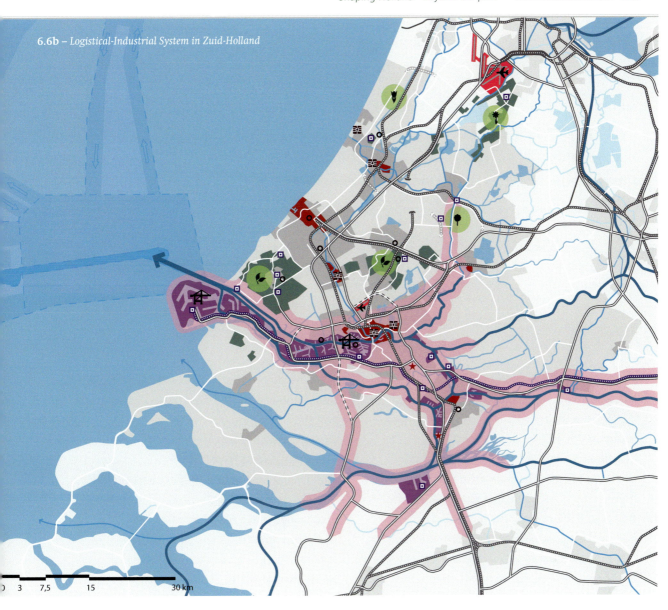

▬	Axis Mainport Rotterdam (indicative)	★	Room for urban development of regional importance
▬	Port-industrial complex	◄	Airport
▬	Greenhouse horticulture clusters	▬▬	Betuwe railway line (freight)
▬	Airport	▬▬	Freight transport on (inter)national public railway network
▬	Urban centres	▬▬	(Inter)national road network
▬	Other built-up areas	▭▭	Missing link (inter)national road network
▫	Logistics transfer point	▬	Regional road network
	Science Park	▭	Missing link regional network
o	Knowledge centre	▬	(Inter)national waterway network
	Mainport Rotterdam	▬	regional waterway network
	Greenport Westland Oostland		
	Greenport Boskoop	▬	Water
	Greenport Bollenstreek	≋	Maritime traffic separation scheme
	Greenport Aalsmeer		

'In an ever more complex world, regional design has to redefine itself. Less of being the designer who determines how things will be, and more a case of showing what is going on and what the consequences are of various development options.'

Frank van den Beuken, planner and strategist, Urban Development Department, City of Rotterdam

The same applied to greenhouse horticulture, although in planning terms the greenhouses belonged to the agricultural sector. The province recognised their economic importance and attempted to contain their spatial impact. In terms of policy, this position meant concentrating greenhouse horticulture in a limited number of designated areas, restructuring where necessary and clearing isolated greenhouses in the landscape. Quality ambitions, other than mitigating environmental impacts, were not considered. Greenhouse horticulture was not a subject for regional design. In 2007, when the total area of greenhouses started shrinking due to urban development pressure, the provincial executive did not look for a political solution in the form of improvement or modernisation, but rather in a quantitative objective: the maintenance of 5,800 hectares of greenhouse horticulture in Zuid-Holland.

Development of the mainport was an exception in so far as it involved a dual objective at the national level. To strengthen the economic structure, continued growth of the mainport was essential, while at the same time liveability was supposed to improve in the region. These goals were linked to each other. The liveability objective manifested itself in a series of projects, both large and small – from quieter asphalt and the renovation of a swimming pool to the conversion of 750 hectares of agricultural land into a nature and recreation area (see Figure 6.5). The government partnership in the region (ROM Rijnmond) saw to the implementation. The province did have a leading role in the larger landscape projects, in line with the provincial landscape policy. However, this interpretation of the dual objective actually emphasised the autonomous character of the port and industrial complex. Improvement of liveability was mainly sought externally rather than internally.

3 _Closer integration of systems

In 2014, the provincial government stopped treating the large economic complexes as autonomous systems. For the first time it drew up a policy vision in which the mainport and the greenports were components of a single integrated logistical-industrial system, together constituting the 'bedrock of the Zuid-Holland economy'. This whole system is shown on a map in the Spatial Planning and Mobility Vision (*Visie Ruimte en Mobiliteit*), which describes the official planning policy (Figure 6.6b). Cities have a complementary role to play

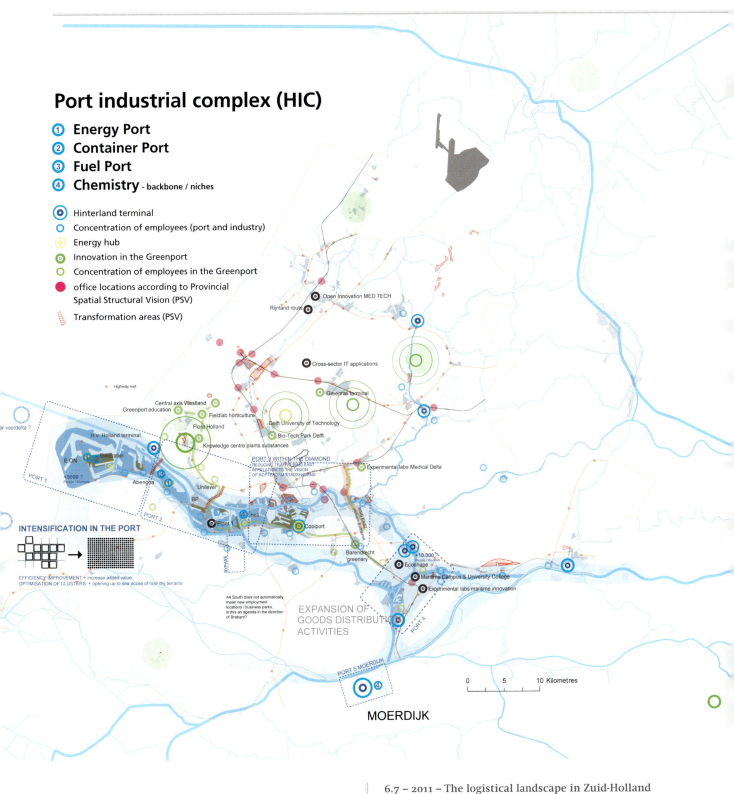

6.7 – 2011 – The logistical landscape in Zuid-Holland

Zuid-Holland is characterised by a unique combination of delta landscape, urban network and complex logistical-industrial structures. The mainports and greenports have large footprints. The associated international infrastructure accommodates extensive flows of goods, raw materials, energy, investments and knowledge.

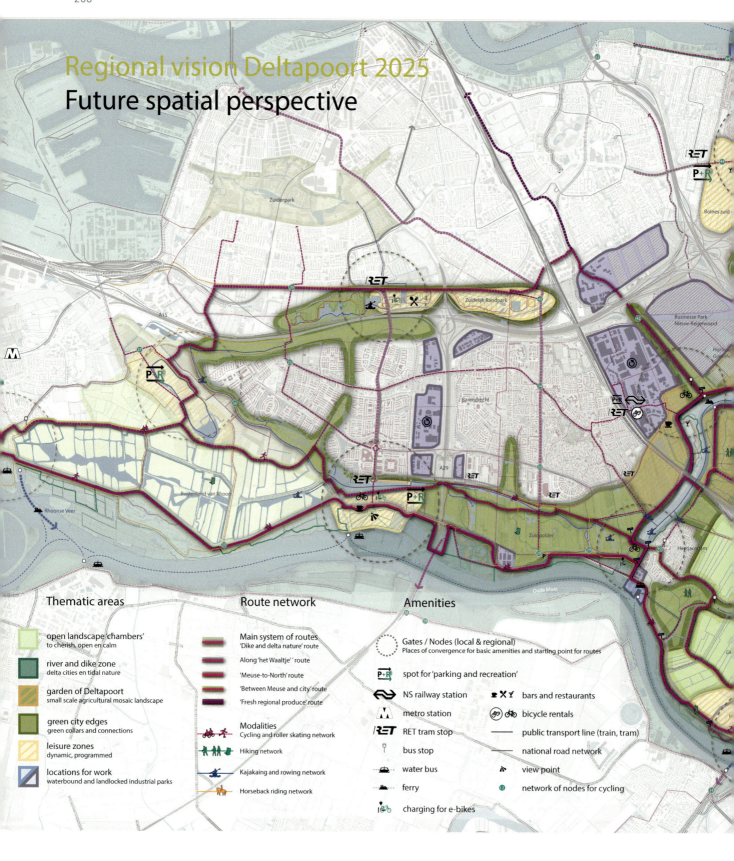

Shaping Holland - Beyond the port   207

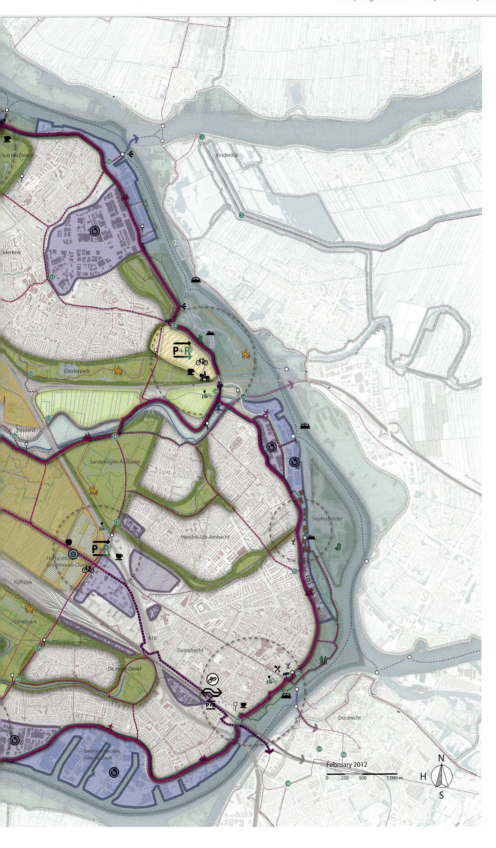

6.8 – 2012 – Regional vision for Deltapoort 2025

Around 2010, Deltapoort was the subject of a flurry of design activity. The area is where the dual objective of a stronger economy and improved quality of life converge. The landscape had become fragmented by the construction of infrastructure and industry. Following the Eo Wijers competition of 2008 and a provincial ambition document of 2010, in 2012, H+N+S Landscape Architects produced this vision for connecting city, countryside and mainport. Ten themes are combined in a single spatial vision. The study was commissioned by the Deltapoort steering committee of representatives from the municipalities, regions, the water authority, the port authority and the province.

6.9 – 2014 – Glasparel development

The Glasparel development integrates greenhouse development, housing and new nature. This unusual combination translates the regional mix of urban and industrial systems to the local scale. It is also one of the projects within the broader Zuidplaspolder development described in Chapter 2.

6.9a – Glasparel spatial vision

here, although no longer in their historical role as consumer markets, but rather as centres of knowledge development and business services (Figure 6.6a).

The integrated nature of mainport and greenports is most clearly apparent from the shared transport routes. In the 2014 Spatial Planning and Mobility Vision, the province observed that 95% of imported fruit and vegetables were already being transported in sea containers, thanks to the advent of refrigerated containers, allowing the greenports to make increasing use of the high-quality transportation services offered by the mainport. Transportation by container enhances the possibilities for inland shipping, short sea, deep sea and rail. A regional port system reaching beyond the port of Rotterdam had emerged (see Figure 6.7). For the greenports, with the greenhouse horticulture of Westland at the forefront, this development has introduced a transformation which is still very much underway. Fruit and vegetables no longer have to actually grow in the greenport to be traded there; imported fresh produce can be ripened, processed and packaged in the greenport. In other words, value is added to the produce. This gives the greenport a position comparable to that of the petrochemical industry, for instance, where imported crude oil is processed into refined, usable products such as petrol.

Trade is not the only factor connecting the mainport and greenports. In its 2014 spatial vision, the province refers to a CO_2 network. Carbon dioxide emitted by companies in the port and industrial complex is transported via underground pipelines to the horticulture complex, where it is used to accelerate greenhouse cultivation. Also, work started in 2014 on a heat network designed for transporting residual heat from the port and geothermal energy from the greenhouse complex to parties requiring heat in the greenport itself and in the urban area. 'The Southern Randstad is ideal for this,' states the province in its spatial vision, 'due to the presence of major urban areas in the proximity of greenhouse horticulture and industrial complexes as well as the potential of geothermal energy' (production of which is profitable in large parts of the Westland).

As had become clear in previous years, the model of two expanding and independent systems in the Zuid-Holland region was no longer sustainable. Systems intersected, and more importantly, this appeared to produce interesting sites and

6.9b – Glasparel artist's impression

environments (see Figure 6.1). At the urban level, Rotterdam set to work on the transformation of the old docks in the city. These still largely active port areas not only took up space and caused nuisance, but they provided atmosphere and inspiration in equal measure. The Deltapoort area between Rotterdam and Dordrecht became the subject of several design exercises (see Figure 6.8). How could this fragmented area with its considerable transit flows grow into a metropolitan park combining green space, water and recreation with logistics and economic activity?

Useful exercises were carried out to investigate possibilities for linking or combining horticulture with other types of land use. Among them were the City Fruitful design experiment (1994), which envisaged combining greenhouse horticulture with housing, and the *Glasparel* (Glass Pearl) design by developers Amvest and Wayland (2008) for a new and sustainable complex with a mix of greenhouses and other types of land use. The latter was part of the Zuidplaspolder development discussed in Chapter 2 (see Figure 6.9a,b); members of the public could become acquainted with modern greenhouse horticulture and bathe in a swimming pool kept warm with residual heat from the horticulture. Many of these initiatives were limited to a local scale. Of the above-mentioned examples, only the Deltapoort has a regional, transmunicipal character.

In 2011, three years before the Spatial Planning and Mobility Vision was published, Xplorelab conducted a more comprehensive study into the opportunities for cooperation between mainport and greenports. As a provincial 'creative workshop', Xplorelab was the successor to the South Wing Studio (*Atelier Zuidvleugel*, see Chapter 5 and interview 'The Director'). It was set up by the province to find a way of formulating a policy that integrates green space, water and the environment. Innovation was sought by working across policy and organisational boundaries and breaking free of tried and trusted working methods and approaches. Research-by-design is a powerful method for this. The study entitled 'From Mainport-Greenport to Growport' was based, among other things, on an exploration of business processes and future agendas of the two economic centres. The mainport was preparing for a transition to a biobased economy, an economy in which maximum use is made of biological materials and fuels. The greenport looked for sustainable solutions in the form of floating greenhouses, for example, and a solution to the brine problem (the salty waste that

F6.3

results when brackish groundwater is pumped up and desalinised for use as irrigation water in greenhouse cultivation). Energy management was a central topic in both complexes. Together with key figures from the greenport and mainport, Xplorelab looked for possibilities to bring the two closer together, drawing inspiration from twenty-four (partly fictional) example projects.

The research resulted in the Growport scenario for 2040 in which mainport and greenport 'together strengthen the Dutch economy' (Figure 6.10a,b). The scenario has four main components:
- Mainport-greenport as global showcase, with world-leading high-quality production and complex logistical processes
- Land reclamation in the North Sea, including artificial islands or floating greenhouses
- ICT-driven logistics, with full integration of the traffic and complex logistical flows (resulting from consumer-driven production)
- Development of a biobased cluster in which mainport and greenport benefit from each other's waste flows; not only CO_2 and residual heat but also biobased raw materials from the greenhouses for e.g. clothing, medicines and chemical products

Many connections between mainport and greenport follow technological lines: IT, renewable energy sources, the materials and value chains that make up a circular economy, etc. Technological developments are now among the main drivers of change. This change is not limited to the logistical-industrial system, but within the province of Zuid-Holland the mainport and greenports will most probably feel the greatest impact. These two sectors face the massive task of giving up fossil fuels and finding their feet in the circular economy of the future. Their future, and therefore the economic and social welfare of Zuid-Holland, depend strongly on the degree to which they succeed in this.

The province has been working on a new generation of futures studies ever since Xplorelab. This type of study was first confined to a studio setting separate from the mainstream organisation, but over the years, futures studies developed as an instrument and agenda-setting working programme with the support of the wider organisation, the Futures Agenda (*Toekomstagenda*). A key study in this development was the 2013 futures study *Zuid-Holland op St(r)oom* (Zuid-Holland Full Steam Ahead – *op stoom* means up to speed and *stroom* means electricity). It proved to be an agenda-setting study exploring policy approaches and

Shaping Holland - Beyond the port

6.10a – Total CO_2 and heat network for Growport

6.10 – 2011 – Xplorelab: Growport 2040

Xplorelab was the innovation studio for the Province of Zuid-Holland in the period 2007–2015. It initiated the 'From Mainport-Greenport to Growport' (Van mainport-greenport naar Growport) project in cooperation with TransForum, the national programme for innovation in the agricultural sector and green space. Other partners were the Municipality of Westland, the Port of Rotterdam Authority, TU Delft, Wageningen University and Research, and the Rotterdam, Breda and Inholland Universities of Applied Sciences. Various civil society partners and the business community were also involved.

Legend:
- Urban area
- Greenhouse horticulture
- Greenhouse with OCAP (CO_2) connection
- Greenhouse with OCAP connection in the 2nd phase
- Industry - CO_2 provider
- Industry - possible CO_2 provider
- OCAP line (100km)
- CO_2 pipes
- Possible CO_2 pipes
- CO_2 transport by sea
- Geothermal heat source
- Planned geothermal heat source
- City heating
- Big possible residual heat source
- Possible cold source
- Grand design heat network
- Beaded cord of heat networks
- Heat backbone in the port of Rotterdam

6.10b – Growport 2040 development perspective

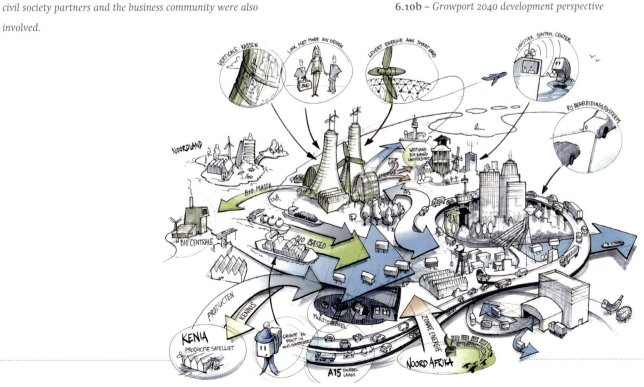

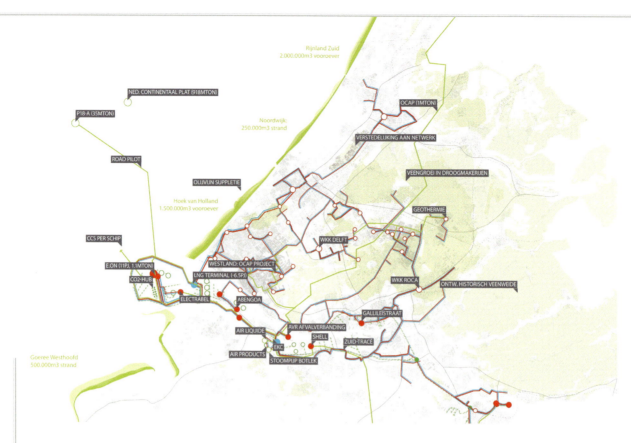

6.11a – *Dutch Energy Solution: a regional heat network*

6.11b – *Smart Thermal Grid 2050: optimising the exploitation and distribution of geothermal energy*

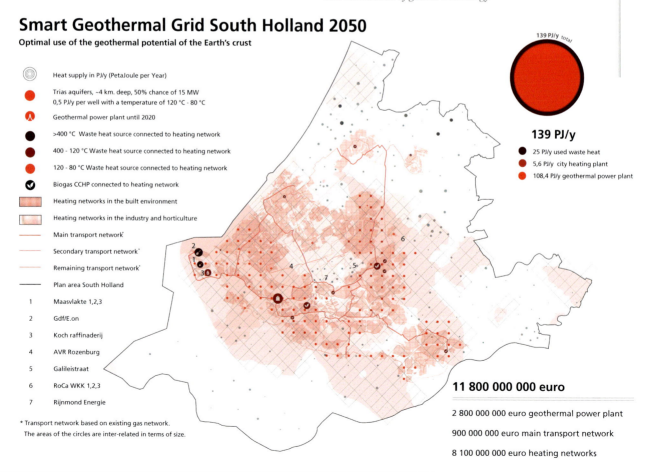

6.11 – 2013 – Futures Study: Zuid-Holland op St(r)oom

'Zuid-Holland Full Steam Ahead' (Zuid-Holland op St(r)oom) was one of the first future-oriented studies within the province's Future Agenda. The study was also one of the first in the Netherlands to visualise the spatial impact of the energy transition and suggest local and regional solutions.

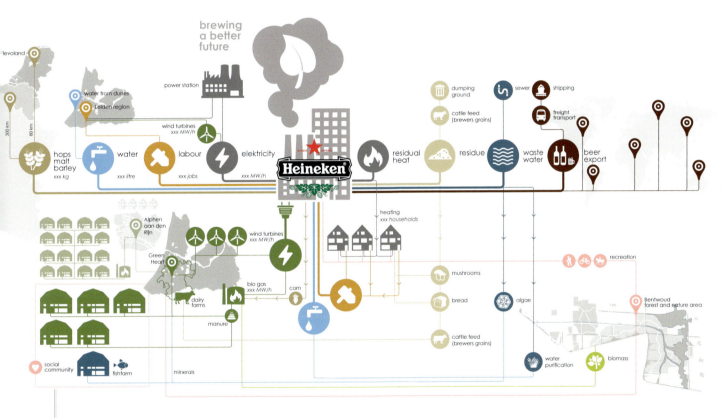

6.11c – *Industrial symbiosis in the Heineken production process*

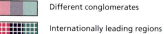

6.12a – Spatial scenario 'World of Conglomerates'

One spatial scenario describes a 'world of conglomerates' in which investments by large, globally operating business conglomerates drive technological developments and the resulting physical developments on the ground.

 Different conglomerates

 Internationally leading regions

 International cluster of greenhouse horticulture run by different conglomerates

Varying agricultural land use, differentiated per conglomerate

 Port divided over conglomerates

 Physically uniform looking recreational areas with use varying relating to augmented reality depending on conglomerate services

Strong migration to central urban areas, densification around cities

 Finer mesh of data networks surrounding urban centres

Overlap of data networks from different conglomerate providers

Intensive use of infrastructure by several, different conglomerates

Large physical, global flows of energy - power generation per conglomerate

6.12 – 2017 – Futures study: societal impact of new technology

Since 2011 the Province of Zuid-Holland has been building a new portfolio of futures studies in which research-by-design plays a significant role. In a study of the social influence of new technology, four future scenarios were developed for Zuid-Holland.

Shaping Holland - Beyond the port   215

Visual legend of Figure 6.12b

① With globalisation and standardisation Westland has grown into a leading region for greenhouse horticulture crops

② Production processes and transport have been fully automated and standardised

③ Only a select number of crops are grown on a large scale

④ Green raw materials for the Biobased Economy, in particular the production of fine chemicals and raw materials for medicine

⑤ With digitisation and robotisation only few people remain, overseeing production

⑥ Increase in scale and expansion of the greenhouse cluster for international markets

⑦ CO_2 and heat is distributed from industries to the greenhouse horticulture complex via the Smart Multi Commodity Grid CO

⑧ Uniform radio masts for a comprehensive coverage of open data networks

6.12b – Westland in the social and technological scenario 'Borderless World'

Current exploratory design uses photomontages at eye level to translate abstract cartographic images to the everyday experiential world. The study into the societal effects of new technology revealed that technological development will have a major impact in Westland. Entrepreneurs are investigating what this could entail for the future. The design process was enriched with interactive sessions with entrepreneurs in order to arrive at these types of images.

'Without all those years of zoning policy, the flow approach would not be possible now. The flows would have been too thin and diffuse.'

Francisco Colombo, urban planner at the Province of Zuid-Holland

regional concepts in light of the transition to sustainable energy sources, building on concepts and working methods developed in the Growport study (see Figure 6.11a–c). The study was an important stepping stone towards incorporating into provincial and regional policies the concepts of circular business development, stronger cooperation between government and businesses, the regional heat network and attention to opportunities for underground renewable energy sources.

Through the debates, research-by-design studies and in-depth investigations in its Futures Agenda programme, the province has been looking for solutions to make Zuid-Holland 'cleaner, stronger and smarter', the motto of the political coalition in the 2015–2019 provincial executive of Zuid-Holland. Mainport and greenports feature regularly in this. Part of this Future Agenda was the study '(Un)limited Technology' on the societal impact of new technology (see Figure 6.12a,b). Will the trend towards open platforms and crossovers between different fields of knowledge and organisations continue or not? Will the economy and society continue to become more international or will there be a resurgence of the local? Four scenarios show the possible consequences for the spatial structure of Zuid-Holland as a whole and

for a number of areas in particular. The Rotterdam port and the Westland area are two of these. The researchers did not state any preferences or put forward any strategies on which to base policy as the purpose of regional design here was not to set out a development agenda or propose specific projects as part of a strategic narrative. Instead, the images make complex, pressing issues clear and comprehensible. They make it possible to conduct meaningful debates across a wide group of interested parties.

4 _Connecting flows

New technologies are central to further development of the logistical-industrial complex of mainports and greenports. The researchers at Xplorelab noted that the use and connection of knowledge flows (knowledge institutions and the business community) remain crucial for encouraging innovation. This is the next level of integration – with the urban economy, in which knowledge, creativity and innovation are key.

'Urban by Nature' was the theme of the 2014 International Architecture Biennale Rotterdam (IABR). One of the project studios focused on the Rotterdam region: city, mainport and greenport.

6.13 – 2014 – Urban metabolism

The City of Rotterdam and the International Architecture Biennale Rotterdam 2014 founded the Rotterdam Project Studio (Projectatelier Rotterdam) to investigate how designing the city's material flows can lead to more sustainable development models. The researchers came up with four interconnected strategies: catalysing re-industrialisation, channelling waste flows, reclaiming raw materials and creating new biotopes.

It investigated strategies for a new 'urban metabolism', a new way to exchange materials in the region (see Figure 6.13). 'From this perspective – the city as an ecosystem – urban development should no longer be about the organisation of sites but rather about connecting and unravelling substance flows,' wrote the researchers in the IABR catalogue. 'In concrete terms, creating connections between flows and ensuring parallel processes, closing recycling loops to avoid waste, and offering alternative infrastructures for spin-off.' The project identified nine 'vital substance flows': goods, people, waste, biota (e.g. movements of plants and animals), energy, food, fresh water, air, and sand and clay.

As with Xplorelab, the heat network and the CO_2 network came to the fore in the IABR project (both being interpreted as energy flows), but also enhancing urban nature by using natural processes of sedimentation, for example. Another proposal was for reusing urban waste as a source of raw materials. Protein from urban biowaste could then be resold to the Westland as a raw material.

The map of the integrated Logistical-Industrial System in the province's 2014 spatial vision (see Figure 6.6a) marks a fundamental but not yet final step forward. It seems a question of time before this system is fully integrated with the other system mapped in the vision, the Metropolitan Zone – the part of the urban agglomeration between Dordrecht and Leiden, centred on Rotterdam and The Hague – where knowledge, urban facilities and the services economy are concentrated (see Figures 6.1 and 6.6a,b). This highly urbanised area is characterised by 'good connectivity, high-quality urban facilities and an internationally recognised knowledge infrastructure comprising universities, knowledge and research institutions and science parks.'

The flows of the metabolism make it clear where the interfaces between the logistical-industrial and urban system are located – in infrastructure, of course. Rotterdam The Hague Airport, for example, serves both complexes, in heating and CO_2, and flows of food, waste, biota and even sand and clay. The tidal park in Rotterdam, a concept repeated in multiple locations as part of a regional programme, shows how the natural sediment flows in the Meuse can be used to create a green riverside urban park (see Figure 6.14). Knowledge too, is such an interface. Innovation centres such as PortXL and the Port Innovation Lab in Delft thrive in an urban environment, but serve innovation in the mainport.

6.14a – The tidal park concept and its development clusters

6.14 – 2015 – Tidal park Rotterdam region

The tidal park is a regional concept for a string of park developments along the tidal river Meuse. The visual planning concept plays an important role in establishing the programme for cooperation and realisation.

Shaping Holland - Beyond the port

3 Cluster Merwehaven - Wilhelminahaven - Heyplaat

This cluster will see a transformation from port area to mixed-use urban area as it is part of the Stadshavens (Port City) programme. Development of the Tidal Park could add a high quality foundation for future urban development as well as an integral approach to dike reinforcement.

4 Maashaven - Nassauhaven

In this area the Tidal Park could be of great significance as inner city public space for Rotterdam South. The Maashaven (Meuse Harbour) remains an inland shipping hub for Rotterdam Port while it can be well combined with a tidal habitat in parts of the basin. With the development of Tidal Park Maashaven, developers can learn from realising the Tidal Park in nearby Nassauhaven. Funding for that location was already made available.

5 Cluster Eiland van Brienenoord - Mallegatpark - Polder de Esch

This areas is already one of the few places where city dwellers can feel 'outdoors in nature'. An ecological 'stepping stone' with recreational and eductional value arises when we expand tidal habitats and connect the area to cycling routes throughout the city. Realisation of nearby Mallegatpark has been funded and construction will start soon.

6 Cluster Stormpolder - De Zaag - Huys ten Donck

Different agendas can be connected in this area: room for maritime development, room for nature development, dike reinforcement and recreational, cultural-historical ambitions. This project first needs further articulation.

6.14b – *Artist's impression of one of the tidal parks within an urban-industrial environment*

'Spatial planning that shifts the attention from sites to flows should go beyond using and connecting those flows. It is legitimate to influence them in the interests of the public domain. This means that we should arrange governance in a very different manner, with an active contribution from the parties that are most closely involved.'

Guus van Steenbergen, formerly Greenports programme manager at the Province of Zuid-Holland

A design approach based on flows rather than locations shows how these ties can become firmly established. It is a precondition for being able to forge the previously relatively autonomous megacomplexes in the province of Zuid-Holland into a single sustainably functioning complex. This emphasises the regional scale, after years in which the international position and local design were in the forefront. Zuid-Holland is turning out to be a field lab in this area. The province gives its own designers and external design firms the opportunity to develop and fine tune their ideas and test them in practice. This helps both the province and the designers to move forward, which in turn helps others, both at home and abroad, to apply and develop the knowledge gained.

5 _The regional design task

From the above we can conclude that the map of the logistical-industrial system in the Spatial Planning and Mobility Vision is set to become a lot busier in the years to come. Described as 'the bedrock under the Zuid-Holland economy', it has the potential to develop into 'the bedrock under the economic transition' to a circular economy, free from fossil fuels and running on raw materials that are biodegradable or reusable (see Figure 6.15). While that is clearly a technological and an economic challenge, it is certainly also a task for regional design, because it brings the main-port and green-port neighbours into a different relationship with each other, bound together by different types of connections.

Within the logistical-industrial complex, regional design has thus far been mainly exploratory in nature. Existing and conceivable cross-connections between mainport, greenport and the city have been analysed in terms of spatial patterns, opportunities and implications. In response to new challenges (such as the current sustainability measures for the logistical-industrial complex) this is an essential preliminary phase.

Despite the integrated system maps in the provincial spatial vision, the flow-based approach has not yet made it into policy. Projects such as the construction of a heat network and exchange of CO_2 are specific applications, but the province is not yet taking them further into a policy for spatial development; they are not connected to any transformations, reallocations or other planned interventions.

F6.4

6.15 – 2016 – New economy

In a proposal for the World Expo 2025, a group of public and private initiators produced a vision of a future economy that was intended to be exhibited in the Rotterdam region. Ultimately, the proposal ran aground due to a lack of commitment from the national government. The region continues to promote itself with ambitious strategies as a torchbearer for the new economy.

Multipurpose growth

New economy
- cross sectoral innovation area
- production techniques

water activitities
cale logistics
, finish, repair, demolish

New energy
- biobased production/storage
- chemicals & fuels
- renewable energy

Innovative
Maritime Delta

6.16 – 2015 – Logistics hubs Greenport Westland-Oostland
In 2015 the Province of Zuid-Holland and the Municipality of Westland embarked on a study that led to a joint development strategy for the future of the Westland-Oostland greenport and an investment agenda for the short term. The first step was to develop a 'snapshot' of the direction in which the area was going, primarily as a source of information for further research-by-design. It was designed in the form of a rich atlas, including attractive infographics, maps and analyses. This drawing shows the horticulture complex as a logistics cluster.

The task of regional design now is not to remain bogged down in research. Designers can take on new relevant and pressing roles: bridging contradictions, facilitating change and making connections. A strategy for the Westland area shows what such a translation into the policy domain can look like. It starts from the premise that large horticulture businesses base their major investment decisions around connections into the transport, water, energy and CO_2 networks (see Figure 6.16).

The province and other authorities steer the development of these networks, indirectly influencing the choices made by the business community. The strategy map of the 2016 'Westland Workbook' (*Werkboek Westland*) shows the spatially distinctive networks, the public investments in strategic components and the differentiation into the expected resulting horticulture environments (Figure 6.17). This map is based on a large amount of data and facts that have been collected in the book for use as a shared knowledge base. Growers who independently opt for different investments will generally not be discouraged from doing this, but they cannot expect the government to provide any facilitating investments.

The transition from research to policy and implementation involves a different set of issues from research into how sustainability can be realised with a flow-based approach. How robust are these flows? Is it justifiable to invest in physical developments to facilitate these flows that involve commitments for many decades to come? Can an implementation strategy be sufficiently flexible and adaptable to accommodate the dynamics of these flows? And how does facilitating flows relate to the quality of the landscape? The peat meadows of Midden-Delfland (see Chapter 5) are situated between mainport and greenport; how will the flows of goods, energy, CO_2 and other substances pass through this area of considerable cultural and historical value? The province can no longer limit itself to facilitating and constraining major economic complexes. It is now about connecting the 'regional metabolism' to the transformation of sites and areas, and a governance that creates the necessary conditions.

Twenty years ago such a flow landscape was in fact designed on the smaller scale of Maasvlakte 2, where logistical and biotic flows determined the contours and layout of the new port area. As a by-product of this functional approach, sites developed naturally that attracted day-trippers

6.17 – 2016 – Strategy map: Westland

The Province of Zuid-Holland and the Municipality of Westland constitute the working group for infrastructure, spatial planning and energy for the HOT coalition for the restructuring and development of horticulture. In this coalition they cooperate closely with the Federation of Fruiting Vegetables Organisations, Royal FloraHolland, Rabobank and the Ministry of Economic Affairs. The Westland Workbook is a partial elaboration of the transition programme Greenport Westland-Oostland 3.0, leading to (1) sustainable production for various markets, free of fossil fuels and based on circular principles, (2) the processing and mixing of home and imported goods into products for consumers, and (3) knowledge and innovation of international significance. This strategy map, the main result of the workbook process, allocates specific spatial strategies for scale of production, infrastructure and restructuring to particular parts of the horticulture region. The aim is to strengthen the sector through smart diversification and modernisation.

Westland Workbook

Spatial Economic Strategy
Greenport 3.0
Satellite Infrastructure-Energy-
Spatial Development

Strategic map

Greenhouse Area

- Large, around 10 ha;
- Mainly fruit vegetable cultivation

- Medium, around 7 ha;
- 50% fruit vegetable cultivation and 50% horticulture

- Small, around 2ha.

greenhouses outside municipality of Westland, preliminary estimate

* study focus area

Accessibility and Mobility

(inter)national roads
inter-regional roads
regional roads

Trade and Logistics

agrological companies
'coolport'

Liveability

residential areas, employment locations and sports
green, recreation area + ecology
transformation zones
ecological connection (water + green)

Energy

heat distribution network

and others. These were then developed as recreational areas to accommodate these visitors. But Maasvlakte 2 was new land. The old land, with its intensive use of space and broad range of natural and cultural values, requires much greater design efforts.

F6.5

The Researcher
Luuk Boelens

Professor of Spatial Planning and Mobility at Ghent University; worked from 1983 to 1998 for the Province of Zuid-Holland and the Randstad Spatial Planning Consultative Group.

Fi.4

Shaping Holland

The early 1980s saw the beginning of an interesting transitional period. We were emerging from a deep economic trough. Following the oil crises of 1973 and 1979, economic development had ground to a halt, and so too had spatial development. Spatial development underwent a period of 'process planning', with a succession of policy documents in which it was more about the documents themselves and playing the process game than the facts on the ground. As for me, I had graduated from TU Delft with a hefty student debt, and no-one was looking for an urban designer or a planner.

In the 1980s, the economy picked up again and there was renewed interest in planning and spatial design. Major cities were advocating the compact city concept of building in and around the existing city. Urban designer Dirk Frieling initiated the design project *Nederland Nu Als Ontwerp* (The Netherlands Now as Design), which resulted in four scenarios for the Netherlands' future, organised around political mainstreams. The landscape architects of Wageningen University saw their opportunity and approached regional design from the perspective of landscape structures.

Zuid-Holland was a pioneer in regional design. I started working there in 1983, spending the first few years working on the designs for coastal expansion on a series of temporary contracts. In those days, inspiration came from outside the Netherlands. The Italian architect Bernardo Secchi, who died a few years ago, was talking about the exploratory power of design, about the designer as a scout, an explorer. Together with a couple of colleagues, he mapped out the Florence-Bologna region in order to better understand the sprawl in northern Italy. In 1987, the architectural historian

228_._Interview_ The Researcher

Ed Taverne introduced Secchi's body of ideas to the Netherlands as the form of research that could bring to light what regular geographic or sectoral research could not.

Following completion of the work on coastal expansion, I got a job at the Provincial Spatial Planning Committee (PPC), where directors and government representatives in the province discussed spatial issues. There too, a conviction grew that we had to start designing again. Urged by and working with the independent members Leo Tummers and Klaus Vollmer, I made an initial detailed plan for urban development between Hook of Holland, Dordrecht and Leiden, an area measuring approximately 50 km x 40 km containing both Rotterdam and The Hague. We saw the small railway line connecting the two cities, the Hofplein line, as the central artery, around which we drew urban, suburban and villa-type environments. This excited the interest of the PPC and provincial executive member Loudi Stolker was enthusiastic, too. This led to a working group headed by San Verschuuren, who drew up the document called 'Park City between Palace and Port?'. Eventually, despite this good work, each town got its own new residential areas, which were all designed as suburbs at a density of about thirty-three homes per hectare. There was little sign of a collective approach, however, and I found that very frustrating. In those days, I still assumed that the design would be implemented much as we had intended it.

At the time, the planning minister, Hans Alders, was preparing the VINEX policy document, the Supplement to the Fourth National Policy Document on Spatial Planning, which set out a substantial housebuilding programme. He wanted to be specific about locations and funding. Loudi Stolker and her fellow provincial executive members De Boer from Noord-Holland and Schapenk from Utrecht offered to draw up a plan for the entire Randstad area. Zuid-Holland was to be in charge, as we already had some experience with regional design. The provinces, however, could not see eye to eye. A report was prepared that contained only abstract maps, some of which were even upside down without anyone having noticed. The provinces could obviously not present this work, but Alders was getting impatient and wanted to see results fast, or else he would do it himself. Needless to say, panic set in. What now? The provincial executive members set their sights on Axel Hartman, head of the spatial planning department, under whose direction I had worked on the coastal expansion research. He asked me to produce an interprovincial vision for the Randstad within two months, otherwise it would be too late.

We set to work with three or four designers. We were given working space in a synagogue in the centre of Amsterdam. Meals were arranged and camp beds provided. We worked day in day out on that vision, while Hartman kept the bickering little groups of economists, ecologists and others at a distance. Within two months, we were able to present a vision entitled 'The Randstad prepares'. This vision was well-received by the executive members. The Province of Flevoland joined us. A lot of this ended up in the VINEX policy document and it laid the basis for the RORO, the Randstad Spatial Planning Consultative Group, a spatial planning team for the Randstad.

In the RORO there were about ten of us working on such subjects as greenhouse horticulture, the Green Heart and the high-speed railway line to Brussels and Paris. However, the results of this were barely incorporated into the spatial plans. Friction arose between those who went to the RORO and those who remained with the province. We were partly to blame, of course. We were cocksure and thought we were more important than our colleagues working in the main provincial government building on things like the South Wing. We should have kept in contact and consulted more, but we were busy working on our own projects and let the others get on with theirs.

After seven or so years, a plan for the bulb-growing area heralded the end of the RORO. The sight of provincial executive members Jaap Wolf from Zuid-Holland and Friso de Zeeuw from Noord-Holland standing on opposite sides of the ring canal surrounding the Haarlemmermeer polder is still fresh in my mind. They waved at each other and announced on camera that they were going to work together. We wanted to relocate the flower bulb industry to the Haarlemmermeer polder, within the Schiphol Airport noise zone. The land thus freed up would become available for new housing. We designed pedestrian pockets around new stations along the old railway line from Leiden to Haarlem, in the spirit of Danish architect Jan Gehl, who approaches urban development from the point of view of cyclists and pedestrians. Unfortunately, the local residents were opposed to the plans. They wanted a real bulb region, not a bulb city brand without real flower bulb production. During the presentation of the plans they hurled flower bulbs at the stage en masse. I picked them all up and planted them in my

garden. I've never had such a beautiful garden before or since! The
municipalities involved and the Province of Zuid-Holland then concluded
an agreement called the Teylingen Pact, which made it clear that the
plans would not go ahead. That singular performance quickly put paid
to the Randstad collaboration.

After all that kerfuffle, I'd had enough. I pursued an actor-oriented approach,
first as an independent advisor and later as a professor in Utrecht and Ghent.
Before you start designing, you have to talk to the regional stakeholders.
What problems or difficulties do they face, and how can you visualise
them? It's all about action and reaction. It's essential to be aware of the
impact your actions have on people, and how they react to them.

This should not be seen as a return to the process planning of the 1970s.
That took place within the government. Nowadays, we work with living
labs, with the people; not in co-production but in co-evolution, trying to
align design, implementation and legislation interactively. That's how we
are making a plan for the area of the Dender river in Flanders, which is
set to overflow as a result of climate change. You may say that it's the
government's responsibility to keep our feet dry, but the prognoses suggest
they won't be able to. That's why we are making sure that people themselves are resilient. People can do a lot themselves. Research-by-design is
still necessary and highly relevant here, not so much within government
for outside consumption, but rather with one's feet in the mud, from the
outside in.

The Advisor
Riek Bakker

Consultant and landscape architect

I learnt early on that direct contact with the executive is essential. As a young landscape architect, I set up the Bakker & Bleeker practice with Ank Bleeker. In the late seventies we designed a cemetery. It was an assignment that meant a lot to me, and I was proud of it. Once the design was ready, a utilities corridor was put straight through the middle of it, just like that. That was disillusioning, to say the least. It then dawned on me that everything is vague and uncertain if you don't bolt it down securely. Politically responsible people are needed to ensure that everything that is put down in black and white also actually happens, and in the right way. I am now two steps further on. I not only want direct contact with the executive, but I also want to know what they are capable of and what they want, and why they are asking for my advice. Sometimes it turns out to be all show. That's fine, but I don't play that game.

For regional design in particular, the question of who you are working for can be complex. In 1996, my practice BVR produced a vision for the Groningen-Assen region, in the north of the Netherlands. A regional vision like that was new in those days. We didn't jump straight into the design work. The basic principle was that all the parties, both large and small, would participate on an equal basis. No one party would be allowed to dominate. But needless to say, some old grudges came up. Rivalries from the past had to be put to bed – between town and country and between neighbouring municipalities. We didn't start with a narrative about the future, but rather with a series of interviews and a conference. In so doing, we laid a foundation for successful cooperation.

That's also how we started, for instance, when Jan Franssen, then
Queen's Commissioner in Zuid-Holland, asked BVR to advise on the form
cooperation in the South Wing should take. Our first task was to create
conditions which would give regional cooperation a chance of succeeding.
We already had some ideas about how the region could develop, but I
didn't reveal them immediately because they would have been rejected
out of hand. Many of the parties were there to defend the interests of their
own areas and were unwilling to hear other people's ideas about them.
The rivalry was unprecedented. We had to cut through that before we could
get anywhere. To arrive at a regional vision, everyone must be prepared to
think at various levels, even if that seems to contradict their own interests.
They have to identify with a common area and look at it in the same way.
Before you can start building that, you need trust. It's a tough battle, time
and again.

You still see that rivalry in the South Wing. The Province of Zuid-Holland
should take a firmer stance in bringing town and country together, without
interfering in matters traditionally the responsibility of the municipality.
National government has given the provinces an important task – that
of looking after and cultivating the bigger picture. There are plenty of
reasons for that. Take the climate objective, for example. You can't leave
that purely to the municipalities. Also infrastructure and subsidence of
peat soils, all those things that have a large-scale impact. Provinces can
make connections between different developments, bring parties together

and encourage renewal. As far as I'm concerned, all twelve provinces should put their heads together and work with civil society to come up with an integrated vision for all of the Netherlands.

The dairy farming industry is also an issue on which the province has an important part to play. It's terrible what's happening. First, farmers were given the freedom to produce as much milk as they wanted, so they bought more cows, but then had to lock them up in the shed because the government hadn't considered the manure surplus this would create. It's a disaster.

I live in the rural Krimpenerwaard area and can see all this happening from close by. A few years ago, my partner launched a regional fund and obtained a lot of money for projects to sustainably develop and manage the landscape and keep it attractive. Last year I felt it was my turn. I made a strategic vision for the future. In recent years, visions have been eyed with suspicion. Our prime minister, Mark Rutte, calls them an 'elephant in the room'. You can't do without them, though. A vision is a shared compass, not a plan that has to be implemented. To organise a joint development process, you need such a compass. Otherwise, nothing will happen and people will be dissatisfied. You can't afford to upset the public.

These days you have to work from the bottom up. Participation is non-negotiable. That's how I approached the Krimpenerwaard area. We worked from an independent location in the middle of the area. But you do need a connection to government, because these types of processes must be based on a broadly supported democratic decision. If it's a close call, it comes back to haunt you. That connection with the public authorities has to be carefully arranged and managed. Parties that want to jointly create a vision need to have excellent communication strategies.

People in the Krimpenerwaard are law-abiding citizens who by nature respect authority. The province represents authority, but it's not an authority that is respected, because every few years the people there are confronted with new regulations and changes to the conditions attached to subsidies. We solved that problem by setting up a committee consisting of four people who have won their spurs in public administration and are of the highest integrity. Jaap Smit, as King's Commissioner, was chair. Residents could approach the committee members with any concerns or requests they might have. Again, it took us the first six months to create the conditions needed to give a regional design a chance of succeeding.

When I was the director of the Urban Development Department at the City of Rotterdam, I worked in a large group on the redevelopment of the former harbour area of Kop van Zuid. A new link across the river was needed to connect the city centre with the much poorer southern half of the city. That, too, was a process of creating trust, talking to people and overcoming ingrained patterns of thinking and behaving. Years later, the day came when the framework of the new Erasmus bridge sailed into Rotterdam on a big ship. That was a beautiful moment I will never forget.

Shaping Holland 237

ii.1 – 1990 – *Patchwork Metropolis (Tapijtmetropool): a radical vision of the fragmented landscape of The Hague–Rotterdam region*

The Academic
Wil Zonneveld

Professor of Urban and Regional Planning, Delft University of Technology, Faculty of Architecture and the Built Environment

Fi.6

'In regional design, comprehension comes first, and intervention follows'

Internationally, the Netherlands is seen as leading the way in regional design. Colleagues outside the Netherlands regard the Randstad as a spatial phenomenon that owes much to design. This perception is based largely on the national policy documents on spatial planning, particularly the 1966 Second National Policy Document on Spatial Planning and parts of the 1988 Fourth National Policy Document on Spatial Planning. The 1988 national policy was preceded by an unprecedented spate of regional design, for example concerning the relationship between the main infrastructure and spatial development and the country's international position. Not much of this was included in the final document, but that doesn't really matter. The design work had an exploratory function.

Designing can be about understanding and intervening. The primary function of regional design is understanding, as a way of discovering regional structures and problems. The 'patchwork metropolis' design by architect Willem Jan Neutelings is a good illustration of this (see Figure ii.1). In 1989 he was asked by the City of The Hague to conduct a study into the possibilities for urban development in the area between The Hague and Rotterdam. Abandoning the concept of clearly defined cities in red-green patterns, Neutelings decided to take a different approach. He explored the area and discovered a whole spectrum of small areas every few hundred metres with different functions and forms. He collected his findings in a

240_._Interview_ The Academic

catalogue of patches in eight different categories, as a classification of the different spaces in the intermediate area. The urban designer Frits Palmboom says that his design for the Ypenburg VINEX neighbourhood in The Hague was directly inspired by this patchwork metropolis model. It would be interesting to see to what extent this concept also influenced thinking at the Province of Zuid-Holland.

The objective of strategic spatial planning is not implementation, but rather to provide a line of reasoning for decision-making, and the same applies to regional design. Its purpose is to improve the quality of decisions. In practice, though, the way it works can be extremely chaotic. As a designer, you can anticipate this by making sure the working and communication process is very well organised. Designers should avoid retreating to a safe haven, but should enter into dialogue with potential users and not shy away from letting their arguments be challenged.

I remember the 'AIR Southbound' exercise from 1998 and 1999, in which several design teams conducted research into the rural Hoeksche Waard area just south of Rotterdam. Almost without exception, the designers made for the drawing board and started assigning identities to the area. But the locals could not relate to any of them. There was one exception to this – Lodewijk van Nieuwenhuijze of H+N+S. The first thing he did was to see how people were using the area, and he did manage to make contact with the locals. That's the kind of attitude you need, setting to work in an interactive manner, investigating how people experience the landscape and its features, and then expressing this in sketches and images. This is likely to result in proposals people have not yet thought of.

Luckily, the territory of the province of Zuid-Holland more or less corresponds to the scale of the functional coherence of the region – the South Wing of the Randstad. However, this region is far more complex than the Hoeksche Waard. In such a situation, you cannot avoid working with a series of cartographic images that represent different perspectives on the region. You then see that various configurations come to the fore, something that is also referred to as 'multiple visioning'. The layer approach also follows this method, although it may have gone too far with its division of the three layers of subsurface, infrastructure and land use. You then also have to superpose the layers: synthesis after analysis. This reveals both the potentials and the conflicts.

Verena Balz worked under me for her PhD thesis on the position of regional design in Dutch spatial planning. We jointly analysed the South Wing Studio. The studio was not part of the administrative system, but was linked to it through personal relationships. Its location helped as it was housed in a conservatory next to a main entrance to the provincial government building. Joost Schrijnen (see interview 'The Director') and Henk Ovink were the protagonists as director and department head. Schrijnen felt that free thinking had disappeared from the organisation and that a space was needed for reflection, sketching and designing the territory of the province. This was held in great suspicion. Efforts to have the studio manned by officials seconded from the South Wing partners failed. They didn't have the capacity, and perhaps not the will. Schrijnen and Ovink left the province almost at the same time, at which point the ties with the administrative system were severed and the studio found itself in a vacuum. We believe that this was the reason the results had very little impact.

As a designer, you need to have the conviction that your perceptions of the regional structure are shared by others. In the case of provincial design, those 'others' are mainly the municipalities. A wide range of factors can be at play here. Municipalities may not identify with a design, and there are interests to be taken into account. However, designers should not be daunted by any potential opposition, otherwise they will restrict their freedom of thought and fail to recognise the structures that can be identified and which can reveal in their designs.

I notice that outside the Netherlands in particular there can be fear of cartographic images. This fear is related to the question of how a design should be used. Is it to provide a motivation and justification for concrete interventions, or as an assessment framework for project applications? In the latter case, the vision is used too instrumentally, which makes people apprehensive. I know of a transnational vision, created within a European investment programme for regions, in which map images were taboo because it was feared they would only lead to arguments and friction.

That's a good way to dismiss many potential ideas and findings out of hand. Analysis and design come about at a global level. As soon as you descend to the level of spatial interventions, you have to keep switching between that specific level and the more comprehensive vision. Back in 1967, the sociologist Amitai Etzioni referred to this as 'mixed scanning'.

Here at Delft University of Technology we have long had a chair for design at the regional scale. In the early days, when Niek de Boer occupied it, it was very much focused on urban structures. In recent years, this has shifted towards 'delta-urbanism' – and this is largely thanks to Han Meyer. The delta offers a different constellation for combining topics. How does the water system work? What is the relationship with the subsurface? How great is the risk of flooding? How do the urban system and infrastructure develop within this constellation? Landscape plays a determining role here. As with infrastructure-related tasks, the water-related task leads more or less automatically to the regional scale.

Regional design is flourishing in the Netherlands, but maybe this is limited too much to the professional domain. The American James Throgmorton called planning 'persuasive storytelling for the future'. He also warned against manipulation by suppressing counterarguments with such a narrative. It's an attractive idea, though – regional design as the art of storytelling.

Regional Design Principles for the Future

This has been a book about narratives. The power of regional design in developing narratives is central, although we have not shied away from moments of weakness. The overarching theme of the book is how the relationship between design and executive government developed over time through various projects and studies. Designers and executive members navigated a delicate course between close association and deliberately keeping their distance. We have seen how tricky it is to keep on finding the right way to go about it.

We have tried to show that regional design is a matter of constantly practising the art of coming up with ideas and working on those ideas for regional *and* local development. The key to regional design is not to be found in individual studies, concepts, plans, or any single moment – a message which comes across in every chapter and interview. A single design is tantamount to no design at all; strength lies in succession. Each design gives new direction to the developing narrative, influenced by emerging issues and changing priorities, or a pressing need to make haste with implementation. At the same time, regional design remains a craft. Visualisation gives it its power.

1 _From functional zoning to connecting narratives

The discipline of regional design has undergone a sea change in the past twenty-five years. It has matured as an instrument for regional planning.

Our background is one of zoning, planning and implementation programmes based on functionality: housing, nature, infrastructure, etc. In regional planning practice before 1990, the Province of Zuid-Holland fulfilled the role one would expect of an intermediate tier of government. The province's task was to translate national spatial concepts into regional plans and policies and to oversee municipal compliance with these planning frameworks. Municipalities had to obtain approval from the province for every single plan. Functional zoning was a suitable planning method for this system because the central problem consisted of conflicting claims on land. Statutory duties and instruments were tailored to implementing this system. This oversight role of intermediate-level government is now outmoded. It has diversified.

The 1990s saw the emergence of strategic regional planning. The provincial government adopted a new way of planning for the future that went beyond functional zoning and legislative regulations. Initially it focused on preparing development perspectives for supramunicipal plans. As time went on it became clear that a robust strategy needed an overarching narrative, and so the idea of the South Wing was born. At the same time, formal regional policy was still geared to the production of regional plans for parts of the province. In the 2000s the strategic approach was first used to produce a strategy for the province as a whole (see Figure iii.1).

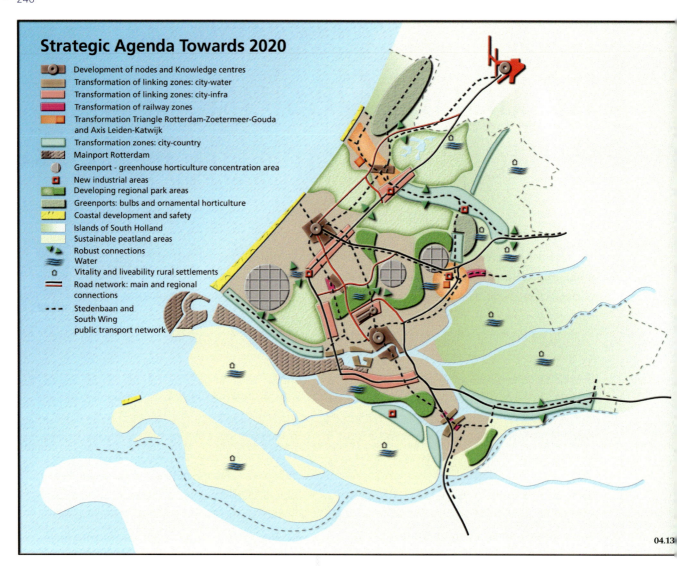

iii.1 – 2004 – The provincial vision for spatial development in 2020

This provincial vision (Provinciale Ruimtelijke Structuurvisie 2020) was the first vision integrating the various regional visions into an overarching provincial policy framework. In line with the vision for the Rotterdam region policy, focus shifted from zoning to strategic planning.

Since the 2010s, national government has increasingly viewed municipalities as the first level of local government. At the same time, such decentralisation means that more initiative is expected from the provinces: they are accountable for the organisation of spatial interests and claims on land, and for the development of economic and ecological core areas. Well-functioning networks and conditions conducive to spatial development have become important components in the spatial policy of provinces. In this book, San Verschuuren refers to the twin concepts of coherence and diversity as an ambition for the 1989 design study Park City between Palace and Port? (*Parkstad tussen Hof en Haven?*). This has lost none of its value.

Besides decentralisation, Dutch spatial planning has undergone a period of deregulation as the ideology of 'small government' has taken root. Over the past few decades, national government has largely withdrawn from the arena of spatial planning and public investment, and subsidies can no longer be counted on. Housebuilding is now dominated by market players – a deliberate choice by national government – which has fundamentally changed the housing market. A broad call for more 'participation' from 'society' requires a form of regional planning which leaves room for initiatives by citizens' groups and market players, and timely contributions from the public.

We are seeing a shift, in fits and starts, towards the use of regional design to explore the scope of planning agendas and identify environmental qualities. Strategic narratives have become increasingly central and the visual language of regional design has changed in step with this. Maps now have different legends from the former regional spatial plans and are arranged according to living environment or spatial development task rather than function. For instance, the coastal towns on the design map for the coast (see Chapter 1) have been divided into five categories: from metropolitan to family resort. The major landscape units of peat, clay and dunes have become visible on maps, while within cities, historic city centres, business districts and areas under redevelopment are highlighted according to the task at hand.

These movements have culminated, for the time being, in the new Dutch Environment and Planning Act (*Omgevingswet)*, which is being implemented in stages from 2020 and centres around local considerations at project level. National government has more or less withdrawn from the sphere of spatial visioning, leaving this almost entirely to the municipalities and provinces. Solutions to major social issues such as sustainable energy and climate change are sought at the regional level. The province, however, has relatively few means of implementation of its own. It does have some for the countryside and for regional infrastructure, but not for urban development (traditionally a matter for the municipalities), the major projects (for which national government is required) and water management (mainly a responsibility of the water authorities).

Where regional initiative is required but there are insufficient means of implementation, thought needs to be given to how such initiatives can be developed and delivered. The implementing parties must be included in the thought processes, and that is only possible if they can see how their own objectives and ambitions connect with the new ideas. Regional design can make that connection by building on strategic narratives with stakeholders. A good example of this is the experience with the coastal defences, as described in this book. National government, the province, the water authority and the municipality coordinated and deployed their implementation tools in a way that delivered exceptional additional qualities to the resorts and the natural environment along the coast.

2 _What makes regional design so special?

The changing practices of regional design have not been ignored by academia. Since 2010, research has taken place at all the different universities of technology in the Netherlands into the function and effects of regional design. For instance, Bart de Zwart (of TU Eindhoven) distinguished in his thesis between the dispositioning, propositioning, problematising and assembling effect of regional design (see Figure iii.2). The different effects of regional design constitute a response to how 'the region' is experienced as context, space, institution or condition.

A prominent example in De Zwart's work is the 2006 area-based strategy for Haarlemmermeer-Bollenstreek as a 'dispositioning design'. He talks in detail about the different perspectives drawn up by the urban design practice MUST for this area, which straddled the provincial borders, for the provinces of Noord-Holland and Zuid-Holland (see Figure iii.3). They appeared about fifteen years after the Randstad Spatial Planning Consultative Group (*Randstad Overleg Ruimtelijke Ordening*) presented a design study into the opportunities for new housing in the Bollenstreek bulb-growing area. Luuk Boelens talks about what happened in the interview with him in this book. De Zwart believes that MUST's perspectives or scenarios aid the debate about the future of the area. Working conferences with interested parties were pivotal points in the design process, which proceeded via an inventory of neutral building blocks through four perspectives towards a consensus – an attractive vision that captures the agreements made. De Zwart describes this process as 'a covenant in the making', closely connected to decision-making.

Elsewhere in his dissertation, De Zwart refers to Luuk Boelens and Joost Schrijnen, who are also interviewed in this book. De Zwart refers to Boelens in particular as a critic of scenario studies, which in the 1990s were liable to become detached from reality. By quoting Schrijnen, he designates part of the essence of regional design as a problematising

	context	**condition**
spatial	**the region as final piece** *regional scale pregnant with solutions, corresponding to scale of problems* regional design as a means to connect sectoral goals and to go beyond conflicting land use claims ↓ producing inclusive spatial concepts	**the diffuse region** *hybridity and overdeterminisation* regional design as a means to to analyse identity and logics of production of a territory as foundation for context-sensitive development ↓ broaching questions and securing spatial quality
institutional	**the region as arena** *decentralisation and deregulation of planning system* regional design as a means to align perception of collective challenges and to seek support ↓ negotiate, shaping consensus and alliances	**the region adrift** *governmental complexity & the regional governance 'gap'* regional design as a means to organise follow-through by mobilising actors, instruments and resources ↓ seeking leverage and connected interests

iii.2 – 2015 – Different roles of regional design

The context of regional design in the early 21st century, as summarised by researcher Bart de Zwart. The overview shows a playing field characterised by various settings, which have repercussions on expectations regarding the roles, capacities and effects of regional design.

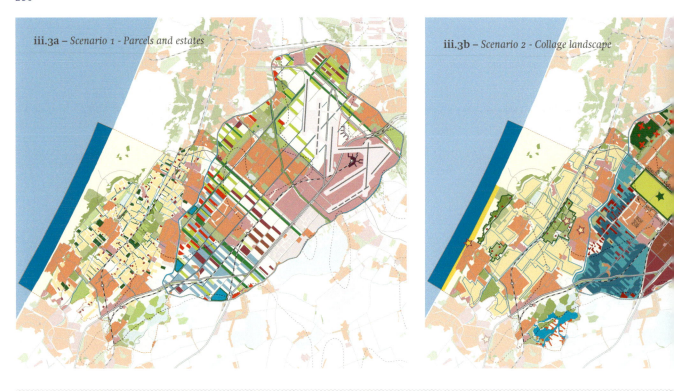

iii.3a – *Scenario 1 - Parcels and estates*

iii.3b – *Scenario 2 - Collage landscape*

iii.3 – 2005 – Explorative study of urban development across provincial borders

Scenarios for future development helped creating an arena to discuss spatial planning in the Haarlemmermeer and the neighbouring bulb-producing region across provincial borders.

base map

	study area "Haarlemmermeer Bollenstreek"
	Area with limitations due to noise 20 Ke 5PK
	area for which housing is excluded
	2010 - railway and station
	2010 - roads
	2010 - Schiphol
	2010 - Schiphol
	2010 - housing
	2010 - economy
	2010 - greenhouses
	2010 - water
	2010 - forest and recreation
	2010 - dunes

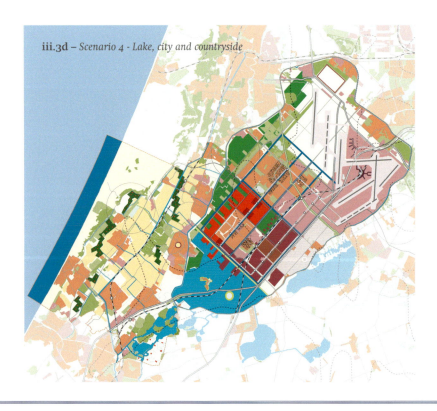

iii.3d – *Scenario 4 - Lake, city and countryside*

Shaping Holland 251

iii.3c – *Scenario 3 - Village and region*

Future scenarios for
Haarlemmermeer - Bollenstreek

activity: 'The act of encouraging spatial proposals in a sense "creates" the task, the assignment and the commissioning party. Herein lies the special potential of the design discipline.'

According to De Zwart, the value of design as a problematising activity lies in its capacity to tap into underlying topics and issues, but he concedes that it can be difficult with autonomous research in labs such as the South Wing Studio (*Atelier Zuidvleugel*) to switch to a more implementation-oriented mode. In other words, it has little if any position in the developing narrative that is constituted by the succession of regional designs. Joost Schrijnen's argument in this book leads to the conclusion that the connection with the administrative and political agendas needs to be safeguarded, also for research-by-design in an independent environment.

Regional design is different from traditional urban design, which focuses on the local level and project implementation. In the past twenty-five years, the differences have become more marked. Regional design cannot be directly interpreted in terms of implementation or investment projects; there is always at least one operationalisation process between the stages, and usually more. These can manifest in many different ways: working out the design, calculating the financial and economic implications, translating the design into regulations or an incentive programme, doing an environmental impact assessment, etc. A good regional design gives direction to implementation and provides

conceptual underpinning through its strategic narratives. So what does regional design actually mean? What lessons have we learnt from the past twenty-five years that we can use for the next twenty-five years? How effective has it been, and why?

In her 2017 PhD thesis Annet Kempenaar examined how much influence regional designers have on spatial planning. Like us, she highlights the fundamental difference between urban design, which is about producing masterplans for new developments and designing street profiles, and regional design, which is concerned with governance and shaping agendas, dialogues and decision-making. The core skill of regional designers is the ability to respond to a multitude of stakeholders. According to Kempenaar, the contours of regional design methodology are:

- Taking a dynamic systems perspective
- Addressing multiple geographical scales
- Looking from past to future, highlighting the long-term and overarching issues
- Creating a continuing dialogue with stakeholders
- Reframing the region
- Sensing and responding (mentioned in almost all interviews in this book)
- Balancing direction and openness

In a 2013 academic paper on regional visioning for peri-urban sites, Terry van Dijk states that 'design-aided visions are essential to peri-urban

iii.4 – 2012 – Regional acupuncture clustered in regional envelopes

Designing for the South Wing of the Randstad as a whole poses quite a challenge. An overall plan as a blueprint is out of the question, being neither desirable nor feasible. A second challenge is creating synergy between local plans with a regional impact. This 2012 design drawing shows how local projects can be clustered to create a powerful regional development perspective. The trick is to address this 'envelope' of projects to the right stakeholders – an approach that had previously been developed in the AReA project (see Chapter 4). The connections between the envelopes are enhanced by diversity: together, they become even more powerful.

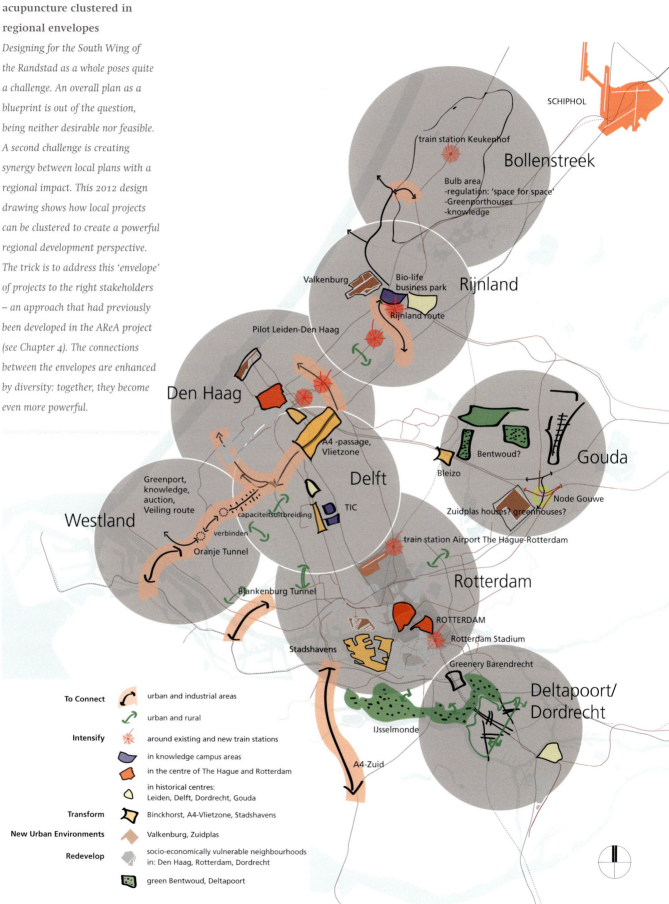

areas because they can unite stakeholders, offer multifunctional, innovative ideas about the future, and provide a framework for experiments that assist in the exploration of the "possibility space" of peri-urban sites.' Expanding on this idea of 'possibility space', Verena Balz, in her 2019 PhD thesis on regional design, develops a theoretical framework for regional design work. She argues that the flexibility for decision-makers to interpret planning concepts generated by regional design is key to an effective use of regional design for regional planning: informing both the argumentation and collaborative nature of rationality between stakeholders.

Balz analyses regional design as a practice, and as such underlines a number of lessons we draw from our experience. She describes regional design as above all a collaborative and social practice. In that context, 'regional design is an argumentative practice that performs in planning decision-making.' This practice, according to Balz, structures knowledge and values through 'spatial concepts' with the aim of either intervening in the spatial organisation of a region or challenging existing views of territories, rules and policy agendas. Regional design practice 'mediates between a collaborative and a strategic rationale of spatial planning.'

'Spatial concepts', described in the 1980s by Andres Faludi and Barry Needham as pre-existing narratives and institutionalised geographies, play a major role here. Regional design continually aims to rethink such narratives and geographies. Design practice introduces new planning concepts when new challenges or new combinations of spatial programmes arise. As Balz says, 'A form of planning that allocates planning resources to some areas while others are omitted, requires a shared understanding of spatial development. [Faludi and Needham] saw explicit (and negotiable) relations between what they called a "spatial order" (autonomous spatial development, motivated by social action) and "spatial ordering" (intervening in spatial development) as a precondition for any approach to strategic spatial planning.' Regional design provides such shared understanding by widening or narrowing the room for interpretation of the task and territory at hand.

Jannemarie de Jonge, in her 2009 PhD thesis on the nature of design in regional landscape architecture, developed her research from a career in design practice. What she brings to the table is the necessary attention in regional design to the physical reality on the one hand and the reality of power relations on the other. Regional design, envisioning what does not yet exist, can only be relevant when it speaks to both of these (see Figure iii.4). By integrating thinking about 'wicked problems' and focusing on design in terms of dialogues, De Jonge comes to the following features of regional design processes as a 'reflective co-design practice':

- The process actively seeks to obtain qualitatively good solutions instead of compromises that reflect existing patterns.

- Participants must have a reflective, learning attitude and represent a wide range of expertise, knowledge and interests.
- Conflict is used constructively as a source of creative transformation.
- Reflecting on real-life situations and concrete cases is crucial.
- The problem-solution space is explored alternately from a solution perspective and a problem perspective, gradually integrating new facts (epistemic dimension) and values (phronetic dimension). The core design activity is using 'creative imagination and reflective judgement' to move towards a central concept.
- Concepts aim to reconcile what are considered to be the key dilemmas and bear the promise of feasible solutions; they represent a reasoned and selective choice of issues and scale within the landscape system.
- 'Tentative decision-making' on concepts, on the basis of wise practical judgement … allows for reasoned revisions or exceptions in subsequent stages of refinement. A distinction is made between a conceptual or strategic mode … and an instrumental or operational mode.

3 _First lesson: Permanent visioning, across all scales

While academic research can help with the theoretical aspects of defining a methodology for and developing methods of regional design, researchers find it difficult to really grasp the obscure workings of decision-making, the position of regional design within a governance context and the craft of design in a process of working with stakeholders that can take many years. From this book, and informed by the different perspectives academia offers us, we draw four lessons from twenty-five years of experience that we hope can bridge the gap between academia and design practice. But however hard researchers seek a methodology, continuous adaptation to unique and changing circumstances as well as geography makes it difficult to pinpoint one particular method of regional design. Nevertheless, from the cases in this book we can draw a number of lessons in which we can recognise some of the points academics have made about regional design.

The first lesson has to do with the diversity of scales in regional design and related levels of abstraction, and the development of a territorial vision over time. A region may consist of a number of provinces, but can also be a transformation zone subject to pressure from many sides, spatially or pro-grammatically. Our account of the history of the A4 corridor is a good illustration of this diversity. Although regional design tends to be on a specific scale, good regional design will always take account of the influences at other scales, both larger and smaller. This makes it possible to shift between scales when necessary. An exploratory design at the Randstad or Delta level is interpreted in terms of regional development for a number of muni-cipalities, which in turn, contributes to a spatial vision for the province as a whole.

In this sense, regional design is never finished. It is a continual process of visioning that constantly switches back and forth between scales, not a one-off exercise for a particular project. Over the years, work has been done on analysing, interpreting and arranging areas and interventions that transcend the local level. Local problems can be solved by placing them in a wider context. Conversely, regional design can break down huge area-based agendas into manageable 'envelopes' of local development programmes. Through the decades, spatial challenges have been found, defined, elaborated or rearranged. It is important to acknowledge that this is a non-linear process.

4 _Second lesson: Attention to governance is essential

A second lesson we can learn from this book is that the dimension of governance is crucial to regional design. Regional design uses the power of visualisation to harmonise opinions, interests, values and qualities across different scales. Previously separate spatial development agendas, such as infrastructure, green space, new housing or water management, 'suddenly' appear to be connected. The 'layers' of the cultural landscape of Zuid-Holland are continuously teased apart and recombined. Through this continuous process of unravelling, recombining and distilling potential new futures it becomes possible to build alliances and enter into partnerships around regional design – to realise physical projects and combine funding,

but often also to put new subjects (or old subjects in new ways) on administrative, political and social agendas.

Particularly where multiple commissioning bodies are involved, such as the province, water authority and municipalities, it can take quite some effort prior to the design process to devise an effective commissioning arrangement. Riek Bakker makes this crystal clear in her interview. The participating parties must be open to regional solutions, and must therefore dare to step outside the range of their own specific interests or territorial boundaries. The success or failure of such 'problematising' design exercises depends on the contact between designers as contractor and the executive as client. If there is insufficient connection between a design study and the assignments as perceived by the executive, the design will be relegated to obscurity.

The closer a plan is to implementation, the greater the role that governance will play – at least in a planning system such as that in the Netherlands. Regional design can then play a part in 'organising the development agenda'. It gives a context to concrete projects and can even launch them. It is essential, though, to 'address' the projects – they need a recipient and an owner. It was not for nothing that AReA (see Chapter 4) spoke of 'project envelopes'. The party concerned must be willing and able to elaborate or implement such a project. Moreover, a regional design must not lead to winners and losers. Former provincial executive member Asje van Dijk makes it clear in the interview with him that the community in the Zuidplaspolder accepted the major development programme through a combination of social awareness and the prospect of being able to profit from it as well (facilities and new nature). Each participant must be able to assume the role most suited to them. The design process puts parties in a position to grow in their role and brings financial or perceived imbalances to light when they can still be corrected.

5 _Third lesson: Start with the layers in the landscape

We have found a common denominator within regional design in the layer approach as an analytical basis (see Figure iii.5). Initially, functional zoning was experimented with by moving from abstract concepts and coloured areas and symbols on maps towards topographically accurate solutions at project level. This has increasingly become a working method which involves making thorough topographical analyses on several levels in order to find connections and structures from which interventions can be derived. In Chapter 3 we saw how two trends reinforced each other. First, the greater emphasis on sustainability brought the natural soil and water systems right back into the picture as structuring elements in spatial development, particularly in the low-lying wetland areas of the Zuid-Holland polders. The peat meadow programmes for Gouwe-Wiericke and the Krimpenerwaard area are derived directly

from this. Second, the landscape took on greater significance as a carrier of regional identity. Historical architectural styles, field patterns and objects acted as a counterbalance to uniform new development and landscape homogenisation. Both tendencies made it imperative not only to think in terms of spatial programmes and developments, but first and foremost in terms of the existing qualities of the area.

The first step is always to establish the physical and environmental make-up of the area: how does it 'work', what flows can be identified, what type of subsurface does the area have? This factual basis gives structure to the complexity. As objective as it is, this first step already gives direction. Depending on the context and the agenda, new layers are added, layers are combined, or the values attached to the factual circumstances are altered. For example, the energy transition means that geothermal energy becomes a relevant element of the subsurface and the heat network becomes a structuring infrastructure – in Chapter 6 we saw how restructuring of the Westland area is related to networks for energy, heat and CO_2. In fact, each chapter of this book reveals a different relationship between subsurface, networks and human occupation.

6 _Making room

In a nutshell, regional design is about switching between scales, continual visioning over time, positioning and agenda-setting in the context of

iii.5a – *Ecomodel: landscape ecological model*

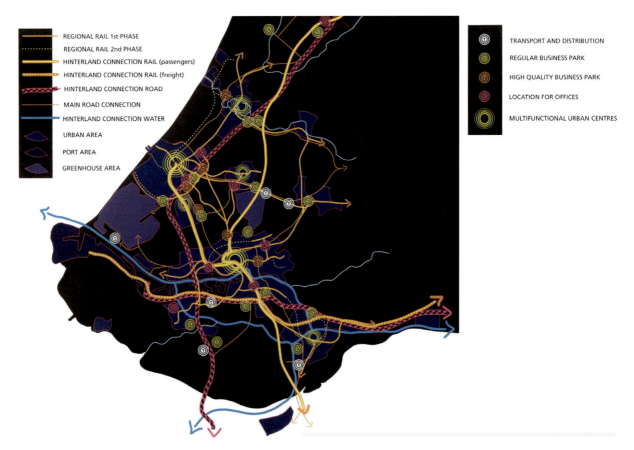

iii.5b – *Network model: economic infrastructural framework*

iii.5 – 1994 – More Elbow Room for the South Wing: regional frameworks for the future

In the mid-1990s, the Province of Zuid-Holland embarked on a new phase in its spatial policy which is still having an effect today. The South Wing was introduced as a planning concept to provide a future compass for governance. A foundation was laid for the transition from functional plans to an ongoing strategic planning of underlying conditions for spatial development. In a spatial study for the future entitled 'More Elbow Room for the South Wing' (Meer armslag voor de Zuidvleugel) designers introduced a planning framework that would later come to be known as the layer approach: the delta and the subsurface provide the underlying conditions for the development of an optimal economic and infrastructure network, which in turn form the skeleton upon which the urban 'carpet' can be laid.

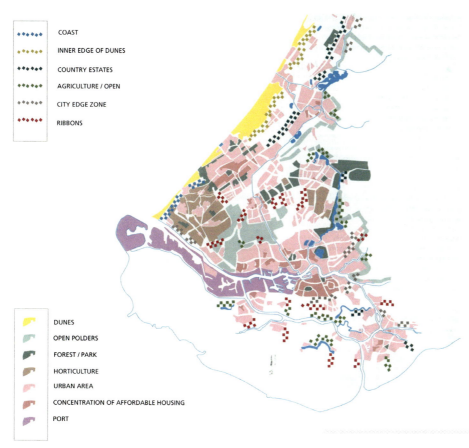

iii.5c – *Living environment model: attractive and varied urban residential and amenity space*

governance, and using layers in the created landscape in order to understand regional agendas. However, there is no magic formula for the balance between these activities; at every step of the way it is a question of looking for the right approach. Design studies do not always get it right straight away. Sometimes the best method and the ingredients needed for the best 'formula' only become clear during the course of the process. Armed with this book, we can underline the importance of both ends of the spectrum of approaches to regional designing that create space for development (although many intermediate forms are conceivable).

The first 'formula', at one end of the spectrum, is 'agenda-setting design'. This design practice centres on an exploratory attitude among clients, designers and stakeholders. This requires room for imaginative thinking, but without losing sight of administrative reality. Input from experts is vital. Agenda-setting design shows how new development agendas can take shape on the ground, which opportunities can arise, the possible links between agendas and between solutions, and the spatial impacts. The results of agenda-setting research, however, are difficult to measure. The effects are often indirect, invisible to those not directly involved, and can take years to emerge. The *Stedenbaan* transport-oriented development concept is a good example of this: some say it has produced little in the way of real results, but the way of thinking has been broadly accepted.

The second formula, at the other end of the spectrum, is 'development-oriented design'. This design practice centres on clients, designers and stakeholders adopting a collegial attitude. It requires political sensitivity, but it must not be allowed to obscure the objective. Input from stakeholders is vital, and it is essential that they are all behind the vision. Ideally, this should involve an implementation programme for the first five or so years. Good examples of this are the integrated development of Delft–Schiedam (IODS) and the Leiden–Katwijk Axis (see Chapter 4). This second example also shows the vulnerability of this formula: one vital link of the public transport plan did not make it to the finish line.

Regional design is a policy instrument, and therefore it serves regional planning. This means that the executive bears a large part of the responsibility for the commissioning of regional design. Will future administrations be prepared to be challenged by thought-provoking or inspiring visual narratives at the regional level? Regional designers now face the daunting task of translating the new challenges of economic renewal, the energy transition, the influence of new technology and climate adaptation into concepts and narratives around which government authorities and stakeholders can align. The main factor for success is creating the mental space for regional design without losing sight of the political and administrative arena.

7 _So what must we do now?

Recent years have seen a shift in which the planning and organisation of land uses has become increasingly less valid as a guiding principle for spatial development. The drivers of spatial development challenges have become increasingly thematic: economic innovation, climate change, the energy agenda. This movement sometimes seems to suggest a return to a new form of silo policymaking, which for decades characterised the compartmentalised sectoral policymaking for infrastructure, housing, the economy and green spaces. There is a growing danger that regional design assignments become limited to finding ways of fitting engineering works into the urban or rural landscape.

This is partly to do with a fear of visioning that has arisen over the past few years, a fear which, in turn, is due to an overly instrumental treatment of visions. This has probably also been fuelled by the traditional task the provinces had of overseeing plan making by lower tier authorities. But provincial visions are no longer created with that aim, or at least they should not be. Visions serve as a compass. They provide direction and ensure that decisions are properly substantiated, as Wil Zonneveld argues in this book. Their power of persuasion should be based on their content and not on the political and administrative power behind them. For this, visioning is again sorely needed, and regional design as well.

The latest generation of research-by-design studies shows that regional design can still reveal surprising and fruitful connections between apparently separate development agendas through the use of new concepts such as urban metabolism and energy landscapes (see Figure iii.6). Since 1990 we have experienced a period of economic prosperity and high growth rates, followed by a deep crisis that derailed all the plans and forced a rethink. We are now at the beginning of a new era. Economic growth is once again on the cards, but we can no longer take it for granted. It is now all about taking a prudent approach to growth and sustainably managing what we have. Moreover, the local scale must be given a clear role in regional design because many groups in society have come to feel that their immediate environment has borne the brunt of larger spatial developments.

Finally, climate change in particular is an increasingly urgent challenge. Measures for limiting and accommodating its effects will change the living environment irrevocably. As a 'delta province', Zuid-Holland will determine the spatial development agenda for the Rhine, Meuse and North Sea more than in the preceding period. It means urban development programmes will have to be combined with strategies for green space and water (see Figure iii.7) In the past twenty-five years we have learnt a great deal, by trial and error, about what regional design can do. We urgently need to take these lessons on board when tackling the tasks that lie ahead.

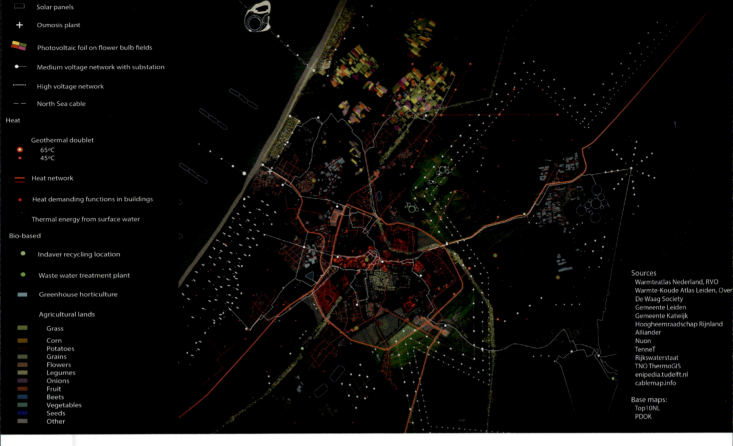

iii.6 – 2016 – An energy-neutral Heart of Holland

Ten municipalities in the Hart van Holland 2040 partnership (Katwijk, Noordwijk, Oegstgeest, Teylingen, Kaag en Braassem, Leiderdorp, Zoeterwoude, Voorschoten, Wassenaar and Leiden) drew up a regional agenda for the Environment and Planning Strategy 2040. The Heart of Holland Environment and Planning Strategy is the first such regional strategy in the Netherlands. It integrates thinking in terms of flows with more traditional planning principles. Extensive preliminary studies, including on the energy system, give a new dimension to regional design. This drawing from the preliminary studies into the energy transition illustrates the ambition of making the region energy-neutral and introduces a new type of map. The study was also a pilot project, supported by the Province of Zuid-Holland and the Ministry of Infrastructure and the Environment, for design studios to develop regional energy strategies.

iii.7 – 2017 – The urban landscape and 'green-blue' structure of Zuid-Holland

This study called South Wing Landscape Park (Landscape Park Zuidvleugel) is aimed at the development of an attractive new perspective for the urban landscape and green-blue structure of Zuid-Holland. It is a response to emerging challenges such as the migration to the city and climate adaptation in an urbanised delta. The vision involves identifying the urban landscape at various scales, visualising various strategic agendas and developing an approach that ties in with the multiple functions and values of the contemporary green-blue structure. The study was made partly at the initiative of the provincial advisor for spatial quality, an institutionalised role for independent advice within the province.

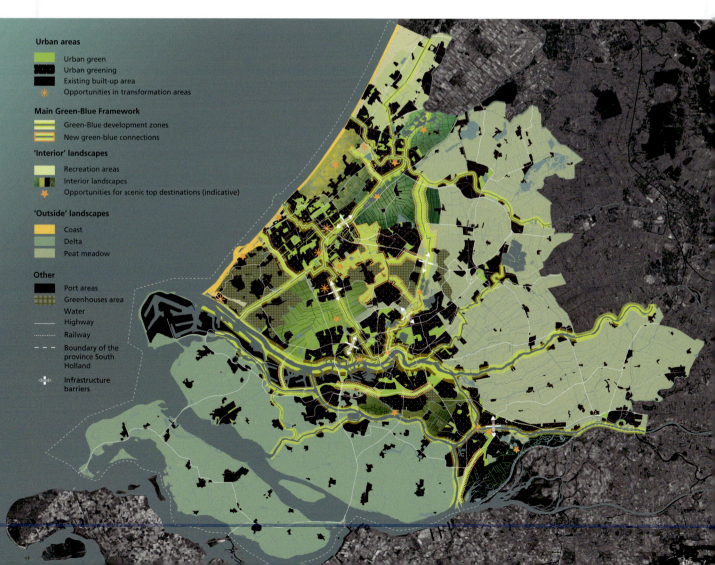

Illustration sources

Photos

F0.1	*Photo: Gerhard van Roon for provincie Zuid-Holland*
F1.1	*Photo: Gerhard van Roon for provincie Zuid-Holland*
F1.2	*Photo: Luuk Kramer / OKRA*
F1.3	*Photo: Luuk Kramer / OKRA*
F1.4	*Photo: On Sight Photography / OKRA*
F2.1	*Photo: Gerhard van Roon for provincie Zuid-Holland*
F2.2	*Photo: beeldenbank provincie Zuid-Holland*
F2.3	*Photo: Remco Zwinkels / Nationale Beeldbank*
F2.4	*Photo: Remco Zwinkels / Nationale Beeldbank*
F3.1	*Photo: Gerhard van Roon for provincie Zuid-Holland*
F3.2	*Photo: beeldenbank provincie Zuid-Holland*
F3.3	*Photo: beeldenbank provincie Zuid-Holland*
F3.4	*Photo: beeldenbank provincie Zuid-Holland*
Fi.1	*Photo: Nicoline Rodenburg for provincie Zuid-Holland*
Fi.2	*Photo: Nicoline Rodenburg for provincie Zuid-Holland*
Fi.3	*Photo: Nicoline Rodenburg for provincie Zuid-Holland*
F4.1	*Photo: Joop van Houdt / Beeldbank Rijkswaterstaat*
F4.2	*Photo: Harry van Reeken / Beeldbank Rijkswaterstaat*
F4.3	*Photo: beeldenbank provincie Zuid-Holland*
F4.4	*Photo: beeldenbank provincie Zuid-Holland*
F5.1	*Photo: Sicco van Grieken for Zuidvleugelbureau*
F5.2	*Photo: Gerhard van Roon for provincie Zuid-Holland*
F5.3	*Photo: Sicco van Grieken voor Zuidvleugelbureau*
F5.4	*Photo: Ton Poortvliet / Beeldbank Rijkswaterstaat*
F5.5	*Photo: beeldenbank provincie Zuid-Holland*
F6.1	*Photo: Gerhard van Roon for provincie Zuid-Holland*

F6.2	*Photo: Wieneke Hofland for provincie Zuid-Holland*
F6.3	*Photo: beeldenbank provincie Zuid-Holland*
F6.4	*Photo: Rob Kamminga for HVC*
F6.5	*Photo: beeldenbank provincie Zuid-Holland*
Fi.4	*Photo: Nicoline Rodenburg for provincie Zuid-Holland*
Fi.5	*Photo: Nicoline Rodenburg for provincie Zuid-Holland*
Fi.6	*Photo: Nicoline Rodenburg for provincie Zuid-Holland*
F7.1	*Photo: Gerhard van Roon for provincie Zuid-Holland*

Images

i.1a-b	*Courtesy MUST, 2004 "Hybrid Landscapes" - Nederland 1860-2010.* *9th Architecture Biënnale Venetië*
i.2a-d	*Provincie Zuid-Holland, Cartography Department, 2021*
i.3a-c	*Provincie Zuid-Holland, 2010, 'Visie Stedelijk Netwerk' (intern study).* *Design by Francisco Colombo and Jeroen van Schaick*
i.4a-d	*Compilation from different studies by Francisco Colombo, OMA en Helmut Thöle*
1.1	*Provincie Zuid-Holland, 2006, design by Arjan van de Lindeloof*
1.2a-d	*Adviescommissie voor de Zuid-Hollandse Kust, 2006, Kustboekje Groeien naar Kwaliteit.* *Design by H+N+S*
1.3a	*West8, 1995, Duindoornstad / Buckthorn City; Manifestatie Rotterdam 2045:* *50 jaar Wederopbouw - 50 jaar toekomst*
1.3b	*Stuurgroep Kustlocatie, 1995, Plan Bhalotra. Design by KuiperCompagnons*
1.3c	*West8, 2006, Happy Isles; in cooperation with Svasek Hydraulics, Coastal, Harbour* *& River Engineering Consultants*
1.3d	*Waterman, R., 2010, Naar een Integraal Kustbeleid via Bouwen met de Natuur*
1.4a-e	*Provincie Zuid-Holland, 2006, Westkust - ruimtelijke kaders Delflandse Kust. Design by MUST*
1.5	*Provincie Zuid-Holland, 2005, Lijnen in het Zand - Integraal Ontwikkelperspectief voor* *de Kust. Design by Bureau Nieuwe Gracht*

1.6	*Provincie Zuid-Holland, 2009, Integraal Ruimtelijk Project Delflandse Kust - Gebiedsvisie Delflandse kust. Design by MUST*
1.7a-c	*Ontwerp voor zwakke schakel Katwijk, OKRA designers, 2016*
1.8a-f	*Provincie Zuid-Holland, Atelier Kustkwaliteit, 2011, Werkboek #4 de toekomst van de stille kustlandschappen. Design by bureau van Paridon x de Groot*
1.9	*Provincie Zuid-Holland, 2011, Strategische Agenda Kust Zuid-Holland*
1.10	*Atelier Zuidwestelijke Delta, 2013, Scenariostudie Zuidwestelijke Delta. Design by BoschSlabbers*
2.1	*Provincie Zuid-Holland (Dienst Ruimte en Groen), 1989, Inrichtingsstudie Tussengebied: Een parkstad tussen Hof en Haven?*
2.2	*Nirov, 1997, De Nieuwe Kaart van Nederland, 1997, Den Haag*
2.3	*Provincie Zuid-Holland, 1994, Stedebouwkundige Verkenning van Verstedelijkingsmogelijkheden tussen Delft en Zoetermeer na 2005. Design by Francisco Colombo*
2.4a-f	*Provincie Zuid-Holland, NIROV,1993, Juryrapport van de eerste fase van de prijsvraag Schakelen & Schakeren. Design by Barbara van Dijk, Egbert J. Broerse*
2.5a-b	*Eo Wijers-stichting, 1995, Juryrapport. Design by VHP stedenbouwkundigen en landschapsarchitecten, winnaar EO Wijersprijsvraag 1995*
2.6	*Design by OMA commissioned by Rijksbouwmeester (in cooperation with provincie Zuid-Holland, gemeente Amsterdam en Rotterdam), 2002, DELTAmetropool*
2.7a-f	*Provincie Zuid-Holland, Dienst Ruimte en Groen, 1994, Meer armslag voor de Zuidvleugel*
2.8	*Provincie Zuid-Holland, 2004, Provinciale Ruimtelijke Structuurvisie Zuid-Holland 2020*
2.9	*Provincie Zuid-Holland, 2003, Ontwerpen aan de Zuidplaspolder 2003-2006. Design by Palmbout Urban Landscapes*
2.10	*Provincie Zuid-Holland, 2013, Internal study for Provinciale Structuurvisie. Design by Francisco Colombo*
2.11	*Vereniging Deltametropool in collaboration with College van Rijksadviseurs, 2014, Duurzame Verstedelijking & Agglomeratiekracht: Casus Zuidelijke Randstad*
3.1	*Provincie Zuid-Holland, 2013, Ruimtelijke verkenningen t.b.v. Visie Ruimte en Mobiliteit. Internal study. Design by MUST stedebouw*
3.2	*Provincie Zuid-Holland, 2007, Dynamiek in de Delta. Design by Francisco Colombo*
3.3	*Provincie Zuid-Holland, 2004, Provinciale Ruimtelijke Structuurvisie Zuid-Holland 2020*
3.4	*Provincie Zuid-Holland, 2004, Provinciale Ruimtelijke Structuurvisie Zuid-Holland 2020*
3.5	*Map by Paul Gelderloos, based on Provincie Zuid-Holland, Cartography Department, 2010*
3.6	*Ambtelijke notitie visie landelijk gebied Zuid-Holland, 1990; personal archive Esjmund Hinborch*
3.7a-c	*Bestuurlijk Platform Zuidvleugel, 1999, Zuidvleugel: Van stedenzwerm naar deltametropool*
3.8a-e	*Provincie Zuid-Holland (Dienst Ruimte en Groen), 1989, Inrichtingsstudie Tussengebied: Een parkstad tussen Hof en Haven?*
3.9a-b	*Gemeente Rotterdam (stadsontwikkeling), 1990, Verstedelijking tussen Den Haag en Rotterdam. Design by Frits Palmboom and Jeroen Ruitenbeek*

3.9c	*Provincie Zuid-Holland, 1994, Stedebouwkundige Verkenning van Verstedelijkingsmogelijkheden tussen Delft en Zoetermeer na 2005. Design by Francisco Colombo*
3.10a	*Gemeente Rotterdam (stadsontwikkeling), 1990, Verstedelijking tussen Den Haag en Rotterdam. Design by Frits Palmboom and Jeroen Ruitenbeek*
3.10b-c	*Provincie Zuid-Holland, 2001, Groenblauwe Slinger - Stad en Land in Balans*
3.10d	*Provincie Zuid-Holland, 2004, De Ontwikkelende Provincie*
3.10e	*Provincie Zuid-Holland, 2001, Groenblauwe Slinger - Stad en Land in Balans. Design by Peter Dauvellier*
3.11a	*Bestuurlijk Platform Groene Hart, 2000, Groene Hart visie. Deel 1: Kwaliteit als basis voor de toekomst. Discussienotitie. Design by Bureau Nieuwe Gracht*
3.11b	*Personal archives Provincie Zuid-Holland*
3.11c-d	*Randstad Overleg Ruimtelijke ordening, 1990, De Randstad maakt zich op*
3.11e	*Regio Randstad, 2003, Ontwikkelingsbeeld Deltametropool 2030. Design by Bureau Nieuwe Gracht*
3.12	*Provincie Zuid-Holland, 2009, Transformatievisie Merwedezone. Design by Francisco Colombo*
3.13	*Provincie Zuid-Holland, 2014, Visie Ruimtelijke en Mobiliteit*
3.14	*Provincie Zuid-Holland, 2012, Gebiedsprofiel Goeree-Overflakkee*
3.15	*Provincie Zuid-Holland, 1988, Randstad Groenstructuur*
3.16	*Louis Bolk Instituut, Vereniging Nederlands Cultuurlandschap, Provincie Zuid-Holland, 2018, Streefbeeld Buijtenland van Rhoon. Design by Peter Verkade Landschaparchitecten*
4.1	*Provincie Zuid-Holland, 2004, Provinciale Ruimtelijke Structuurvisie Zuid-Holland 2020. Design by Francisco Colombo*
4.2	*Provincie Zuid-Holland, Noord-Holland, Rijkswaterstaat en Ministerie VROM, 2000, AReA: Aanpak van het gebied tussen Amsterdam, Rotterdam en Antwerpen. Design by Eric Luiten*
4.3	*Rijkswaterstaat Steunpunt Routeontwerp, 2008, De Deltaroute A4*
4.4	*Interne studie provincie Zuid-Holland, 2003. Design by Francisco Colombo*
4.5	*Rijkswaterstaat Steunpunt Routeontwerp, 2008, De Deltaroute A4*
4.6	*Provincie Zuid-Holland, 1999, Corridors - een (ruimtelijk) discussiekader, een deelstudie van het project "Noord-Zuidcorridor". Design by Francisco Colombo*
4.7a	*Provincie Zuid-Holland, 2008, 'Dubbelstad' design by Francisco Colombo*
4.7b	*Buck Consultants, 2004, Economische effecten A4 Delft - Schiedam. Belang A4 voor de regio. Design by Francisco Colombo*
4.8	*OMA commissioned by Ministerie VROM, 2002, Atelier DELTAmetropool*
4.9a	*Ministerie Verkeer en Waterstaat, 2007, Programma Randstad Urgent*
4.9b	*Ministerie VROM, 2008, Voorstudie voor Randstad 2040*
4.10	*Provincie Zuid-Holland, 2001, Integrale Ontwikkeling Delft-Schiedam (IODS)*
4.11	*Provincie Zuid-Holland. Workshop A4 corridor, 2017. Design by Francisco Colombo*

4.12a-b	*Provincie Zuid-Holland, 1996, Interne studie: stedebouwkundige verkenning van mogelijkheden tot overbrugging van rijksweg A4 tussen Leidschendam en Leidschenveen. Design by Francisco Colombo*
4.13	*Gemeente Den Haag, 2010, Werkboek A4/Vlietzone, op weg naar de Nota van Uitgangspunten*
4.14	*Provincie Zuid-Holland en regio Holland-Rijnland, 2006, Ontwerpen aan de oevers van de Oude Rijn. Ontwerpatelier As Leiden-Katwijk. Design by BVR Adviseurs*
4.15	*Gemeenten Leiden, Leiderdorp, Zoeterwoude, Provincie Zuid-Holland, Rijkswaterstaat, Ministerie VROM, 2001, Ontwerp Masterplan W4*
4.16	*Provincie Zuid-Holland in cooperation with gemeenten, 2005, Strategisch Masterplan Knoop Leiden-West. Design by West 8*
5.1	*Interne voorstudie voor Provincie Zuid-Holland, 2005, Stedenbaan Zuidvleugel - Van Idee tot Programma. Design by Francisco Colombo*
5.2a-c	*Provincie Zuid-Holland, 1994, Stedebouwkundige verkenning van verstedelijkingsmogelijkheden tussen Delft en Zoetermeer na 2005. Design by Francisco Colombo*
5.3	*Platform Zuidvleugel, 2003, Stedenbaan. Design by Walter de Vries*
5.4	*NS en Bureau Stedenbaan, 2007, Folder Regionaal OV Zuidvleugel. Design by Movin Systems in cooperation with Rodenbröcker&Partner*
5.5a-b	*Provincie Zuid-Holland, 2002, interne studie. Design by Francisco Colombo*
5.6	*Provincie Zuid-Holland, 2004-2005, Milieudifferentiatie langs de Stedenbaan. Design by Urban Unlimited en Universiteit van Utrecht*
5.7a-b	*Bureau Zuidvleugel in cooperation with Vereniging Deltametropool, 2013, Zuidvleugel Stedenbaanplus Monitor 2013*
5.8	*Platform Zuidvleugel, 2007, Ruimtelijke ambitie Stedenbaan 2020. Design by Francisco Colombo*
5.9	*Provincie Zuid-Holland, 2006, Ruimte en Lijn. Design by Atelier Zuidvleugel*
5.10	*Provincie Zuid-Holland, 2006, Ruimte en Lijn. Design by Atelier Zuidvleugel*
5.11a-c	*Provincie Zuid-Holland, 2006, Ruimte en Lijn. Design by Atelier Zuidvleugel*
5.12	*Provincie Zuid-Holland, 2011, Atlas Research & Development - Verkenning van de ruimte voor Innovatie in Zuid-Holland. Internal study*
6.1	*Provincie Zuid-Holland, 2011. Internal study. Design by Helmut Thoele*
6.2a-c	*Rijk and Zuidvleugelpartners, 2013, Adaptieve Agenda Zuidelijke Randstad 2040*
6.3a-b	*Provincie Zuid-Holland, 2004, Provinciale Ruimtelijke Structuurvisie Zuid-Holland 2020*
6.4	*Provincie Zuid-Holland and Stadsregio Rotterdam, 2005, Ruimtelijk Plan Regio Rotterdam 2020*
6.5	*DCMR, 2017, Integrale Rapportage Visie en Vertrouwen - Afsprakenkader Borging Project Mainportontwikkeling Rotterdam*
6.6a-b	*Provincie Zuid-Holland, 2014, Visie Ruimte en Mobiliteit*
6.7	*Provincie Zuid-Holland, Internal study Havenstudie Rotterdam. Design by Helmut Thöle*

6.8	*Stuurgroep Deltapoort, 2012, Gebiedsvisie Deltapoort 2025. Design by H+N+S*
6.9a-b	*Amvest and Wayland developers, Glasparel, 2008-2010. Design by BVR*
6.10a	*Provincie Zuid-Holland, Xplorelab, 2011, Van Mainport-Greenport naar Growport. Design by Zandbelt & Van den Berg*
6.10b	*Provincie Zuid-Holland, Xplorelab, 2011, Van Mainport-Greenport naar Growport. Design by JAM Visual Thinking*
6.11a	*Provincie Zuid-Holland, 2013, Zuid-Holland op St(r)oom. Design by Fabrications in cooperation with H+N+S*
6.11b	*Provincie Zuid-Holland, 2013, Zuid-Holland op St(r)oom. Design by Studio Marco Vermeulen*
6.11c	*Provincie Zuid-Holland, 2013, Zuid-Holland op St(r)oom. Design by POSAD*
6.12a-b	*Provincie Zuid-Holland, 2017, (On)begrensde Technologie - Maatschappelijke Invloed van Nieuwe Technologie in Zuid-Holland. Design by Studio Marco Vermeulen in cooperation with DRIFT*
6.13	*Projectatelier Rotterdam, IABR 2014. Design by Fabrications*
6.14a-b	*Stadsregio Rotterdam in cooperation with WNF/ARK, 2015, Getijdenpark Brienenoord - De Esch. Design by Florian Boer, De Urbanisten*
6.15	*Stichting Rotterdam World Expo, 2016, Bidbook Expo 2025 Rotterdam. Design by POSAD*
6.16	*Provincie Zuid-Holland, Gemeente Westland, 2015, Gebiedsfoto Westland-Oostland: de Greenport in beeld. Design by MUST*
6.17	*Provincie Zuid-Holland, Gemeente Westland, 2016, Werkboek Westland. Design by Francisco Colombo, Bart Goedbloed and Wibo Lenting*
ii.1a-b	*Project Tapijtmetropool / Patchwork Metropolis, 1990 in cooperation with Gemeente Den Haag. Design by Neutelings Riedijk Architects*
iii.1	*Provincie Zuid-Holland, 2004, Provinciale Ruimtelijke Structuurvisie 2020; Strategiekaart. Design by Francisco Colombo*
iii.2	*Zwart, B. de, 2015, Republiek van beelden: de politieke werkingen van het ontwerp in regionale planvorming. PhD Thesis Technische Universiteit Eindhoven.*
iii.3a-d	*Provincies Zuid-Holland, Noord-Holland; gemeenten Haarlemmermeer, Bennebroek, Regio Holland-Rijnland en Hoogheemraadschap van Rijnland, 2005, Discussienotitie Gebiedsuitwerking Haarlemmermeer-Bollenstreek. Design by MUST*
iii.4	*Provincie Zuid-Holland, 2012, Internal study. Design by Francisco Colombo*
iii.5a-c	*Provincie Zuid-Holland, 1994, Meer armslag voor de Zuidvleugel*
iii.6	*Alliantie Hart van Holland, 2016, Omgevingsvisie 2040. Design by Fabrications, POSAD, Evolv and Buck Consultants*
iii.7	*Provincie Zuid-Holland, 2017, Verkenning stedelijk landschap en groenblauwe structuur Zuid-Holland - naar een schaalsprong voor een metropolitaan landschapspark. Design by Marco Broekman*

Acknowledgements

We would like to thank Delft University of Technology and the Province of Zuid-Holland for funding and support to make this English edition of our book on regional design possible. We are grateful for all those regional designers who delved into their analogue and digital archives and helped us collect an impressive and unique visual overview of regional design practice in Zuid-Holland. In particular we thank the interviewees for sharing their personal insights and stories about what happened behind the scenes while shaping Holland. We thank Eric Luiten who helped us develop and structure our narrative. Translator and editor Derek Middleton's work on the final version of the manuscript was invaluable to improve readability. Finally, we thank all those who gave their time to attend the working sessions that formed the basis of this book in 2017: Abe Veenstra, Alex Bruijn, Arjan van de Lindeloof, Barend Jansen, Caroline Ammerlaan, Dries Zimmermann, Donald Broekhuizen, Edith van Dam, Ejsmund Hinborch Eric Luiten, Frank van den Beuken, Frank van Pelt, Gerard Wesselink, Gielijn Blom, Guus van Steenbergen, Hans Kleij, Helmut Thoele, Isolde Somsen, Jack Vessies, Jan van der Grift, Jan Ploeger, Klaas Hilverda, Koos Poot, Marcel Wijermans, Marco van Steekelenburg, Mark Reede, Paul Gerretsen, Peter Verbon, Ronald Löhr, Steven Slabbers, Tanja Verbeeten, Tony van der Meulen, Twan Verhoeven, Walter de Vries, Wim Keijsers and Wil Zonneveld.

Project team Kracht van Regionaal Ontwerpen / Shaping Holland
Francisco Colombo, Jeroen van Schaick,
Marleen Verton, Peter Paul Witsen

Text and research
Peter Paul Witsen, bureau Westerlengte
Jeroen van Schaick, provincie Zuid-Holland

Idea, research, editor and image editing
Francisco Colombo, provincie Zuid-Holland

Photos and images
Jeroen van Schaick, provincie Zuid-Holland
Marleen Verton, provincie Zuid-Holland

Consultant
Eric Luiten, landscape architect

Design supervision
Sacha Beusen, provincie Zuid-Holland

Translation and editing
Talencentrum UvA Talen
Derek Middleton, Text Compilation Editing Translation

Design
Corps Ontwerpers, Den Haag
ref. 201201572

Amsterdam/Den Haag, 2017-2021